Whitetail Nation

Books by Pete Bodo

NONFICTION

Pelé's New World

*The Courts of Babylon: Tales of Greed and Glory in
the Harsh New World of Professional Tennis*

*The Atlantic Salmon Handbook: A Compact Guide to
All Aspects of Fly Fishing for the King of Game Fish*

*A Champion's Mind: Lessons from a Life
in Tennis* (with Pete Sampras)

*Hardcourt Confidential: Tales from Twenty Years
in the Pro Tennis Trenches* (with Patrick McEnroe)

*Whitetail Nation: My Season in Pursuit
of the Monster Buck*

FICTION

The Trout Whisperers

Whitetail Nation

MY SEASON IN PURSUIT
of the MONSTER BUCK

PETE BODO

HOUGHTON MIFFLIN HARCOURT

BOSTON   NEW YORK   2010

For information about permission to reproduce selections from this book,
write to Permissions, Houghton Mifflin Harcourt Publishing Company,
215 Park Avenue South, New York, New York 10003.

www.hmhbooks.com

Library of Congress Cataloging-in-Publication Data
Bodo, Peter.
Whitetail nation : my season in pursuit of the monster buck / Pete Bodo.
p. cm.
ISBN 978-0-618-96996-8
1. White-tailed deer hunting—United States. 2. Bodo, Peter—Travel.
3. United States—Description and travel. I. Title.
SK301.B644 2010
799.2'7652092—dc22   2010011519

All illustrations by Glenn Wolff
Book design by Brian Moore

Printed in the United States of America

DOC 10 9 8 7 6 5 4 3 2 1

The names and identifying details of some of the
persons in this book have been changed.

FOR LUKE

In the hope that one day he, too, will feel the joy and experience the wonders I've known, out there . . .

Contents

PROLOGUE 1

PART I

1. ALL ROADS LEAD TO ANTLERS 13
Andes, New York, October 12, 2008

2. BLOOD TRAIL TO NOWHERE 32
East Arcade, New York, October 12–13

3. THE MILKWEED FACTOR 51
East Arcade, New York, October 13–14

4. PANCHO AND LEFTY, REPRIEVED 67
Delhi, New York, October 20

PART II

5. GRAVITY IS A BUZZKILL 93
Andes, New York, October 22

6. THE WHITETAIL EXPRESS 119
Great Falls, Montana, October 24–28

7. LORD OF THE PLAINS   140
Rudyard, Montana, October 26

8. THE BIG EMPTY   154
Rudyard, Montana, October 30

PART III

9. LOVE AND WAR IN THE WOODS   179
Andes, New York, November 5

10. THE MILLION-DOLLAR FREE THROW   202
Fredericksburg, Texas, November 7–11

11. KNOW WHEN TO FOLD 'EM   233
Bovina and Andes, New York, November 16–19

12. A NIMROD'S LAMENT   265
Galilee, Pennsylvania, November 26–28

AFTERWORD   297

GLOSSARY   301

ACKNOWLEDGMENTS   305

Prologue

As I opened the passenger-side door of the pickup, a blast of frigid air rushed into the cab and snow crystals danced in the glow of the dome light. Paul, my driver, guide, and host at his deer camp in southern Saskatchewan, leaned over and pointed at a wide trail leading arrow-straight through black walls of pine trees. A foot of snow, ice blue in the moonlight, lay on the trail that faded into a void.

"The stand will be on your left about half a mile in, at the edge of the alfalfa field," Paul assured me. "I'll be back 'round for you at eleven."

I struggled to swing my legs out of the truck, feeling a little like a turtle stuck on his back. I was bound up in layers of wool, all of which I would need if I were to make it through my early shift in the Texas tower, a small, Spartan wooden shack resting on top of a metal tripod fifteen feet off the ground.

I watched Paul pull away, the snow boiling up around his tires until his red taillights looked like a pair of malevolent eyes twinkling in a mist. Then it was dark. And cold. And all around me it was silent.

Working in the lime green glow of my flashlight, I shucked myself into my daypack, jumping in place to get it up and properly set on my back. I decided to load my rifle, despite the lack of visibility. A false sense of security is better than no sense at all. The weapon felt puny and sticklike in my heavily gloved hand. I trudged through the freshly fallen snow, feeling the air on my face as if it were solid—some elemental substance that, were it greatly compressed, would become steel.

I flicked off the lamp; the snow reflected enough light to illuminate the trail. Stars burned in the black sky overhead, and a shimmering platinum band surrounded the moon. Trudging through the woods at night when it's fifteen below is weird, but in a good way.

I stuck to the middle of the trail between the conifers. It was easy, quiet going, the silence interrupted only by the swishing of my boots in the fine powder snow. This was the first morning of my first hunt in a place famous for its monster whitetail bucks. Although I'd hunted whitetail most of my adult life, I'd never been obsessed with killing a giant buck. I wasn't purely a "meat" hunter, quick to shoot the first legal deer I encountered. But I was content hunting average whitetail with friends, mostly in New York and Pennsylvania.

However, I'd always hoped to shoot a giant whitetail buck, a legitimate trophy. And while a fair number of such deer are killed in New York and Pennsylvania every year, I had never managed to get one. Many of my regular hunting buddies, being either more obsessed with killing a trophy buck or just wealthier than I, routinely booked hunting trips to exotic places in hopes of slaying a brute of a whitetail. I held out against joining them.

I took the Zen approach, known in some circles as "the lazy guy's way to true enlightenment." My day would come, I reasoned. Every dog has his day, I told myself. Even a blind pig eventually finds an acorn. One day, one of those eyebrow-raising bucks that survives a couple of seasons of intense northeastern hunting pressure would step out in front of me and—*bang!*

The next thing you know, my neighbors, admiring the eight- or ten-pointer hanging in the yard, would whistle and ask, "Where's that guy been hiding?" It was just a matter of time and patience: being in the right place at the right time.

For a while I also held out against entering the world of pay-to-play hunting. Including travel and license fees, you can expect to drop about six or seven grand on a seven-day white-tail trip, which sounded an awful lot like you're just buying a trophy buck. Who's going to spend that kind of dough just to go sit and freeze his ass all day, sustained by chili, bacon, and whiskey? It wasn't like you had to go to the boreal forests of Saskatchewan, the densely foliated river bottoms of Montana, or the crop fields of Illinois to shoot a big deer. Big deer were everywhere. Just never in front of my gun. It was like some big, terrible mistake.

But I always felt a twinge of envy as my friends returned from hunting trips to Kansas, Alberta, or Wisconsin, goofy grins plastered on their faces, bubbling over with tales of big bucks they'd shot, or at least observed. So I finally caved and booked a trip to Saskatchewan with a regular hunting buddy, Chris Ingvordsen. *I've got plenty of antlers on my wall, but nothing really special*, I figured. *Let me put that issue to rest by splurging on this trip and then get back to business as usual.*

That all happened well over fifteen years ago. And that's how this whole thing started.

When I came to the end of the trail, my stand was visible against the night sky, like a Porta-John hovering in the ether. I stripped off my pack, emptied the gun, and tied everything to the nylon haul-cord with fingers that worked just long enough before they went numb. But it was easy climbing up the metal ladder and through the trapdoor in the floor of the wooden hut. I sat down on the aluminum-framed kitchen chair. The mice had been at it, mining almost all the cotton out of cracks in the Naugahyde seat.

I studied the landscape before me. I was in the corner of an enormous rectangular field, with the woods directly to my right and left. The field before me was mostly flat, but soon I made out a few black stains on the purple plain in the predawn light. They were patches of brush. The deer presumably were out there, pawing the snow away to get at the alfalfa. Soon they would be making their way to the safety of the woods, where they would spend the day bedded down, rising only to stretch and get their thick blood circulating as they nibbled leafy browse on another short, cold day.

The body heat I generated walking and climbing into the stand dissipated quickly. As I withdrew further into my parka, tucking my chin into the high collar, I wondered if I'd last until eleven. I wondered if Paul had ever returned to pick up a client who had frozen to death. Periodically, I scanned the field with my binoculars, peering through the horizontal shooting windows.

For someone accustomed to the northeast, where an eight- or ten-acre field is substantial, the sheer scale of the landscape was intimidating. Back home, a four-hundred-yard shot was likely to cross a town line and put out the window of the local Presbyterian church or a tire dealership. In Saskatchewan, you had to man up; taking a four-hundred-yard shot was the equivalent of trying to scale a card into an upturned fedora. Even if you missed, it was no big deal.

I was shivering and not yet able to assemble all the vague shapes lying out there into a coherent landscape. But far to the east, the backs of long, low-lying hills were outlined by something that was trying to become light. I set aside the field glasses and balled my fists around my chemical hand warmer long enough to enable me to light a cigar—a De Nobili, which looks like a section of gnarled tree root and is manufactured in Scranton, Pennsylvania. It did nothing to make me warmer.

Wait. Something doesn't look quite right out on the field.

I almost toppled from my chair grabbing for the binoculars. I trained them on the area and located a dark shape barely discernible against the smoky pink background. It sure looked like a deer. Or was it someone's stray pony? There were no antlers. Did it move, or was that my hands shaking?

What the hell is that?

A whitetail buck. It appeared in the glass, just like that, alongside the doe. It wasn't just any old buck, or even a representative Saskatchewan cockwalloper. It was something else. Outlined against the rosy backdrop, the antlers of the buck were jet black, towering, and symmetrical, with four tines, each seeming a good foot in length and tapered to a point, rising skyward from the main beams. How those heavy antlers stood out, so big and conspicuous that they made the giant body beneath them look small, like that of a cartoon buck.

The deer were walking. The buck appeared to wobble slightly beneath the weight of its antlers. The image shimmered, a snow country mirage, grainy, dark, sepia toned. Alongside the buck, the doe looked tiny. I made a move for the gun leaning in the corner but stopped. The deer had to be four, five hundred yards away and the light was poor. *Don't panic*, I told myself. *Don't do something stupid and blow it.*

The deer made their way across the field at an angle, coming no closer. If I stayed in the tower, well-concealed, maybe they would veer my way and provide a reasonable shot instead of a prayer. If they remained on course, I would mark where they slipped into the woods and track them later, an easy job in fresh snow. I had them, bang to rights.

This Saskatchewan hunting ain't so bad, I thought. My face was cold and brittle; the shit-eating grin could wait for now. But where would those gigantic antlers look best, in the living room above the TV, or in the hallway entrance, where even a neighbor borrowing a cup of milk would have to see them? Would the buck make the Boone and Crockett Club record book? You bet.

I watched. The two deer drifted to a patch of brush and disappeared into it. This was getting even better. I had them trapped on a quarter-acre island in the field. I could wait them out. A tide of pale yellow light advanced toward me, from far across the field, slowly eating up what was left of the darkness. The distant green hills were already bathed in it.

The brush offered scant cover; they couldn't stay in there too long, and with the improved visibility, I might take that long shot after all. It was a still day, I wouldn't have to worry about bullet drift in the wind, and my 7 mm. Remington Magnum could deliver a bullet just two inches below my point-of-aim over the four hundred yards between me and the deer. I checked the gun over, reengaged the safety, and rested it crossways in my lap. I watched.

The minutes slipped by peacefully but slowly. I fidgeted in my chair. *Stay ready,* I told myself. *They might pop out at any time . . .*

I relit my cigar. It was broad daylight now. Would the deer have the gall to stay holed up in the brush for hours, hiding in plain sight? Whitetail deer are crafty bastards, with instinctive genius for melting into a landscape. That uneasy feeling in my gut? I put it down to nerves.

After all, here I was, in the northernmost reach of the range of *Odocoileus virginianus,* or whitetail deer. These were the ur-deer of the species, robust survivors of a harsh process of selection that took place over the course of eons and, as is the case for most mammals at the extreme margin of their habitat, they had eventually become the largest representatives of their kind. In colder climates, survival is often determined by body mass, and that yields a proportionate gain in brute power and antler size. And these were deer that still might have to fend off wolves, or bears.

I was determined to play it cool, Clint Eastwood cool. Hell, I even had an Eastwoodesque cigar, and I smoked it down to a nub, never taking my eyes off the island of brush. But as my vigil lengthened, I increasingly sensed that something was not quite right. The feeling grew in my stomach like a loaf of bread baking in an oven. I felt self-conscious, although I was alone in the middle of nowhere. But that changed in a moment, as Paul's truck came blasting out of the woods and slid to a stop in a shower of snow beneath my stand.

I got up and stuck my head out the window, grinning.

"Did you see him?" Paul was agitated. "Did you see the Picket Fence?"

The Picket Fence? You mean that buck has a name?

"He walked into that patch of brush yonder," I said, casually. "I'm waiting for him to come out."

No sooner were the words out of my mouth than I was filled with dread.

"'Waiting for him to come out'?" Paul repeated, looking astonished. "Why the hell didn't you shoot? Or get down out of there and cut him off at the pass? He isn't coming out. He's long gone!"

"Long gone?" I muttered. "That can't be . . ."

"It is. Get down out of there. Hurry."

I moved as swiftly as I could in my dense cocoon of wool.

When I made my two-point landing, Paul sniffed the air. "What the hell are you doing, smoking?"

"It's a cigar," I said, stupidly adding, "Deer don't mind the smell of tobacco."

That was how I felt about it, anyway, but the exasperated look on Paul's face suggested he didn't share the opinion. He let it drop, though, as he explained that the patch of brush in question was on the crest of a rise. The ground behind it drops off gradually into a shallow wash. In the poor light, it might have *looked* like the deer walked into the brush; what they really did was walk down into the swale behind it. Then they stole along the bottom, out of view, toward and into the woods.

Paul had seen it all, from far in the distance where he'd parked the truck on a rise of land to watch, waiting to hear the report of my rifle at any moment.

All was not lost—at least that's what I told myself, feeling humiliated. *The Picket Fence. It's kind of a stupid name . . . a cliché. Who would give a big buck such a name?*

"We've watched that buck all fall. He's definitely a Booner," Paul said, tersely. A "Booner" is a buck that would qualify for a place in the record book of the Boone and Crockett Club, which keeps the official big-game hunting records as diligently as the *Congressional Record* keeps track of the doings of the thieves in Washington, D.C.

"Let's go," Paul ordered.

We jumped in the truck and went to collect Chris and his guide, Lance. Paul saw where the Picket Fence had slipped into the woods, and he knew that unless harassed, the buck was unlikely to travel far in broad daylight before bedding down. We still had a shot. That made me feel better. Maybe I wasn't so wrong after all, if we had him pegged in the woods.

Four hours later, my face scratched by briars and my watch cap and wool parka festooned with all kinds of seedpods, the four of us sat on the tailgate of Paul's truck, exhausted, sipping hot lemon tea. Paul had positioned Chris and me in various stations while he and Lance literally beat the brush, whacking trees with clublike batons, trying to roust out the Picket

Fence and drive him toward us. We'd walked, circled, crawled, climbed, and skulked in deadfalls. We watched clearings in the woods and natural gas pipeline cuts that ran straight and treeless for miles. We found plenty of tracks, many of them fresh. We found fresh scat, trophy-sized deer poop, suitable for mounting. (How would that look in my main hall? "See this hunk of deer shit? It's from the Picket Fence, the legendary Saskatchewan buck!")

We never saw another deer that morning. But I would see the Picket Fence in my fantasies, in my dreams, in my reveries, for weeks, and months, and, finally, years—long after I returned home from Saskatchewan broke, ready to be haunted.

PART I

1

All Roads Lead to Antlers

I T WAS THE SECOND week in October, the Year of Our Lord 2008.

I took extra care in preparing and packing for opening day of bow season. I dug through all the hunting gear piled helter-skelter in the big wooden box in my mudroom and washed all the clothing in a scentless detergent. Then I sprayed it all down with Autumn Blend, a commercially made scent-masking agent that smells like wet leaves and soil, and goes for $11.99 for a mere twenty-four ounces.

The clothing all went into a giant, industrial-grade Ziploc bag, and then into an airtight plastic container. It keeps the clean clothing safe from the unwanted odor of cheeseburger, cigar smoke (I caved on that after Saskatchewan), or wet dog, all of which deer are thought not to like.

I packed the rest of my gear, as usual, by smell. Anything that stank to high heaven of Doc's Extreme Heat Double Doe Urine, or Team Fitzgerald's Rampage Dominant Buck Lure, went into my duffel bag. I wouldn't need much of that odiferous stuff until weeks later, at the arrival of that period in early November that the magazine editors ominously call "the pre-rut lull." After that, everything I use smells like the pee of a whitetail doe in estrus or a dominant buck, including (according to my wife, Lisa) kitchen utensils, my wallet, the doorknobs.

In a new season, nothing is ever where it will end up by the time you've put in some time afield. Certain pockets—and Lord, do you have pockets on those "Deep Timber" camo-pattern fatigue pants, or your "Bow Hunter Extreme Special Legends Edition" jacket—are more accessible than others, and you've got to give your critical stuff time to migrate there.

I fished out a small Ziploc bag and dropped it, horrified. But that thing that looked like a shrunken head was just an apple that had been sitting in my pack for about eight months, since last deer season.

This year, I had vowed, it was going to be different. Instead of stealing away in some helter-skelter fashion to hunt when I could, I was going big. I wanted to shoot a big whitetail buck; I felt I needed to shoot a cockwalloper. Maybe not one like the Picket Fence (nobody ever did get him, I'd heard years earlier, and that was some consolation), for that Saskatchewan hunt was too rich for my blood. But I was determined to get a monster buck, because I'd grown tired of expecting to stumble on one by chance. And because time was running short.

When I turned the significant corner of fifty years, a sense of urgency began to work at me. I'd hunted as steadily as I could, for a man with a job, a family, and some sense of responsibility to both, for more than a quarter of a century. It was unlikely that I could hunt another twenty-five years. I'd shot quite a few bucks, including some good ones. But not a great one. And I couldn't shake that image of the Picket Fence, sauntering across the frozen plain. Another year slipped away, then another. The birth of my son, Luke, was a joyous occasion, but afterward it was even tougher to focus on hunting. I had to face the facts; I was getting older, the law of diminishing returns was kicking in. It was time to man up.

Over the years, my aims and ideas about deer hunting also had changed. I never fancied myself a "trophy hunter," but I ingested all of the books and magazine articles outlining the strategies for ambushing a big deer, learned all there is to know about hunting transition zones between feeding and bedding areas.

I spent enough time in the woods to be able to tell whether a track in three inches of snow was relatively new or old. Over time, I accumulated a bewildering assortment of calls meant to mimic deer vocalizations, from the lost fawn bleat to the aggressive buck's grunt-wheeze. I bought rattling antlers that promised to lure dominant bucks to the sound of combat between two younger peers, and camo everything.

I had everything but the buck.

But in this year, the Year of Our Lord 2008, it was going to be different. I was going to take up every invitation that came my way, from hunting acquaintances and friends near and far, and make as much time as I could—without having to consult a divorce lawyer—to get myself a wallhanger.

Now, on the brink of another opening day of another deer season, one that I wanted to be different from the ones that had come before, I was getting on my game face.

I admired a new addition to my bow hunting kit: a very light, wide-mouth, one-quart plastic jar that originally contained peanuts. It was filled with miscellaneous small but critically important items: a mini Allen wrench (for repairs to the bow), spare bowstring, a variety of arrowheads . . . I was tired of slicing fingers on those nasty-sharp objects that poked a hole through whatever I put them in and made me bleed like a stuck pig every time I reached into my duffel.

Hunters take an absurd amount of pride in DIY brain-storms, and the magazines we read are filled with "how-to" features that will teach you, among other things, how to create a rifle cartridge holder from a bar of household soap (not a bad idea at all: when you shoot up all your bullets, you can wash off the stench of failure), or fishing lures out of your wife or girlfriend's pantyhose—preferably after she's vacated them.

"Who's the man?" I cried, shaking and admiring my "everything" jar. Did I tell you that I don't even have to open the lid on my magic jar to make sure it contains what I'm looking for?

Hello, nasty-sharp broadheads. You can't touch me now!

I answered myself in a voice so confident it would have scared the kids, had any been around: "You are. You're the man."

According to *American Hunter,* a publication of the National Rifle Association, 10.7 million Americans hunt big game (out of a grand total of 12 million hunting-license purchasers). And the whitetail deer is—far and away—the most widely beloved and sought after of North American big-game animals.

The whitetail also happens to be about the most perfectly realized of God's creations, and this sometimes gets underplayed simply because deer are so abundant. Imagine bumping into a couple of Angelina Jolies or George Clooneys every time you popped into a convenience store. Would they still seem so exotic? So . . . beautiful? Deer hunting in northern states generally begins with a bow season sometime around mid-October, and it peaks with a general firearms segment during, or right after, the mating season, the November rut. But you'll still find scores of hardy souls out there in January, toting their smoke poles, or muzzleloaders, thanks to the late "primitive firearms" season, or some variation thereof. Deer seasons have grown longer in recent years, opening greater and greater windows of opportunity, thanks to a burgeoning deer herd, wiser manage-

The whitetail deer gets its name from its dazzling tail-flag with which it signals other deer and alerts them to danger.

ment of both public and private land, and increased demand for hunting opportunity. Word is that an early Pennsylvania blowgun season is in the pipeline—boo-yah!

Hunting your way through three months or longer takes stamina, fortitude, and a pretty strong stomach, but don't underestimate the grit—or plumbing—of a dedicated deer hunter. Come October, he morphs into a Ho Ho and convenience-store microwave burrito–fueled doomsday hunting machine. He's unstoppable: he'll switch from bow to gun to smoke pole, acquire the slew of special permits and licenses required to transition from one to the other, and write the name of his wife on a Post-it note—just in case he should forget. When he uses up his sick days, instead of returning to work with his head bowed, wondering just where he ranks on the boss's shit list, he just calls in dead.

Think I'm kidding about that? According to U.S. Labor Department statistics published by the *Milwaukee Journal-Sentinel,* Wisconsin traditionally leads the nation in an odd but recurring spike of unemployment claims filed for the week when the rifle season for deer begins. Wisconsin claims jump by more than 15,000 filings, fully five times greater than the next biggest leap, by Arkansas. But I could have told you that whitetail deer are more bewitching than catfish.

The sense of fraternity among deer hunters has never been stronger, and it isn't because all those unemployed guys in Wisconsin have nothing better to do than hang out, giving each other man-hugs between hunting sessions. It has something to do with our times. Deer hunting has become, to use the inescapable word, a "lifestyle"—one that's predicated on reconnecting with nature and traditional virtues and pursuits, including competence in the natural world, self-sufficiency, providing for the family, even understanding the role of death and killing in some vaguely felt natural order of things. The Spanish philosopher José Ortega y Gasset put it best when he wrote: "I don't hunt to have killed. I kill to have hunted."

Hunting is about the things we witness and feel in the woods and meadows, usually alone, often at times of the day or under ambient conditions when nature is at her spectacular best—or worst, if you prefer feeling comfortable, warm, and dry. Deer are most active at daybreak and nightfall, before most bird watchers, hikers, or fly-fishermen are out, and after they're back in front of the fireplace. Deer become active on the leading edge of a cold or storm front. You don't have to endure four or six hours of misery to feel truly alive, but it's a better way to get there than spending that amount of time staring at a computer screen.

This way of thinking seems ingrained in the American character, insofar as there still is such a thing. *The Journals of Lewis and Clark,* one of our nation's iconic texts, is, as much as anything else, a *hunter's* diary. It includes details like the white man's first recorded encounter with a previously unknown species, the grizzly bear (it was up near the Great Falls of the Missouri, in present-day Montana), and the men of the "Corps of Discovery" hunted and feasted upon deer, antelope, buffalo, black bear, wolves, and elk galore. Hunting was central to life in nascent America; it was a symbol of the pioneering, adventurous spirit of a new people, and often a necessity for survival.

The pendulum swung away from that kind of thinking as our culture matured, but it still has a strong gravitational pull for many, and that's not just a matter of nostalgia. The number of immigrants, like my own father, who leap feet first into the hunting culture as soon as they settle here is impressive, if difficult to quantify in numbers and statistics. And the blowback against hunting from scolds and "enlightened" urbanites in our time has created some unintended consequences. Nothing will galvanize a group of like-minded people and encourage them to define themselves better than a threat to their common interest.

Starting in the 1960s, antigun, antihunting, and, a little later, "animal rights" sentiments began percolating in elitist circles, especially so in cities and suburbs. The rise in crimes committed with firearms completed our transformation from gun-toting to gun-fearing folks. Hunters were often caricatured or scorned by the well-educated citizens who fell out of touch with the natural world, except in a sentimental way. The mainstream media merrily fueled the fire. When did you last see a PBS or HBO special on, say, the ritual of opening day in a deer hunting epicenter?

But persecution is a powerful tool for community building, so hunters quietly began to push back, aided by powerful organizations like the National Rifle Association, Ducks Unlimited, and the Rocky Mountain Elk Foundation. It's hard to define a group as large and diverse as deer hunters a subculture, but castigating or ignoring them effectively made them one.

A growing industry also fueled this process. Entrepreneurs flocked to two distinct hunting product categories—the gear, and the dream. Even big-box stores that somewhat hypocritically refused to sell firearms began to stock their shelves each fall with massive quantities of doe-in-heat urine, camo thermoses, and even ammunition. And roofers and insurance claims adjustors started brown-bagging it all year in order to afford a one-week, six-thousand-dollar "dream" hunt in Canada and elsewhere.

In recent years, the tide of public opinion has been turning in favor of hunting, mostly due to the self-interest of nonhunters. Problems like deer-automobile collisions, the spread of Lyme disease by deer-borne ticks, and the destruction (by out-of-control deer herds) of the forest understory combined with a better understanding of the role "recreational" hunting plays in wise herd management to soften up some of the resistance to the hunting and killing of deer.

My "Deermobile," a 1991 Jeep Cherokee, would need a seven-digit readout on the odometer to display the number of miles it's traveled. In an earlier life, it bore a bumper sticker: I SMOKE AND I DON'T VOTE. But after 9/11, I peeled it off in favor of a pair of small American flag decals, one in either lower corner of the liftgate's rear window, and a big white decal depicting a magnificent buck.

Driving down the long hill below my farmhouse in the Catskill Mountains town of Andes, New York, I noticed two people on the dirt road. I took them for the young couple renting a nearby cottage. I'd heard that these folks were vegetarians, or vegans, who came up weekends from the city, slept late, and spent most of their Sundays holed up with the massive Sunday *New York Times*, emerging now and then to tend their garden.

They were pretty well bundled-up and visible from a great distance thanks to their blaze-orange hats and jackets. They stood huddled close together like refugees right in the middle of the road. Maybe they were afraid that if they strayed too near the woods, some yahoo operating on a beer breakfast might mistake them for deer and take a poke.

I almost pulled over to put their minds at rest; it was only going to be *bow* season. Bow hunters are a lot like fly-fishermen — dedicated, conscientious, responsible, image-conscious, and more than a little proud of their prudence. More important, for my vegan friends, a bow is effective only out to about forty yards; at that range it would take a dose of something much stronger than beer to mistake a lanky slacker from Brooklyn for a whitetail deer.

The scowls of the couple dissuaded me from stopping; let them figure it out for themselves. I waved halfheartedly and goosed the accelerator. It must be tough, being a vegan during deer season.

The Deermobile hummed along, heading for Interstate 88 and the upper Susquehanna River valley. Although we'd enjoyed a sultry Indian summer, the previous night had brought lashing rain and a biting cold front. That was good—it would get the deer moving and feeding. The skies were still threatening, though; it was a day of autumnal war games. Giant raindrops exploded on the windshield intermittently, and a strong gust pushed the Deermobile toward the shoulder. What did I care? I was warm and cozy, listening to a country music station on the radio; the coffee in my thermal cup was still warm.

Underneath it, though, I felt simmering anxiety. Ordinarily, I would be hunting on opening day on my own property, where

I could screw up in any way imaginable and who was going to know?

But I was spending the opening weekend as the guest of Tom Daly, at his farm up near Buffalo. This was the first and, in some ways, most delicate leg of my quest. For bow hunting demands a greater degree of skill than hunting with a firearm, and a far greater level of attention to details such as wind direction, human scent, and the entry-level skill—judging distance accurately while in the grip of high anxiety, often from an extreme angle fifteen or twenty feet above the ground. Bow hunting offers myriad opportunities to make a hash of things, and for that reason the chance of killing a trophy buck is diminished.

The bow hunter has two big advantages, though. Because bow hunting is allowed earlier than gun hunting, he's in the woods long before the opening day army of gun hunters puts the deer on red alert for the remainder of the season. And in October, the deer are still in their summer feeding and bedding patterns. A diligent, stealthy bow hunter has the woods mostly to himself, and he can "pattern" the deer over the weeks and months leading up to the season.

I stopped in the town of Walton to tank up and bought a Vanilla Coke and a ceremonial bag of Cheez Doodles, because it comes in the hunter's color, blaze-orange. Somewhere west of Harpursville, I passed a freshly killed red fox. The bright blood still trickled from its nose, adding to the expanding black patch on the tarmac. I felt bad for the poor critter, but for me roadkill is a life-affirming experience—a testament to our abundance and a viscerally experienced index of the local wildlife. If roadkill creeps you out, you can move to Europe, where the general lack of furry creatures solves that problem.

My route took me to Corning, the "Crystal City" where the eponymous glass and cookware company is based. More important, this prosperous, neat town is on the eastern edge of

Steuben County, which consistently tops New York state when the annual, official deer harvest numbers are compiled. Corning sits on the bank of a Susquehanna tributary, the Chemung River, which gets its name from the Iroquois language. It means "big horn" or "horn-in-the-water." I clearly wasn't the only hunter to pass this way and think *whitetail* when I beheld those brushy, riverside draws and poplar and willow bottoms.

What is it with antlers, I found myself wondering again. *Why does the single element that distinguishes a "trophy" buck from any other deer seem to mean so much?*

You probably have to observe a buck in his full majesty to understand. His antlers, lacquered by sunlight, are heavy; they protrude on either side of his forehead and curve forward gracefully, sometimes to the point where the tips almost touch. The main beams are picketed with tines, each of which can be eight or ten inches long and tapers elegantly to a fine tip as sharp as any dagger. Sometimes, the tips are as white as ivory and contrast handsomely with the caramel or mahogany tones of the main beams and tines.

Antlers have had a mysterious, remarkable hold on man's imagination for time immemorial. Back in the day when people ran around in pelts and believed that giant nets to the east and west kept tossing the sun back and forth at twenty-four-hour intervals, antlers were associated with the Sacred Tree and the mysteries of birth, death, and regeneration—the latter because a buck sheds its antlers every winter, and spends most of the spring and summer growing new, bigger ones.

As far back as the Paleolithic era, man was busy producing symbolic images incorporating antlers and assorted cervids (the Latin genus to which whitetail, mule, and less common deer belong). Human skeletons were sometimes represented wearing a crown of antlers, suggesting a primitive belief in regeneration. Antlers are a potent symbol partly because it's awfully hard to pin down exactly what they represent, but as someone once observed, there has to be a reason people have been nailing them up above the barn door for centuries.

The association of antlers with virility is obvious, and that may explain why so many of the ad pages in the back of hunting magazines are devoted to human potency-enhancing therapies and drugs, like Viagra. It's rich Freudian ground, but I couldn't care less. I don't need to know everything; I've moved on. I'm just glad that the Chinese, many of whom believe that consuming ground-up rhino horn can make an impotent old lecher pop a woody like there's nothing to it, haven't shifted their attention to deer antlers. Deer horns cause enough problems as it is.

The white and black markets for antlers are well-subscribed. George Waters, an Iowa taxidermist, wound up in jail when he and an accomplice were convicted in Colorado of killing at least forty-two huge whitetail, eleven bull elk, and six mule deer estimated by federal officials to be worth $338,000. The Boone and Crockett Club (of which President Teddy Roosevelt was a founding member, and an outfit of which many of our proto-conservationists and environmentalists were proud members) is America's official keeper of big-game hunting records. In Whitetail Nation, the club's record book may even rank ahead of the Second Amendment of the U.S. Constitution as a sacred text and lodestar for hunters.

The B&C Club inadvertently opened a Pandora's box in 1932 when it came up with a scoring system for measuring antlers. The system is precise and complicated, with the final "score" of a given set of antlers determined by the total inches in length and girth of the main beams and all the tines—with penalty deductions for irregularities. The entry-level score is 160.

The club distinguishes between two types of antlers—typical (symmetrical antlers) and nontypical (those antlers have significant variations, including palmated growths and drop tines, which grow downward off the main beam instead of up).

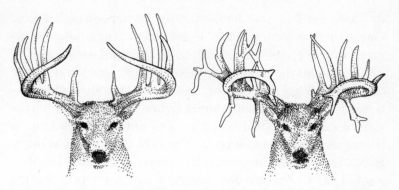

Typical antlers are symmetrical, with the same number of tines on each of the main beams, and no individual features or odd growths. Nontypical antlers have features such as drop tines (which grow down from the main beam, instead of up), stickers (short growths of antler on beams or tines), or other significant antler deformations.

Exceptional antlers have become more than the traditional ticket to bragging rights at the gas pump. They're a highly desired commodity, subject to the usual market forces. Antlers can bring Big Money. According to a report in *American Hunter,* a single, shed antler thought to be from the famous Lovstuen buck (a nontypical whitetail shot in Iowa in 2003; B&C score: 307⅝) was put up for auction on eBay with a starting bid of just under $4,000. The same article reported that the full rack of the Lovstuen buck was ultimately bought by the Bass Pro Shops retail chain for a figure reported to be over $200,000.

Antlers have been the source of all kinds of chicanery and woes, including expensive court battles and intense, multigenerational family feuds resulting from disagreements over just who owns the dusty, decrepit head mount of the buck Grandpa shot in 1934—which turns out *still* to be the second or third largest buck ever taken in the state.

In 1932, an Alberta man, Ed Broder, shot the world record nontypical mule deer (B&C score: 335⅖); in 2007, his descendants were still in court wrangling over ownership of that rack. One of the rival parties landed in jail for ignoring a judge's command to give up the rack, which he had stashed somewhere.

There's also the more contemporary phenomenon of antler chic, which triggered crises of conscience at the always busy intersection of fashion and animal rights. Unbearably hip, typically antihunting fashionistas noticed antlers showing up in boutiques where they shopped or worked (how could so many girls who claimed in their high school yearbooks that they wanted to become "marine biologists" go so wrong?). Stuffed deer heads—Ralph Lauren himself had them at his designer ranch!

Weren't hunters just those Elmer Fudds you saw in the scary parts of the nation where they didn't even have the basics, like cell phone service and a decent tapas bar?

In the cowboy-chic world, antlers began to compete with the bleached-out skulls of longhorn cattle. The market was flooded with antler-themed goods and patterned fabrics, suggesting common ground between an interior designer toting a man-purse and the mill worker trudging to his tree stand wearing a camo fanny pack.

Hunters with good radar for political correctness will often take the path of least resistance when asked the silly, loaded question: Why do you enjoy killing those beautiful deer? They answer, truthfully, that it's not about the killing, and trot out the familiar justifications for hunting. But the eight-hundred-pound gorilla in the conversation is antlers.

Let's face it, nimrods don't walk into taverns with their chests flung out to prattle on endlessly about the spiritual experience they had shooting an antlerless doe, although it might have been something like that. They gather to talk about antlers, not the variety of fungi they discovered on some log trail (as pleasant a discovery as that is), and they're bewitched by legends of great bucks like the Picket Fence or Old Mossy Horn (every rural county has one), who invariably makes his appearance at dusk, just after shooting light, down in the cedar swamp. The one thing all those legendary creatures have in common is big antlers. A deer gets a name only when it has a rack deserving of one.

Technically, any hunter who refrains from killing the first legal deer he sees because he thinks there might be a better specimen to be shot is a trophy hunter. He's out for antlers. Granted, there's something cold and remorseless about hunting for the sole purpose of killing a great deer with impressive headgear, as if it were just an interesting, machismo-driven game. Charlie Jeffers, the owner of a three-thousand-acre ranch in the Texas Hill Country, made this intriguing comment to a wildlife official: "My personal feeling is that the emphasis on the size of the antlers has shifted the emphasis to be on the animal harvest, rather than the hunting experience."

In other words, antler obsession is decadent; it strays far from the fundamental purposes and value of hunting. And on top of that, killing the biggest and best bucks was long thought to have an adverse impact on herd quality—theory being that those animals were the ones that ought to be doing the most breeding.

But on-the-ground realities emerged to challenge those assumptions. Bucks within reach of a reasonable number of hunters rarely attain full maturity; in some places—like much of my own state and neighboring Pennsylvania—nearly *90 percent* of the bucks born in any given year are killed at eighteen months, which is when they usually first have visible antlers. That's a staggering waste of, among other things, young life, and it represents an enormous waste of reproductive energy and labor.

Trophy hunting, with its premium on big antlers, is most viable only where a reasonable number of deer manage to attain full maturity (roughly three to six years) and antler growth. It's an admirable and perhaps even morally commendable approach: allow deer to live full lives before dropping the curtain. Everybody wins, including the deer.

And if you think old age is a drag for us humans, imagine being a nine-year-old deer in the dead of winter, too enfeebled to feed or move, patiently awaiting death as a pack of coyotes tears at your hocks and intestines.

Recent science also challenges some of our received wisdom. A highly controlled scientific study of whitetail breeding in Texas and other southern whitetail precincts showed that, contrary to cracker-barrel opinion, the biggest, most dominant bucks—the specimens that theoretically carry the integrity of the herd in their loins—were not nearly as dominant or prolific as everyone imagined, at least not by the time they attained trophy status.

The study demonstrated that relatively young (two-and-a-half- and three-and-a-half-year-old) deer were the most active and successful breeders. And those "decent" bucks, which usually have more than single-spike antlers, but not necessarily trophy racks, are the ones that most hunters simply won't pass up. The guy holding out for the monster buck has science on his side, in terms of herd health and genetics, because Old Mossy Horn is done as a vigorous breeder, if not as a wise, stealthy ghost of the woods.

The chance that a buck will make it to old age in areas accessible to hunters is slim to none. Yet even on my own home grounds, the grapevine every season hums with reported sightings of a few bucks in the 140 or even 150 B&C class—the baseline for a whitetail trophy-seeker in the northeast, even though antlers of that score fall at least 10 points short of making the revered B&C book.

I would take a buck like that in a heartbeat, for my own

plight was a sad one. I've always been so fearful that no buck I've shot would break the 100 B&C mark that I'm scared to score them. I was aiming to fix that.

I stopped to poke around in Corning and found it well-kept and pretty, with a gauntlet no tourist could resist: antique shops alternating with jewelry and crystal boutiques, leather-goods shops, emporiums offering the "world's best" homemade fudge, and art. But something was missing, amid all the handsome gaslights, colorful flower boxes, and reproduction turn-of-the-century storefronts: there was no "sporting goods" store of the kind that once was a regional magnet for folks interested in guns, ammo, duck calls, crusher hats, and woolen long johns.

The American sporting goods store has given way to the year-round "Christmas Shoppe" (*Over four thousand orna-ments in stock!*) and other specialty units. The few old-school stores that deal in guns and fishing tackle have been driven into shabby and decaying strip malls on the fringes of town, to hud-dle alongside the Chinese takeaway restaurant, the "Images" hair salon, and the Brazilian waxing parlor.

I picked up some Scotch and a few bottles of wine for Tom Daly and pushed on, feeling a little nervous. I'd never hunted with Tom, but he's one of those guys who seems to have it all figured out. He's a painter (canvas, not house) who specializes in landscapes and still lifes, in both watercolors and oils.

I've been an admirer of Tom's work for a long time, and fi-nally met him the previous fall at a conservation-related dinner. We struck up a conversation about deer hunting, and I learned that he isn't just a deer hunter, he's an archer—part of that splinter group of bow hunters who eschew modern compound bows, like my own Mathews, in favor of "primitive" or "tradi-tional" instruments, including the longbows once toted around by Robin Hood and his band of merry men. (Some of those outlaws were also hunters, and ended up slightly less than ecstatic when they were caught poaching deer on the king's land. They were then hung by the neck—often from their own bowstrings instead of rope.)

These days, the compound bow, which looks more like some weird electronic musical instrument than that thing you made as a kid with a stick and some string, is such a refined and technologically superior killing instrument that, despite its obvious lineage, it's really more like a firearm, albeit with a drastically reduced range.

A good compound bow, with all the requisite accessories, also can cost well over a thousand dollars—nearly twice as much as a high-quality rifle. Compound bows appeal to hunters who have a zest for "fair chase" (the ethic that attempts to keep hunter and hunted on a relatively level playing field) along with an interest in high-tech articulations of low-tech, traditional weapons.

Tom, by contrast, comes by his bows the old-fashioned way. He makes them—from scratch. After our conversation in New York, I decided that I couldn't imagine a more fitting way to open the bow season than in the company of Thomas Aquinas Daly—painter, outdoorsman, and traditional archer. If I were going to go all out this year, I might as well cover all the hunting bases and immerse myself totally in the deer hunting subculture.

What I didn't really envision was that Tom would think this was a good idea as well and invite me up for opening weekend.

I got off the interstate at Dansville and crawled through the small country town, exchanging a friendly wave with an elderly gent in porkpie hat sitting in a folding aluminum beach chair, just watching the cars go by. I guess there's only so much whittling a man can take in any given day.

Soon I was on a winding roller coaster of a two-lane black-top lined with yellow "deer crossing" signs, each bearing the image of a leaping buck. I fell in behind a beater pickup truck, with a gun rack and a decal of a wind turbine with the familiar European-style red circle and slash. A few miles on, I passed a large piece of plywood propped roughly on a lawn, bearing the legend: NO WIND TURBINES.

I was looking for the town of Bliss, where I would pick up a dirt road on the last leg of my trip. Semidistracted, I pulled up a long incline and . . . *Wham!* Wind turbines—giant three-hundred-foot-tall towers, with propeller blades like long, freakish steak knives—towered over me. And I knew, viscerally, that if I lived in this place called Bliss, I'd be thinking, like the guy in the pickup I passed miles back: *What the hell are the environmentalists doing to my town?*

About five hours after I left Andes, I pulled off the road and onto a crushed stone driveway alongside a well-maintained barn. A good portion of the structure's south side was covered in dark green ivy, a handsome contrast to the deep red siding. The ivy rippled in the breeze, the golden highlights of the afternoon sun crossed it in waves. Nearby, trees towered over a dark, pretty little house with mullioned windows. It was the kind of well-kept place that belonged to someone who cared deeply about details.

Sweet, I thought. *I sure hope it's the right place.*

2

Blood Trail to Nowhere

EAST ARCADE, NEW YORK, OCTOBER 12–13

TOM DALY, SLIGHTLY BUILT but obviously fit, emerged from the mudroom at the back of his house, wearing blue jeans and a simple gray cotton sweatshirt. He's light on his feet, even though his hair and neat beard are almost pure white. Tom is fair-skinned, with the watery blue eyes that are familiar to anyone who's spent any time in an Irish tavern. Only Tom is an Irishman who hardly drinks. What he does is paint—and hunt whitetail deer.

He greeted me warmly, showed me into the house, and introduced me to his wife, an attractive brunette named Chris. They have two dogs and two grown children, gone from the nest.

It's always a good sign when a guy's barn is bigger than his house and contains more stuff. Tom's has been transformed into his art studio, a stable for Chris's three horses, a garage for his boat and trailer (his spinning rods were still rigged with the summer's Mister Twister plastic crappie baits), and four or five additional rooms providing plenty of space for a man who's got his own personal lathe and all the tools required for (among other things) carving wooden decoys, working on an outboard motor, making long and recurve bows and split-cane bamboo fishing rods—and even a little recreational welding.

"I don't know about you, but I get obsessed when I get into something," Tom said. "I tend to go full bore. I did a lot of trapping before I took up bow hunting about twenty years ago. I used to see such big bucks back then . . . and I never cared. It was actually funny. Bow hunters sometimes stole foxes out of my traps, so I hated them."

Tom's barn also contains an indoor shooting range, where he can fire off arrows from as far away as fifty or sixty feet—distance enough for keeping your eye and form intact year-round.

My bow is a compound, so-called because the bowstring isn't attached to the bow, but rides in a loop of pulleys at either end of the bow. Also, the three-piece frame is made from different materials. The two limbs are made from graphite and fiberglass, and attach to a stiff, central aluminum piece called the riser, at the center of which is the grip.

The limbs of a compound are so stiff that they can launch an arrow at 315 feet per second—at least twice the speed of a traditional archer's bow. But it takes nearly superhuman strength to fully draw and hold an arrow against the resistance, hence the ingenious feature called "let-off."

As you approach full draw (just before your arms begin to quiver and turn to Jell-O), the pulleys rotate and, because of the camlike shape of the wheels, the tension suddenly lets off—not entirely, but enough to allow you to hold at full draw for as long as eight or ten seconds. In deer hunting, that can be an eternity, and it allows you to wait for a good moment, if not forever, to shoot.

Tom's bow is a handsome recurve (the tips at either end curve out and away from the shooter) that he made in 2001,

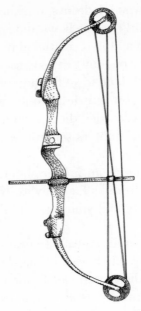

A compound bow, with the cams and cables that create "let-off."

at about the same time I bought my compound. I admired its beautiful curves and lustrous finish. He said, almost apologetically, "When I took up hunting with the bow, I bought a compound and killed a deer with it. But all the while I was thinking, *This is a little strange, what the hell is this thing?* It just didn't feel right in my hand. So I decided to make my own traditional bow."

I self-consciously slipped on my release, a glovelike device with a mechanical trigger that clips right onto the bowstring. A compound shooter doesn't even draw his bow the old-fashioned way, with his fingers; he clips the release onto the string and uses—and needs—the strength in his arms and back to draw back to the point of let-off.

I slipped one of my thin, ultralight carbon arrows into the arrow rest, clipped on the release, and settled myself with

A recurve bow.

feet and shoulders perpendicular to the target. Taking a deep breath, I drew back and, as the let-off kicked in, I peered through the peep sight at the uppermost of three pins made with light-gathering, fluorescent fiber-optic wire. Each adjustable pin represented a different distance; mine were set to ten (green), twenty (orange), and thirty (red) yards. But I flinched as I squeezed the trigger, and the arrow flew about two feet high and to the right of the bull's-eye.

I glanced at Tom, who was trying to hide his skepticism.

I muttered something about being a little nervous. After that, though, I was okay. I shot eleven more arrows, most of which landed within inches of each other in an area about the size of a dinner plate, which is roughly the size of the area you need to hit to make a clean, quick kill on a deer standing broadside.

Then it was Tom's turn. Instead of an engineered release, he slipped his fingers into a small leather pad. He took one of the arrows he assembles himself, from store-bought materials (although he prefers barred turkey primary feathers for vanes). I noticed that he had glued a small hank of soft, fluorescent orange polyester fibers to the nock-end of the arrow. "They're like tracer rounds in a gun," he said. "The contrast against the brown hair of a deer is so striking that you have no doubt about where your arrow hits."

Tom's traditional style was markedly different from mine. He crouched as he drew, rotating his shoulders toward the target with the bow roughly at forty-five degrees to the ground. In one smooth, fluid motion, he released the arrow. Who knew I'd be hunting with an Irish Indian? "It's instinctive shooting," he explained. "A compound is like a rifle; you draw, aim, and fire. This is more like pulling a six-shooter in a gunfight." Who knew I'd be hunting with an Irish cowboy?

We still had a little daylight left, so we hopped in Tom's truck to do a little scouting. Tom's property of two-hundred-plus acres is ideal whitetail habitat, featuring a big cornfield as well as a hay meadow rising to a forested ridge that curves around a steep, U-shaped basin with a creek, a swamp, and dense cover at the bottom. The deer use the ridge to travel between feeding and bedding areas down in the basin.

We threaded our way along an obvious deer trail through a stand of mixed pines and hardwoods; Tom wanted me to see the tree stand from which I'd be hunting in the morning. He stopped and gestured toward a twisted trunk hardly larger around than a telephone pole. I had rather expected something a little more . . . artistic. Perhaps a neat little hut perched on stilts, with thatched roof and a Swiss cuckoo clock?

A series of evenly spaced screw-in steps—each about the size of a railroad spike—led up the trunk of the tree about fifteen feet, to a steel post with a fold-out platform about the size of a doormat.

"That's my basic tree stand," Tom said. "I have a bunch of them all over the place. I bought a commercial one a few years ago for about eighty bucks and decided what the hell—I can copy it and weld up a bunch easy enough."

He paused. "Hell, I didn't even know how to weld." Reading my mind, he quickly added, "They're sturdier than they look. It's just that I like to keep a low profile."

I took a deep breath and clipped my safety harness onto the Prusik hitch tied onto the heavy nylon safety rope. The Prusik hitch moves easily on the rope, but in the event of a sudden downward tug caused by, say, a guy falling out of the tree, it locks up and prevents the knot from slipping. Of course, this leaves said guy dangling and twisting on the safety rope, screaming for help while alone in the woods. But you cross that bridge when you come to it.

I felt apprehensive about the ascent, but begging off was not an option. This is part of the nimrod's code. If your host advises you to shimmy up that three-hundred-foot-tall flagpole in front of the Dodge dealership and sit there in the dark, with the wind blowing at twenty-five miles per hour, you just say: *Great! See you back at the truck at dusk . . .*

I had to do a little twisting and ducking, but I got to the top step, flipped down the platform, and, hugging the tree with one arm, took the last and most unnerving step—out onto the platform with nothing beneath it but air. It felt solid. I folded down the tiny seat at the top end of the center pole and sat down with my back against the tree, noticing hooks where I could hang things within easy reach higher up on the tree.

The stand overlooked a trail coming off the steep slope and the basin below. There were two apple trees nearby, and a section of snow fence.

"I put the fence there," Tom said, his eyes twinkling. "It funnels the deer toward the tree."

Strategically, the setup was perfect. *Would this be where I killed my big buck,* I wondered, as the smoky haze of nightfall enveloped us.

Tom's taillights disappeared in the dark and I was left standing by the road, bow in one hand and backpack in the other. It was opening morning of bow-hunting season. I started down the trail to my stand, clutching my LED flashlight.

Has any piece of gear changed for the better more dramatically than the common flashlight? Yesterday's heavy war club, with its tube full of weighty D batteries that projected an anemic, flickering yellow light, is a thing of the past. Today, you get eight or ten times the illumination with a stylus-type flashlight that's the size and shape of a number two yellow pencil and clips to the brim of your cap.

I found my way to the tree stand. The gray light was sufficient for climbing without a light. By the time I stepped onto the stand, I was perspiring. I sorted my gear and hung it from various hooks and nubs on the tree. I nocked an arrow and pushed the graphite shaft into the arrow rest.

I was all set, and the woods were slowly coming to life. Indiscernible objects materialized before my eyes. A bump on a tree morphed into a porcupine, a mottled shadow emerged as a deadfall. The first birds began to twitter and to the east, the distant ridges and treetops were limned in buttery light.

I was lightly dressed under my camo fatigues, but I was still warm. Before long, a red squirrel got busy on the ground below me. It raced up and down various trees, pausing on a limb here and there to sound a shrill, chattering call.

Unable to rouse a playmate, the squirrel finally settled on breakfast. It skittered up the gnarled old apple tree about twelve yards out and below me, and selected a dented yellow fruit. The apple had to be at least three times the size and weight of the squirrel's head, but the little guy lifted it with ease and ran down the tree, carrying it in his mouth. Then it ran up my tree and, pausing on a branch below me, set the apple into the crotch and ran off again.

The leaves were still pretty thick on the shrubs and hardwoods, forcing me to rely on my ears more than my eyes. Overhead, above the perforated, pale green canopy, the sky was delicate blue tinged with orange as the day poured light into the sky. I heard turkeys fly down from their roost beyond the dropoff into the basin, and the distant uproar of crows.

It was very quiet, and probably too warm for deer to be moving much, a disadvantage of the early season. But I sat with my arms folded, allowing my mind to drift this way and that as I waited, watching and alert. I was moving into slow time—hunting time.

The longer you sit, the more your mind wanders, until after a couple of hours on a really quiet day, you're apt to find yourself wondering what would have happened if America had been discovered by a Polish guy instead of an Italian, or what Madonna would be doing today if she had been born into a humble family in Uzbekistan instead of Bay City, Michigan. Eventually, you fall into a semiconscious state comparable to meditation, but without the chanting and funky sandals.

I contemplated the strange disconnect between so many "smart" people, who revere and romanticize all things Native American, but ridicule deer hunting and the role it plays in our culture. Indians lived to hunt; they were ecstatic on the buffalo trail, and scores spent the bulk of their days hunkered down in swamps or crouched behind deadfalls, patiently waiting to kill something. That's deer hunting in a nutshell, and today's version isn't all that different from the original. Oh, sure, today we hunt less from necessity than from a hunger for the experience, but which plays a greater part in anyone's life anyway?

When someone asks me why I hunt, I'm always tempted to

say something insufferably arrogant, like: "Because I'm haunted by the spirit and imbued with the instincts of the Iroquois who used to live yonder, where those McMansions and that thirty-seven-screen multiplex cinema now stand. And who are *your* spiritual forbears, the Rat Pack?"

My idle thoughts vanished as I heard the telltale shuffling of hoofs through dry leaves. It came from just over the lip of the basin, probably on the main trail. I snatched the bow from the hook and checked to make sure my arrow was properly nocked . . . I slowly rose from the small seat, hooked my release to the bowstring, and went through a mental checklist: *Don't rush . . . draw at the right moment . . . take a deep breath as you draw, hold just back of the buck's front leg . . . buck? Gosh, what if it's a buck—a really big buck!*

Slow down, hoss . . .

The deer walked over the crest, right where I expected. It was a doe, a nice, fat, healthy one. I waited for fawns or other deer to appear behind her, but she was alone. Her black eyes caught the gleam of the sun and her olive gray coat was flawless.

Over breakfast, Tom had told me he was in the habit of annually donating the meat of a doe to a family just down the road from his place. Maybe I could save Tom the trouble of field-dressing and dragging out a deer for them; it would be a nice gesture on my part, and I would get a chance to test my skill.

In New York state, rifle season is restricted to killing bucks only, although special "doe tags" are available in many areas. But the bow hunter may kill a deer of either sex, because the hunt is used to keep deer populations in check. So while this wasn't the big whitetail buck I longed to meet, the conditions for making a clean kill were ideal: she would pass fewer than twenty yards from me, broadside.

The doe paused to browse some briars. A moment later, she turned slightly and lowered her muzzle to nose for forbs at ground level. Out of her line of vision, I drew the arrow. Broad-side again, she took three steps. I thought a quick prayer and settled my green pin just back of the top of her left leg. I gently squeezed the release.

The arrow hit with a dull *whap!* The stillness was shattered by a sharp bleat. The doe went down, kicking clods of dirt and grass, and then she slithered off under the nearby deadfall and disappeared from view on the other side. I carefully marked the spot in my mind.

I didn't see exactly where the arrow hit. But I was trying for the preferred double-lung shot. An arrow, unlike a bul-let, doesn't kill by inflicting massive trauma and shock, which is why the instant kill shot is rare. The typical arrowhead, or broadhead, is basically an elaborate two- or three-sided razor-blade that kills by slicing. The vital organs of a whitetail are packed in the area just behind the top of the front legs, some-what protected by the rib cage.

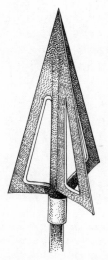

The broadhead is attached to the front tip of the arrow shaft.

A well-placed arrow will often pass clear through a deer, and so quickly that the animal may just buck, as if stung by a bee, look around, and casually walk away. Meanwhile, the entry and exit wounds left by the arrow, and the damaged organs inside, are hemorrhaging. A deer may lose enough blood to die in just minutes; a shot that gets a piece of the heart can put the animal down where it stands, although even that isn't guaranteed.

The vital organs of a deer. The double-lung shot is the preferred goal for gun as well as bow hunters, partly because it may also destroy part or all of the heart. Shots to the stomach or intestines will often mortally wound a deer, while giving it enough time to escape a hunter.

Even with a killing shot, a deer may run off and go for more than a hundred yards before it piles up. At other times, it might go just a short distance and, growing weak, lie down and expire. But even a badly wounded deer will find the energy to leap up and flee if it's still alive when you approach. For that reason, you don't come down from your stand until a good forty-five minutes after the shot, no matter how curious you are, or how certain that you made a good, clean kill. It was 9:10 A.M., and Tom wasn't picking me up for about two more hours. I was in no rush to recover the deer.

I grew anxious as I sat and reviewed the situation. The reaction of the deer made me worry that I'd shot too high and missed the lungs. Dealing death entails certain responsibilities, chief among them the ability to deal it with a good purpose, respectfully, competently, and swiftly. I was okay on the first two fronts; it was the latter two that concerned me.

I gave it about fifteen minutes, then very quietly climbed down, knowing that I could approach the point-of-impact without making any noise. And what breeze there was would carry my scent back over my shoulders. The place where the doe fell was scuffed up, but the blood, a fair amount of it, had been absorbed in the soil. I spotted a bright green vane poking out of the grass ten feet distant and retrieved the arrow.

I was using a "mechanical" broadhead with three blades that open on contact, like an umbrella activated by pushing its tip against something solid. The blades were bloody, and one of them was bent almost in half. The shaft of the arrow was smeared with blood, but none of the greenish matter that suggested the worst-case scenario, a gut shot that leads to slow death without impairing the animal's strength or stamina in the short term.

The absence of blood on the vanes was discouraging; there was no way the arrow went clean through the doe. The bent blade suggested that the arrow hit, stuck, and twisted loose as the deer fell on it. My spirits sank, but they lifted when I found significant blood splashed on the ferns and shrubs around the deadfall.

I sat on a stump for twenty minutes, thinking. The slope fell away quickly on the far side of the deadfall, just fifty feet away. I'd have a good view of the wooded slope beyond. Maybe I'd find the doe expired, or a good blood trail. It would be wise to wait for Tom, so he could help with the tracking, but I was unsettled. I decided to steal over and stealthily scan the slope.

I painstakingly worked my way through the tangle of underbrush, on hands and knees, delicately moving small branches and twigs out of the way in order not to snap them. Beyond the thickest stuff, a hummock of grass partly blocked my view. I began to get up on my knees—and froze. The doe, lying down and leaning against the trunk of an ash tree, stared at me with those black, moist eyes. She was just beyond the crest of the swale. I melted back to the ground, rolled onto my back, closed my eyes, and silently cursed myself out.

I heard shuffling in the leaves. Did the doe get up, or was it my imagination? A heavier sound followed; maybe the weakened doe had stood—and collapsed. The one thing I knew was that if I alarmed the doe any further, she would find the adrenaline to run.

My only option was to go out to the road and wait for Tom. *The road to hell is paved with good intentions,* I thought bitterly. So much for providing meat to the neighbors.

Tom didn't see much on his own hunt, and he listened to my summary and confident prediction that the doe would be lying dead not far from the ash tree. He unrolled a long length of toilet paper, shoved it in his jacket pocket, and asked me a few pertinent questions, among which one struck me: "Did you aim for the lower third of the body? That's the best way to make sure you hit in the kill zone."

I hesitated before answering, "I think so."

We returned to the ash and examined the large crimson smear on the bark; we also found blood where the doe had walked away, downhill. But the trail went cold quickly. We fanned out, inspecting the ground for blood. Finally, Tom called me over. Using a thin stick about the size of a conductor's baton, he pointed out a single, glossy red droplet of blood on a yellow maple leaf. "She went off the trail," he muttered. "No wonder we lost her."

Tom took out his toilet paper, pinched off and rolled up a small piece, and laid it on the leaf. Then we resumed looking. We found a succession of ferns and leaves with a bit of blood on them, and followed the trail easily for about forty yards. Tom left a pinch of paper at each sign. But we ran out of luck again. Tom looked back up the way we'd come, ticking off our toilet paper markers as he pointed to them with his baton and tried to read something into the path of travel.

We spread out and began looking again, often getting down on our hands and knees to determine if a red mark was blood or just seasonal pigmentation in the fallen leaves and undergrowth. Tom gently poked leaves this way and that with his stick. My hopes were fading, quickly, and I felt guilty about wasting Tom's time on opening day. But at one point, he muttered without looking up: "This is what I love doing most. For me, it's not so much about the actual hunting as the woodsmanship and the skills that come into play at every stage of a hunt."

Thanks mostly to Tom's forensic work, we picked up the trail again. We had blood for another sixty yards, but the trail led into a stony thicket of thorn apple trees, where we no longer had contrasting leaves. The trail of toilet paper zigzagged up the incline behind us, without rhyme or reason. And there was no sign that the deer had stopped. She seemed to be walking, not running—perhaps she was conserving her energy.

The meager signs led us to an old skid road. Try as we might, we found no blood in the track, where it would have been easy to pick up against the lime green moss. And we found none along the far side of the trail. It seemed as if the deer had come to the edge of the road and—vanished.

Ninety minutes had gone by since we started looking, and the truth was becoming inescapable. Finally, Tom straightened up. He said: "I think we've run out the string."

He toyed with his baton and added, "It happens."

I knew he wasn't just saying that, but I hated to give up. I hated to face the truth: I missed the easiest of shots. This was a nightmare scenario at the best of times, and an awful way to embark on a year when I hoped to put all my knowledge and what I thought were reasonable skills to the ultimate test. A guy just going out to get a deer to put in his freezer could not have done worse.

"I've lost my share, too," Tom said, trying to console me. "But I think she'll recover, because all the signs indicate a flesh wound . . .

"We might as well be optimistic about it."

We followed the trail of toilet tissue back up to the top of the ridge and walked back to the truck, each of us lost in his own thoughts.

Tom's bow-making workshop is tidy and Spartan, with various bows, some half-completed, lying here and there. He carefully removed an old recurve from a shelf and, with the vaguely surprised look that I would come to know pretty well, said: "I made this one out of Osage orange, and I killed the first eight deer I shot at with it. That's an incredible streak. I still can't believe it myself."

An experienced bow maker, or "bowyer," can shave out a serviceable longbow (or "stickbow," in the archer's lingo) in as little as a day. It's nothing more than a straight piece of high-quality wood (the yew tree is the traditional favorite) with a handle built up around the middle and notched ends to accommodate the string.

The recurve bow represented a great technological leap, taken in the second millennium, B.C. (that's Before Camo). The tips on either end of a recurve curl away from the archer, and the physics therein enable the bow to store greater energy more efficiently and allow for the bow to be shorter and more maneuverable—significant advantages to the hunter-warriors among people like the Mongols, Scythians, and Hyksos.

But because of the greater strain on recurves, barbarians often found themselves holding a handful of splinters at the most inconvenient of times. They soon discovered that bows incorporating laminations—thin, flat layers of various substances (animal horn, different woods, or leathery sinew) bound or bonded together—were far stronger, and the concept of a composite bow was born.

Tom's own bow began as a block of red elm three feet long, two inches wide, and eight inches deep, a few thin strips of fiberglass, and a block of bocote, or Mexican rosewood, about the size of a loaf of bread. For starters, Tom shaved six thin laminations out of the elm, spliced them together into three sixty-inch by two-inch lengths that resembled strips of stiff ribbon. Then he cut two strips of fiberglass to the same dimensions and sandwiched the three strips of elm between them. The thickness of the bow, front to back, determines its draw weight, or the power required to pull back the string—a factor expressed in pounds.

The block of bocote would become the handle, incorporating the arrow rest. Tom chose that wood because it's extremely hard and also looks sharp—it has a warm, golden glow and interesting, variegated markings. The handle must fit the shooter's hand comfortably, and it has to join with the limbs smoothly. On Tom's bow, the bocote wood is so thin where it meets the limbs of the bow that it's semitranslucent. Shaving it that close calls for a steady hand, while marrying these components into a bow calls for wearing a hazmat suit.

With the basic pieces ready, Tom mixed up a big batch of a heat-activated epoxy. He set up his mold, a rectangular, two-part box in which the bow would be made. He lined the bottom of this long, thin box with Saran wrap, to keep the epoxy from seeping out of the laminations and fusing the bow to the mold. He assembled the components in the mold, lathering them with epoxy.

"It gets messy," he explained. "You just have to keep gluing and adding, gluing and adding. You have to have faith, because all the pieces are sliding around and sometimes it's hard to imagine how anything useful can come out of it."

With the components glued up and secured in the form, Tom carefully smoothed out and laid a section of fire hose over the entire works. He placed the lid half of the form on top, tightened down the screws, and, with the help of an air compressor, inflated the hose through the same kind of valve used in tires.

Tom's eyes grew big as he confessed, "The whole works, box and all, gets so tight from the air pressure that you think the whole frickin' thing is going to blow up. It scares the shit out of you."

The entire mold goes into a wooden box containing four two-hundred-watt light bulbs. It's basically a homemade plywood oven in which Tom cooked the ingredients for four hours, using an oven thermometer to make sure he never exceeded the 150-degree mark. If the temperature crept too high, Tom eased off on the screws and placed spacers under the lid of the box, allowing cooler air to enter.

Fresh out of the mold, the bow looked woeful, but that's when, as Tom said, "The fun begins." That is, if your idea of fun is, say, whittling a bar of soap into a replica of the Taj Mahal. It isn't easy to shape something as large, curved, unwieldy, and symmetrical as a bow, but it's critical to get the proportions exactly right; otherwise, the bow either won't shoot straight, or it will quickly break under stress at its weakest point. Tom calculated the precise dimensions and drafted a template that he taped on the rough bow. Then he went to work with a scriber and a band saw. When he was finally finished with the tracing, shaping, and details, he hung the bow from a string and applied four coats of polyurethane. "A hard lacquer is better," he conceded. "But working with that stuff . . . it *will* kill you."

While commercially made traditional and recurve bows are now comparable in price to compounds, Tom estimates that his cash outlay for the bow was fifty, sixty bucks. The finished product is elegant, unique, and—to its maker—priceless. You can't tell Tom's bow from a commercially sold one without resorting to a magnifying glass.

The scary part is that in his own mind, Tom doesn't believe that any of this is all that difficult: "I'm into aesthetics, I suppose. But it's not like I'm against technology. For chrissakes, I use an electronic fish-finder in my boat! I guess I just felt that there was a right way to do this. And look—I could have gone totally primitive, made my bow out of a stick, using sinew for string, and chipping out my own obsidian arrowheads. What do I look like, some kind of wacko purist?"

But all the while, as Tom walked me through his bow-making process, my mind kept returning to the morning's events. A clean kill represents closure in more ways than one. Wounding an animal leaves a hunter with grating doubts and feelings of shame.

Hunting with the rifle is a less intimate, intense experience, with a lower premium on skill and stealth. Any nimrod can hit a pie plate at a hundred yards with one of today's highly accurate rifle and scope combinations. But the price for leveling the playing field, which falls under the general philosophy known as "fair chase," can be high, and I'd just paid it.

Guilt is a modern conceit, and part of my legacy as a twenty-first-century man. I never mistake myself for a Lakota Sioux, but I also know that back when hunting was a less complicated thing—back before guns and trucks and scopes and compound bows and the birth of an entire culture dedicated to trophy hunting, just for sport—the only remorse felt by native hunters who pin-cushioned a grizzly bear or watched an elk run off, festooned with arrows, was that the critter got away.

I could imagine a Piegan Blackfoot or Nez Perce hunter feeling foolish, incompetent, or angry. But I can't imagine him ever feeling guilty.

3

The Milkweed Factor

EAST ARCADE, NEW YORK, OCTOBER 13-14

L ATER THAT SAME DAY, Tom took me to a piece of flat woods surrounding a black pond filled with teal and geese. It was a warm afternoon, bright with golden autumn sunshine. I enjoyed it while I could, for Tom had plans. He was sending me to hunker down in a ground blind that he had excavated in the giant root ball of a long-fallen tree.

The blind was surrounded by dense brush, including a fragrant wild rose. Entering the blind was like going down a rabbit hole, but once I squeezed inside, the foam seat on a thick ledge of root was comfortable, and I had a perfect window out of which to watch, or shoot. The forest before me was mature, with significant gaps between the maple, ash, and pine trees. It was a hiding place worthy of an Indian.

Shortly after I settled in with bow in hand, a partridge flushed and, rocketing through the trees, almost crash-landed in my face. It veered away from my window so late that I felt the breeze of its passing on my cheeks.

Because of how things had gone earlier that morning, I knew

that if I had another shot at a whitetail, I had to make it count. And I wasn't going to play the great provider this time. I would only draw on a big buck. Judging from the quality of the rubs on some of the nearby trees, where a buck had lacerated the bark with his antlers, I might have the chance to do just that.

But it was so warm that the deer were likely to remain bedded until the cool of evening descended on the forest. I sat back and drifted off into the deep time of the hunt. At dusk, I crawled out of the root ball and walked the short distance to the pond. Tom was already there, patiently waiting, part of a scene he might have painted himself. He was still as a heron and holding his recurve loosely by his side. The sky behind him was silver and in places almost entirely black with flocks of honking geese.

Back in the barn, changing out of our hunting garb, Tom remarked: "I think this whole camo thing has gotten pretty silly."

I felt a little weird, given that I was sporting an Advantage Timber camo backpack, Tru-Leaf matching camo fatigue pants and jacket, a camo Boonie hat, Mathews bow with a camo riser and limbs, and a knife with a camo handle. If I went in for nail polish, I suppose that would have been camo, too—perhaps Trebark, to offset the lighter tones of my backpack?

Tom himself was wearing heavy gray woolen pants, the kind old men wear with the waistband just south of their armpits, and red suspenders.

"What exactly do you mean?" I said.

"Well, if you stand in front of me wearing camo, you still have the outline of a human being. That's the big thing, I think. If you really want to be hidden, you have to do like certain African tribesmen. You want to paint yourself vertically, half-black, half-white. Now *that* really breaks up the human silhouette."

Tom is full of tricks and sly, wise ideas. He showed me a stick that he'd whittled himself in the shape of the small letter *t*. He explained that it was a tool he used to simplify the most un-savory part of field-dressing a deer—removing the intestinal plumbing and anal canal without leaking toxic feces or undi-gested matter onto the meat.

The stick works like a corkscrew. The first thing you do af-ter the deer is down is insert it in the anus, cross-end first, and twist about half a turn. When you withdraw the stick, it pulls out enough of the elastic anal canal to allow you to snip and tie it off. That way, when you slit open the belly to excavate the or-gans, you can pull out the stomach, intestines, and entire anal tract without having the mess you get if you cut the canal.

"I call it the ace in the hole," Tom said, with a straight face. "And I heard they make something like it now, in orange plastic."

"Does it come in camo?"

Tom laughed. "If it doesn't yet, it will . . . it will."

Of that I had no doubt. Nothing captures the entrepreneurial genius of the hunting industry, or the sensibility of deer hunt-ers, better than the history of the camouflage clothing indus-try. Camo has evolved from practical field gear into a symbol, a declaration of values and lifestyle. That's why you commonly see people walking around the mall on a Wednesday afternoon in much of America dressed in Mossy Oak Break-Up, or any of the other dozen or so camo patterns on the market.

Jim Crumley is the founding father of this oddball industry, and he put it this way when we spoke: "Flying the flag—that's what camo is all about now, especially at a time when people are worried about losing their hunting rights and their guns."

Crumley began his career in camo in 1972, while he was still a marketing-education teacher in the Alexandria, Virginia, public school system. A bow hunter, Crumley knew the value of camo, but he was dissatisfied with the standard woodland green and tiger-stripe patterns developed by the U.S. military.

He'd noticed that the dominant colors in the woods during hunting season were mostly black, grays, and browns—and no military camo mimicked that.

Crumley often hunted on the Quantico Marine Corps Base in Virginia, where one of his companions was a beefy, gruff, cigar-chomping drill instructor. They were walking down a tank trail after hunting one morning when Crumley's companion had a *Eureka!* moment. He stopped in his tracks and, according to Crumley, said: "I've got it! I know why this camo is lousy for hunting. The U.S. military has never designed a camo made for warfare in the United States."

It was an excellent point, but there was something else. The military wanted its soldiers to look like . . . nothing. The idea, Crumley explained, was for soldiers to just melt into the landscape. But for a variety of reasons, including gun safety, hunters would be better off if they were able to blend into the environment, without actually seeming to disappear. In other words, the ideal hunting camo shouldn't be *too* good.

Crumley, who hunted only in the eastern forests, knew that most hunters commonly positioned themselves with their backs to tree trunks on or above the ground. "The human body is very nicely designed to blend with a tree trunk, and that suggested camo with a vertical design."

After mulling over the problem for months, Crumley took the plunge. He bought some Dickies work clothes and gray Rit dye, and before you can say "bathtub disaster," the world had its first camo pattern developed exclusively for hunting. He fine-tuned the design and colors and came up with a predominantly gray and black pattern that simulated the bark of the most common hardwood trees (maple, ash, and oak).

For the next several years, while he worked as a school administrator, Crumley took the same roller coaster ride as many other small-business entrepreneurs. He had trouble figuring out how to get his pattern printed onto fabric; he had trouble finding a textile manufacturer who would make the relatively small amount of Trebark fabric (for that was the name he settled on) he needed to get started. Crumley had to work out how to sew the material into clothes that fit. He didn't have enough money, so he went into hock. But he finally got enough Trebark coveralls sewn up to test the market. He took out an ad in *Bowhunter* magazine in July 1980.

Crumley rented a special post office box for his budding business. Within a few weeks, he received the issue of *Bowhunter* containing his ad. Every day from then on, he rushed home after work to check his p.o. box for incoming orders. He always found it empty. After fourteen increasingly depressing days, he finally had a single piece of mail. It was the bill for his ad.

Crestfallen, Crumley called *Bowhunter* to see if anything was wrong and was cheerfully told that the magazine he received had been a courtesy advance copy sent only to advertisers. The actual magazine would not go out to subscribers or the newsstands for another week.

About ten days later, Crumley went to his post office and found another slip summoning him to the front desk. When he presented the slip, the clerk disappeared into the back and soon reemerged—with an official U.S. Postal Service canvas sack filled with mail, most of it orders for his suit. He was a made man.

Crumley quit his job in 1981 to concentrate on his booming Trebark business. Within six years, two competitors emerged, and they quickly moved in to dominate the market: Bill Jordan (Realtree) and Toxey Haas (Mossy Oak). Crumley, an amiable, gregarious man, has no hard feelings about that, and he's remained friends with both of his original competitors. As he said, "The product is pretty simple. This business is about marketing and packaging to the nth degree, and those guys are great at it. The way I see it, I planted the field and they reaped the harvest."

In early 2000, Haas (Mossy Oak) bought Trebark, retaining Crumley within the company. The original Trebark pattern vanished (literally) from the market. Crumley has kept his hand in the business, though, and recently he brought back the original Trebark pattern—unchanged, but for the addition of a few rust-colored leaves in the pattern.

Since then, Crumley has shipped at least one order to every state in the union, and he believes that every one of those customers is over forty years old. "We're talking about guys who shot their first deer, maybe their first squirrel, wearing Trebark camo. Now, for the first time in fifteen years, they can get it again. There's a nostalgia factor there. Like I said, a lot of this is just plain marketing."

Indeed. Back in the day, one of the first places Crumley looked for a licensing deal for his Trebark pattern was with Easton, the company that has dominated the hunting arrow manufacturing field. Upon hearing Crumley's sales pitch, the president of the company said, "Wow. Camo arrows. It's a no-brainer. If we can keep these guys from finding their arrows in the woods, it's a gold mine!"

The camo market is "mature," perhaps overripe. You can get almost anything in camo, including toilet paper, and that begs the question: Is there anything you *don't* necessarily want in camo?

One of Crumley's new businesses is C.A.M.O. Enterprises, an outfit that can apply a high-quality, custom camo finish on firearms (or any other object, although he draws the line at dogs, kids, and wives). Periodically, Crumley gets a call from an embarrassed hunter who confesses that he laid down his Camonet-treated rifle to go behind a bush to answer the call of nature. But upon finishing, he was unable to find his firearm.

· · ·

A freak accident had knocked out the power to Tom Daly's big shed, where he does his barbecuing, so in the evening we stood in just the pale glow emanating from the grill as he cooked steaks.

The corner of the shed was piled high with traps—scary, medieval-looking steel contraptions, powered by giant springs. Next to trapping, even a blood sport like hunting may seem about as visceral an enterprise as rhythmic gymnastics. At one time, Tom ran traplines on as many as thirty farms, targeting beaver, fox, and coyote. He showed me a special slip-rig that allowed whitetail deer, for which he had a soft spot long before becoming an archer, to slip out of a trap unharmed (the law prohibits trapping game animals, like whitetail).

Guys like Daly and Jim Crumley might butt heads over the philosophy of camo, but both have found a way to live the dream, incorporating deer hunting into their daily lives in a way most nimrods can only fantasize about. Tom secured his two-hundred-acre piece of deer heaven through his art in a surprisingly direct way. When he put in a bid on the old farm he now owns, the owner called and suggested that instead of paying cash, Tom pay in paintings.

"I held the phone away from my mouth so the guy couldn't hear and practically hollered, 'Yes! There really is a God!'"

That wasn't the first manifestation of Providence in Tom's life. As an infant, he was abandoned and left somewhere in the town of Albany, although the precise details never were made clear to him. He didn't even have a proper birth certificate. He knows only that John and Grace Daly of Niagara Falls traveled to Albany to claim him as a son and give him a name. He was baptized Thomas Aquinas Daly in Albany's Chapel of the Maternity Hospital and Infant Home, and the baptismal certificate was the only form of identification he had for most of his young life.

John Daly was an undertaker, and when Tom was young he

was frequently summoned to help his father flip over a corpse that was being dolled up for his farewell party. It takes a man with a pretty strong stomach to think up a tool (as well as the name) like the ace in the hole.

John Daly had connections in Niagara Falls politics, which earned him a plum patronage position as the city's director of housing. When he wasn't taking care of some stiff or fulfilling his civic obligations, he was getting tight at the gin mill; according to his adopted son, you could find John with the regulars down at the local every night, including Christmas Eve. Grace Daly dealt with all this in the accepted fashion of the time. "She went to church daily," Tom said. "It seems she found something bad to pray about every day."

Although John Daly secretly hoped that his son would excel at football, the boy preferred riding his bike and fishing in the local creeks. Tom grew up very close to Niagara Falls, and the base of the thundering cascade was something like his local swimming hole. There was a big eddy about a quarter of a mile below the falls, he remembered, and it was a gas to just jump in and allow the powerful current carry you far out into the broad river—and then bring you back in a lazy arc and deposit you right back where you started.

"It was stupid, on the whole, because there was a very bad rapids right below the eddy. But we were young people, we didn't care. I basically lived down there. We had BB gun wars. We'd shoot each other. We were lucky nobody had an eye put out . . ."

Tom trained the barbecue fork he was using right between his own eyes. "*Poof!*"

John Daly often brought home yellow legal pads, which Tom promptly filled with drawings. He created his own baseball-themed comic strip featuring Vic Wertz and Johnny Rhodes, and his first "commissions" were pictures he drew for the nuns at his elementary school, Sacred Heart.

Tom soon discovered Buffalo's own Bob Kuhn, a gifted animal painter well-known for the illustrations he did for the popular outdoor magazines, like *Outdoor Life* and *Field and Stream.* "I got juiced up by that kind of stuff when I was fifteen, sixteen years old. I did a ton of paintings. You know, I'd put a leaping whitetail buck in the foreground, and under his belly you could see a guy in the distance, with his rifle up."

Tom planned to study fisheries biology at Cornell, but a Sacred Heart priest prevailed upon the Dalys, convincing them to send Tom to art school. Instead of Cornell, he enrolled at the University of Buffalo and eagerly absorbed everything he could about painting, drawing inspiration from the likes of Winslow Homer, Edward Hopper, and George Inness.

Tom worked for twenty-two years at a printing firm and raised a family (he has a total of six kids from two wives and "a pile" of grandchildren). But he always painted in his spare time, refining his technique and vision until he quit his day job in 1981 to concentrate exclusively on painting. His pictures are mysterious and confident testimonials to and about the natural world, and moods or beauties deeply felt and understood in his woodsman's heart. "I kind of have a feeling and try to convey that in the shape of some clouds, or the way a dead partridge looks hanging on a barn door. And you can always tell if you nailed it or not. That's the job of the artist—to convey feeling."

These aren't the best of days for guys whose pictures move you to say, "Wow, that's beautiful." Most of the stuff out there is more likely to make you think, *What the fuck? My six-year-old can do that!* Or as Tom said, "These days, you paint pictures of animals, and in the art world you're basically dog shit."

On that note, Tom grinned and raised his wineglass in a toast.

I took a sip of my Scotch and asked Tom about trapping. Back in the day, he got as much as sixty-five dollars for a red fox, forty for a gray. He also caught mink. "It was pretty good, for a while. I made a few thousand bucks. You know, Christmas money."

But Tom learned a great deal about animals as a trapper, and he chuckles to himself when he hears deer hunters bragging about their scouting prowess. The ways of deer are obvious and well-documented; they're stealthy, but not necessarily furtive.

"The life of a fox—now *that's* a big secret," Tom said. "A fox is something else. When I got one in a trap, I'd usually find it all curled up, asleep. Like the fox was just waiting for me to come wake it up. Killing it was the tough part. You stepped on its rib cage, hard, to crush the heart or liver. It's brutal. But that's the way you do it."

Tom poked a steak, frowning.

"What kind of bait do you use to trap a fox?"

Tom described his lure of choice: squares of woodchuck meat, "seasoned" in a tightly sealed glass jar, left out in hard sunlight for the length of one day. Any longer, and the bait would turn so putrid that even a fox would just roll in it, like a dog.

"Well, these steaks are just about done," Tom said. "You ready to eat?"

Tom was still trying to figure out which stands to hunt as we finished breakfast the following morning. It promised to be still and warm—an unlikely day for an encounter with a monster buck, but that was all right. It was just the second day of hunting season.

Theoretically, the deer were still following their normal summer routine when it came to feeding and bedding, but out in the fields at night the social interactions among the deer were subtly changing. They were sizing each other up for the rapidly approaching rut, or breeding season. Tom had told me there were a few dandy bucks running around, but they weren't likely to be wandering about in broad daylight. Older, wiser bucks often become almost exclusively nocturnal.

Tom decided to put me in a stand on the back side of his big meadow, where the land fell away toward the swamp. "There's some apple trees down in there, near thick brush," he explained. "You may catch a deer coming off the meadow, stopping to feed before he sneaks back into the swamp. Or sometimes, they'll come out of the thick brush for a snack."

Tom fiddled with a small Ziploc bag containing something that looked like giant, dried-out pea pods. He passed me one; it was a pod from a milkweed plant, a common noxious weed. It was already cracked open, and some of the silky white spores were beginning to separate from the rest. The spores open up like puffballs and float away on the wind like tiny parachutes— each of them a brave traveler intended to establish a new milkweed colony wherever the wind might take it.

Wind is the dominant factor in any whitetail bow hunt, and most gun hunts. A deer relies heavily on scent; its nose is a few thousand times more sensitive than ours. Wind-borne scent can drastically diminish your chances of even seeing a deer, at least if you're hunting outside that suburban bubble in which the odor of humans, dogs, hamburgers, plastic, and diesel fumes is an omnipresent fact of a whitetail's life. Thus, hunting upwind (where the breeze can carry your scent to the deer) is a cardinal sin. But while a strong blow is easy to read, zephyrs are endlessly tricky, and a wind direction indicator can show you that twenty yards from where you sit, the direction of the air currents suddenly changes.

Although a single milkweed pod contains a near-lifetime supply tightly packed and ready to use, the market teems with commercially made and marketed "windicators." These include ultralight polyester yarns (in blaze-orange, of course; camo remains a dream of yarn engineers), wispy fibers that you tie to your bow or gun, like little windsocks, and powder in a small plastic squeeze vial.

As far as I can tell, that powder is simple talc, so the only difference between the Whitetail Magic Industries product and a generic container of talc from Walgreens is that the former goes for about $4.99 for a third of an ounce, while Walgreens will sell you something like two pounds of talc for $1.89. But it doesn't come in a conveniently small container with the image of a monster buck on it.

It was still dark when Tom dropped me off. I slipped over the edge of the meadow and down a short, steep incline. I had no trouble finding the cherry tree where the slope leveled off along the fringe of an old, overgrown apple orchard.

Once again, I was hunting over a strategically placed section of snow fence meant to funnel deer past my tree. Instead of cutting clear shooting lanes in various directions, Tom had used wire and even sections of heavy, dead limbs to push or pull obstructions out of the way, leaving me with a nice web that kept me well-hidden but contained numerous windows for launching an arrow.

The stand was ideally located for watching the scrawny apple trees corkscrewing out of ground so stony than nothing else had the tenacity to poke up through the carpet of leaves. The mini-orchard was almost entirely surrounded by brush so dense that the three or four trails used by the deer were rutted. It was as good a setup for close-quarters bow hunting as I've seen.

I released one of the milkweed spores—it rose slightly and drifted off over my left shoulder. The air was perfect; any deer approaching upwind would surely turn and skedaddle without disturbing the orchard or brush beyond. The morning was cold and still. As the first rays of hard, clear light hit the side of a mountain visible beyond the treetops, I opened the thermos Tom had thoughtfully provided.

This fox-stomping former trapper with the ice-blue eyes was the same guy who painted one of my all-time favorite pictures, depicting a partially skinned buck hanging from a gambrel in a barn in soft, almost holy light. The hide hanging from the deer eerily resembles the skirt of a hand puppet. It beautifully represents the wonder of life, transcending the fact of death. Something a hunter understands.

While we had been talking about why we hunt, Tom gave me his version: "It's way down deep, it comes out of God knows where. It's primitive, but it's very real. Shooting the deer is the climax, but what I love is all the stuff that comes before, during, and after that moment. I love taking care of the animal, I really relish it. What I always wanted was to be really competent at all aspects of this—that's about as close as I can come to explaining my motivation. Gutting, skinning, cooling a deer— aging it, butchering it. I do all those things with equal pleasure. They sound simple. They are simple. But you'd be surprised how many people don't know how to do those things."

White fog hung over the swamp not far away, contrasting handsomely with the reds and yellows of the hardwoods on the slopes of the mountains beyond. I enjoyed the perfect autumn scene, but my reverie was interrupted by the unmistakable snort-wheeze of a deer. It's an odd sound, a cross between a brief, guttural cough and a cat's angry hiss. Sometimes it resembles the high-pitched hiss made by one of those annoying "whizzer whistle" toys.

The vocal language of a whitetail is primitive, consisting of four basic sounds, with a few specialized variations on each of them. The most distinctive is the burplike grunt of a buck, which he uses to contact does, or in a slightly softer modulation when he's tending a doe. The blat is a doe's vocalization, and she makes a slightly different blat when she's in estrus and seeking attention from a buck, alarmed, communicating in a social group, or trying to locate another deer (usually her fawn).

Fawns of eighteen months or under bleat, either a high-pitched squeal to signal distress, or a softer sheeplike bleat to signal hunger. When a fawn bleats, does will respond and investigate, and during breeding season opportunistic bucks may also be called in, knowing a doe must be nearby.

The snort-wheeze is the sound all deer make when a human or some other threatening critter manages to penetrate their envelope of security. The snort-wheeze is often accompanied by an indignant, firm stamp of a front hoof. Both behaviors are meant to warn you, as well as alert other deer in the area. Usually, a deer will bound away very soon after snort-wheezing.

The deer wheezed again; this time I felt pretty sure it came from the direction of the swamp. It's unusual for a deer to wheeze more than two or three times, but this one continued wheezing; it sounded desperate. I couldn't imagine I was the cause of the creature's alarm; I was too far away. Could it possibly be the deer I hit yesterday, mortally wounded, trying to keep a pack of coyotes at bay as she lay somewhere nearby? It was an awful and maybe even far-fetched idea, but I couldn't dismiss it.

That deer had never been too far from my thoughts for almost a full day. Our eyes had met, it had a claim on me, unlike all those unremarked deer that get whacked by eighteen-wheelers, torn apart by domestic dogs that, by day, lick children's faces and retrieve tennis balls, or the deer that topple over from starvation following a final, ill-timed March snowstorm.

I wished the wheezing would stop. I considered climbing down and going to investigate. What good would it do? And then, as suddenly as the deer began wheezing, it stopped. But I had a feeling that I wasn't alone.

Sure enough, a deer stood there under one of the apple trees, no more than fifteen yards from my stand. It had wandered in silently, over leaves that were as damp as wet tissue paper. It was a small deer, with the stout, squared-off body of a six-month-old button buck. I could hear him chewing apples, and I saw the telltale bumps (or "buttons") on his skull, just forward of the ears, where in twelve months' time he might have his first set of antlers.

A hoof clicked on stone. Another deer appeared, the button buck's apparent fraternal twin. The new arrival stopped and stood at the edge of the clearing, sizing up the situation. Satisfied, he took two or three bounds to join his brother. The ground was littered with yellow apples, and the little bucks ate the apples as if they were candy, although it was a messy business, a little like watching toddlers eat spaghetti. As the bucks snapped up and tried to pulverize the fruit, entire sections of apple fell from their mouths. A deer's teeth are designed for ripping and grinding forbs and brushy browse, not taking bites out of apples.

I scanned the brush nearby, sure that the mother doe had to be in the vicinity. I finally picked up a patch of brown through the pale green screen of brush at the edge of the orchard, and saw the flicker of an ear. Slowly, the doe moved into the opening at the end of the trail. My eyes, having grown accustomed to the young bucks, weren't quite ready for her size; she looked as big as a horse, and olive brown. She had a typical doe's long, thin face and slender legs. If I wanted to shoot a mature deer in peak physical condition, this was a chance.

But I resisted. If I shot this deer, my hunt would end. And I liked my setup in the orchard; the dense brush around me was ideal cover for a big buck. I had a few more hours to go before I'd have to call it quits.

Besides, this was a good-looking little family. I didn't really want to turn those button bucks into orphans, when the doe could teach them so much about surviving the harsh north-eastern winter. I relaxed and moved the bow in my lap. The doe ducked her head, and I knew she had detected the slight movement.

That was unusual, because the main advantage of hunting from a tree stand is that while deer have acute vision, they rarely look up. The days when they had to fear cougars leaping onto them from overhead branches were long gone. The body language of the doe suggested that she was trying to work out what it was up there in the cherry tree. The game was over.

She stiffened and backed away, high-stepping like a drum majorette, her body fairly trembling with watchfulness. She stamped her foot, stood frozen, and regarded me again.

The greedy little bucks ignored the thud of her hoof on the soft soil. One of them walked even closer to my tree. She stamped again, more forcefully. They couldn't be bothered. The next time she drove her hoof into the ground with great force, and they finally noticed. The twins lifted their heads and looked over their own backs at her, immobile as marble statues. They waited for some further cue from the doe.

Finally, one of the little bucks started for her, lifting each leg high with each slow step. His ears were upright and dialed out in both directions. In one explosive moment, all three bolted, disappearing into the brush, and I was left staring at a handful of slender, yellow, banana-shaped leaves falling from a nearby tree, rocking as they drifted to the earth.

Those were the only deer I would see that day.

4

Pancho and Lefty, Reprieved

DELHI, NEW YORK, OCTOBER 20

WHEN I WALKED into the Spring Valley Sportsman, Mark
Finne's archery pro shop, indoor range, and techno-hunt
setup, the proprietor was in his usual post, sitting before an
elaborate aluminum contraption bristling with carbon arrows
in various states of assembly. He was gluing fluorescent green
vanes onto an arrow while holding the phone pinched to his
cheek, talking to his wife, Patti.

It was a sultry Indian summer afternoon, just a few days after I got back from Tom Daly's place. Ostensibly, I was picking up half a dozen new arrows Mark had assembled for me,
but I was also curious about his techno-hunt and deer-farming
activities. And I wanted to check my bow for accuracy on the
heels of my disaster at Tom's.

Mark greeted me with a wave and bellowed into the phone:
"Wait, Patti. Patti? Don't forget, I need that codeine!"

From somewhere far back in the long, rectangular building
attached to his shop, I heard the heavy *thwock* of an arrow as it
hit the screen on which a techno-hunt projector cast images of

whitetail, bear, antelope, sneaky coyote, and even grouse and wild turkey. The sound recurred at intervals of about twenty seconds; it sounded like a boxer thumping the heavy bag.

Mark told me he was on codeine because, just the day before, he had rolled his all-terrain vehicle on the steep hillside inside the fenced enclosure where he keeps his herd of nearly thirty deer. He was hurting all over but, as he said, "At least nothing got busted, then I woulda really been screwed."

I've known Mark casually for some years and didn't think codeine, or any other opiate, would do much to slow him down. He's a bearish fifty-year-old with a helmet of dark hair showing some gray, chestnut-colored eyes, and a thick Zapata-style mustache. He's outspoken, hotheaded, strong as a bull, and good with his hands—the kind of man I could imagine Meriwether Lewis or William Clark, shrewd judges of male competence, choosing to take on their historic American adventure.

Thwock.

Mark is deaf in one ear, but suffers no comparable handicap when it comes to speaking. He's given to exclaiming, "Don't get me started!" but it's like the blast of a foghorn warning that . . . he's about to get started. Mark is an equal opportunity ranter, ever ready to call out bureaucrats, the media, bow manufacturers, politicians, hunting guides, New York state conservation personnel—you name it.

I set my bow down on the counter and asked about using the range to try my new arrows, but before he could answer, the phone rang again. This time, it was a customer seeking advice on scent-suppressing clothing for his upcoming dream hunt to the latest monster whitetail hotspot, the "golden triangle" area of Illinois. Meanwhile, I examined a picture of Mark on the cover of *New York Sportsman* magazine, hanging framed on the wall. The cover line blared: "Is This the Best Bow Hunter in New York?"

Mark grew up in the suburban community of Southville, on New York's crowded Long Island. He always was more interested in hunting squirrels and rabbits and camping in his backyard than school. "I won the Sportsman Award in high school, but that was the peak of my career as a scholar. I had a hard time, until they started this early release program for high school juniors. That got me out of school early to go work as a carpenter's helper, at sixteen. I never wanted to go to college. I was like a cutup, a joker. I thought I knew more than the teachers. You know how that is."

After a stint in Illinois, where he met and soon married Patti, Mark moved his family back to Long Island. Eventually, he was able to buy a plot of land just outside the Catskill town of Delhi, along with a pop-up camper that would become their weekend retreat. One night, his toddler daughter's pillow caught fire and almost sent the entire camper and its occupants up in a synthetics-fueled, iridescent ball of flame. That was it. Soon thereafter, Mark leveled part of his hillside property with a bulldozer, built a home with his own hands, and moved the family upstate permanently. He abandoned carpentry to become a deer-urine farmer and archery shop owner.

Delaware County can be a tough place to make a living if you aren't a county employee, a (cow) semen salesman, or a mechanic. But thanks to second-home owners and the growing popularity of bow hunting, Mark has survived and even flourished. It helps that modern bow hunting is a costly and gear-intensive recreation. The same high-tech features that turn off a purist like Tom Daly help Finne survive.

Thwock.

Mark hung up the phone and picked up my bow, about the way a dog walker might pick up a plastic baggy full of warm poop. "What's the matter," I asked. "Don't you like Mathews bows?"

"Don't get me started on Mathews," he growled.

Thwock.

Mark's delivery on a rant is exquisite and deliciously predictable. He starts quietly, from a solid base of morose contemplation ("I guess it's an okay bow, but . . ."). Then whatever is bugging him starts to get the better of his self-control. His level of agitation rises and gracefully transitions to perplexity ("Lemme ask you this: Why *should* anyone spend that much more on a bow?"), which easily leads to anger ("Hey, you know why they get great reviews? Who do you think *pays* for all those ads in the magazines, huh?"). And finally, there's a grand, defiant, sweeping excoriation ("They're all full of shit—all of them!"), after which his excitation ebbs and he returns to peaceable brooding ("It's all bullshit. How you been, anyway?").

Thwock.

Patti opened the door between the shop and their living quarters, and two fluffy little black dogs appeared, yapping and boiling around Mark's feet. "Patti," Mark hollered. "The dogs are being a pain in the ass!"

We escaped them by going into the indoor range, where I explained how I wounded and failed to recover the doe at Tom's. I shot half a dozen arrows, putting each one in the lethal zone on a paper target at twenty-five yards. "Guess what, pal? You just missed. It looks like you just had a case of buck fever. On a doe."

Mark's tone was sympathetic, though; the "can't miss" miss is inevitable for the bow hunter.

Mark's techno-hunt theater looks a lot like one of those small galleries where they show "art" movies. It's a long, narrow space, about seventy-five feet by twenty feet, with a black screen made from a special heavy fabric at the far end. The ceiling and sides of the gallery are draped black, and the floor is covered in dark carpet.

I slipped in just in time to see a pretty college-aged girl, wearing the obligatory low-rider sweatpants and flip-flops, draw her compound bow as a squirrel appeared on the screen and began to dart around. "Why me?" she wondered.

One of her fellow cyber-nimrods whispered, "Take your time, Steph."

It was dark, but Steph's painted toenails were aglow in the ultraviolet light—the "black light" familiar to any stoner. What the black light does best is highlight every single speck of lint on whatever article of clothing you're wearing, but on a techno range it also supercharges the fine fluorescent, fiber-optic cables used in a sight, and it makes the bright vanes on the black carbon arrows stand out as if they're floating in thin air.

I stood just behind Steph and her two middle-aged male cohorts, Mack and Herm. At my shoulder, a projector beamed the film clip of the squirrel downrange. A squirrel is a tough shot in a scored techno-hunt because, while many times larger than life, it's still smaller than the other targets.

Thwock! The arrow hit the screen and bounced back.

"Shit." Steph had missed clean; an icon on the screen showed exactly where the arrow hit, after which a digital readout flashed her ID and score: *Hunter no. 1: Zero.* The screen refreshed to show her group's total scores for the round thus far. It refreshed again, advising Hunter no. 2 to get ready.

Mack stepped forward, his arrow already nocked; the plastic vanes glowed a pleasant Chernobyl orange and green. Techno-archers shoot their basic hunting arrows, but they remove the broadheads (which are used only for actual hunting) and replace them with a special blunt tip that won't pierce the expensive screen. In the new video clip, a handsome whitetail buck wandered among some trees.

"You've got to be kidding," Steph muttered, saying what we all must have thought: *How come I never see a buck like that where I hunt?*

Mack's challenge was tricky: he had to make a snap decision to shoot before the deer disappeared behind the next tree—or the system timed out because he waited too long for the right shot. Dawdle too long and the screen goes blank, you get zero points, and your companions roar with laughter.

Thwock! Bull's-eye! The screen displayed the point-of-impact and identified the shot as a direct hit to the vitals, worth the maximum number of points.

"Nice shot," Steph sniffed.

Hunter no. 3, Herm, shot from a seated position, as if he were in a tree stand or seated in a ground blind. Of course, he wasn't wearing four layers of clothes, his teeth weren't chattering, and his seat wasn't swaying in the wind, so you couldn't really call it authentic hunting conditions.

The program presented him with a mighty Cape buffalo. Standing by, Steph was impressed, but unnerved. "I wouldn't go in there after I killed that thing to drag it out of a swamp like that."

"That's what they have natives for," Herm reminded her. And, clearly addressing me, he added, "By the way, feel free to pick on Stephanie."

It went on like that, through an array of targets, the archers teasing each other and cracking corny jokes. When a gorgeous full-curl bighorn sheep appeared, Steph grumbled, "You just watch. Even if Herm shoots him in the ass, the computer will *still* give him a bull's-eye. He's got some kind of in with the machine."

Near the end of the round, a scrawny little spike-horn buck appeared on the screen. It was Steph's last chance to redeem herself.

"Now that's a New York state buck," Mack said, dryly.

"If I didn't have my bow drawn, I would tell you to fuck off," Steph whispered.

They all laughed, and Steph finished her round with a nice shot that collected body points, but not the elusive "vitals" bonanza.

After they finished, Herm showed me the computer room and a printout of the score sheet. An integrated techno-hunt setup, which costs about $40,000, can handle all kinds of statistical chores, including league play, for dozens of individuals. At the peak of his league business, Mark had over one hundred and twenty archers—most of them willing to brave anything on a weekly basis, including treacherous winter weather that turns the Finnes' steep driveway into something like an amusement-park-worthy, frozen water slide.

It takes about fifteen minutes for an individual to shoot a techno round, so a foursome eats up an hour, and then there's the socializing over pizza. "The nice thing is that you can talk while doing this," Steph said. "You can't do that when you're really hunting, sitting all alone by a fence."

Mark also organizes an annual mid-winter techno-hunt awards banquet, where trophies and prizes are given out. "It's not just small stuff, either," Mark told me. "We've given away boats with outboard motors, ATVs, fancy hunting rifles. But we only draw for those now. It got a little crazy with the competition when guys knew they could win a bass boat."

Stephanie told me she's a biochemistry major at nearby Hartwick College, as well as a cheerleader, firefighter, and, at the time, studying to be a paramedic. Mack and Herm are part of her extended family: she attended high school with Mack's son, and she drank her first glass of wine under Mack's supervision (at a family function). Herm is retired from the Air Force and now drives a school bus and looks after a small local museum.

These were people outside the urban bubble; many of them still dial just seven numbers when they make a telephone call, wave to anyone they pass driving on the road, and, thanks to the Internet and satellite television, they know something they don't often get credit for: they know what you—if you're inside that urban bubble—are thinking. And how you view them.

And guess what? They couldn't care less.

The big-city politicians who show up to bowl or throw back whiskey shots with these folks in Whitetail Nation may secretly hold them in contempt (or worse, pity) and suspect they're bitter, just clinging to guns and religion out of despair. But these pumpkin rollers know that's all bullshit, plain old laugh-out-loud, if-they-only-knew, what-a-bunch-of-arrogant-dipshits-they-really-are bullshit.

Country people have the confidence that comes with independence and competence; they know how to change a tire, plow a driveway, or fix a leaky water faucet. They don't have doormen carrying their parcels, or professional walkers for their dogs. And these seemingly bland folks, considered unenlightened by many of the urban elites, are capable of doing amazing things—it's been proven time and again in places far more dangerous than a sushi bar. Come to think of it, the only time they might *not* rise to a challenge adequately is when it comes to having to decide between the yellow fin sashimi or the avocado-and-spicy salmon skin roll. But they know from killing and butchering that great gift of protein, a whitetail deer.

Of course, the allure of techno-hunting might render that last skill irrelevant. As Herm said, "This is just addictive. I'm not even sure I need to go out in the woods hunting anymore."

At least one entrepreneur had the jump on that idea. He figured out a way that a "hunter" sitting in an easy chair in the comfort of his own living room could remotely kill a real deer coming to a feeder on a Texas ranch four thousand miles away. It isn't all that difficult; all it takes is a movable firearm and webcam in a blind, linked to a computer via the Internet.

Thankfully, the public outcry (the protest was led by hunters) against this creepy idea led to almost instantaneous legislative action banning remote, computer-based killing. I guess that Deer Hunter II, a runaway favorite video game featuring only virtual deer, will remain the gold standard—for now.

If Saxton Pope, the undisputed father of bow hunting and the author of the bible of the sport (*Hunting with the Bow & Arrow*, 1923), were brought back to life and shoved into a technohunt theater, fancy compound bow in his hand, it might still rank as just the second-most improbable experience of his life. For Pope's life and legacy were inextricably bound up with the remarkable story of Ishi, who earned a melancholy distinction as the last "wild" Indian when white men discovered and captured him in the Mount Lassen region of northern California in 1911. Ishi's entire Yana tribe had been persecuted for generations and finally he was—literally—the last Yana left.

At the time, Pope was a prominent physician from a wellheeled family, working at the University of California, Berkeley. Shortly after Ishi gave up his life in the wild and turned himself in to white men, a UC anthropologist was able to communicate with him via the few words he knew in the Yana dialect. Ishi, whose age at the time was somewhere between forty and sixty, was transported to the Museum of Anthropology in San Francisco, where he became a subject of study. Pope, a longbow enthusiast and instructor at the University Medical School adjacent to the museum, became Ishi's physician as the Native American battled one infection after another, all stemming from contact with white civilization.

And this is where the events that would alter the face of hunting in the United States really began. Ultimately, Ishi was employed at the medical school as a janitor. (As Pope wrote, without a trace of irony: ". . . to teach him modern industry and the value of money.") This enabled Pope to build a relationship with Ishi, who adapted admirably to the new ways. It took the physician no time at all to work out that Ishi was an extraordinary man. Pope wrote: "Though very reserved, he [Ishi] was kindly, honest, clean and trustworthy. More than this, he had a superior philosophy of life, and a high moral standard."

Pope could justify making such judgments because he learned the Yana dialect from Ishi and spent many days in his company. He came to believe that Ishi "knew the history and use of everything in the outdoor world" and it was proven to him, often in dramatic fashion, when the two men hunted together. Pope claims that Ishi "spoke the language of animals" and that he taught Pope to make bows and arrows, and how to hunt "Indian fashion."

The friendship was most decidedly a two-way street: after three years in San Francisco, Ishi's white wardens took him back to his own country—territory where he'd killed and roasted a bear, where he could still point out sites where ancient Yana chiefs made their villages, where for centuries his own people had ambushed deer. "But," as Pope wrote, "he did not want to stay [in his ancestral territory]. He liked the ways of the white man, and his own land was full of the spirits of the departed."

Ishi shared his hunting secrets with Pope. His bow, which Ishi called *man-nee*, was forty-two inches long and made of mountain juniper backed with sinew. He shaped the instrument by rubbing it on sandstone, and created the mildly recurved tips by bending the wood over a heated stone. Ishi took the leg tendons of deer and chewed them until the fibers separated, softened, and became adhesive. He used those fibers to make the "backing" that gave his bow strength, and attached it to the bow using glue made from boiled salmon skin. He wrapped additional tendons around the nocks (the two places where the bowstring is attached), and wrapped the finished bow tightly in long, thick strips of willow bark, which he peeled away several days later, after which he smoothed and polished the bow with sandstone.

Ishi kept his bow in a case made from the skin of a cougar's tail. He fabricated his bowstrings from the finer tendons of a deer's shank. I omit some details, but the finished product had a draw weight of about forty-five pounds, and it could shoot an arrow two hundred yards. The "savage" Ishi believed that a well-made strung bow made a musical note when it was tapped with an arrow.

Pope wrote: "This was man's first harp, the great grandfather of the pianoforte." Ishi sometimes put one end of his bow to the corner of his open mouth and, tapping the string with an arrow, made pleasing music that Pope likened to "an Aeolian harp." When inspired to do this, Ishi would sing a Yana folk song telling how birds came into being. A great warrior shot an arrow at the sun, put out its light, and the only way men avoided freezing in the cold and dark that followed was by growing feathers. Thus were birds, our brothers, conceived.

For an arrow (*sa wa*) shaft, Ishi preferred witch hazel with a six-inch "foreshaft" at the tip, made of heavier wood (usually mountain mahogany). He painted his shafts to make them visible in the woods and to distinguish them from those of others. His paints contained red cinnabar, black pigment from the eyes of a trout, and vegetable dyes of green and blue made from roots and wild onions.

Ishi preferred obsidian over flint for his arrowheads. But it still took expertise to flake out the tip and point—something he did while his face was thickly smeared with mud for protection from the flying chips, which were razor sharp. Pope wrote that in half an hour, Ishi was able to make "the most graceful and perfectly proportioned arrowheads imaginable." In his new life, Ishi came across magical materials—using his tried-

and-true method, he flaked out equally impressive arrowheads from old beer bottles.

Ishi felt that the longbows used by Pope and his cronies were inferior ("too much man-nee"). He frequently missed a four-foot target at the same distance from which his white friends shot, offering the novel excuse that the target was "too large," and the bright colored rings around the bull's-eye diverted his attention. But, oh, what a hunting machine he was! Pope saw Ishi kill ground squirrels (gophers) at forty yards and professed astonishment at his accuracy in the field.

Ishi's patience as a hunter was such that Pope wrote: "Time meant nothing to him; he would watch a squirrel hole for an hour if necessary, but he always got the squirrel." While they were hunting, Pope wrote, Ishi would sometimes stop and say things like, "The squirrel is scolding a fox."

At first, Pope told Ishi he could not know such things. But, challenged to remain in hiding to prove his point, the men would invariably see a fox on the move. It got to the point where, when Ishi told his white companions that the raucous jabbering of a blue jay meant "Here comes a man," they would all desist hunting for a while. Pope believed that Ishi could speak "a half-dozen sentences" to quail.

Ishi was apparently able to smell deer, cougar, and foxes; often, it was the first thing that alerted him to their proximity. He studied every aspect of the environment, taking important clues and cues from landscapes to watering holes, and when hunting he was always keenly aware of wind direction, as well as the position of the sun.

For twenty-four or more hours before the day of a hunt, Ishi would avoid fish and tobacco, odors he felt could be detected from afar. The morning of a hunt, he rose early and drank water, but still avoided food. He bathed in the creek and rubbed himself down with aromatic yerba buena leaves. He wore only a loincloth because he felt clothing made too much noise.

Ishi contracted tuberculosis before he could help Pope fulfill his dream of killing a deer with a bow. Pope and Ishi's other caretakers did all they could, but the disease rapidly ravaged the slight Indian. Feverish and unable to eat, he suddenly developed a massive pulmonary hemorrhage. Pope was at his bedside to the end.

Not long thereafter, Dr. Pope finally got his first deer. He went on to become the founding father of bow hunting, along with his companion, Arthur Young. Together, the men performed remarkable feats, and today the Pope and Young Club is the official keeper and arbiter of bow-hunting records (it is the bow hunter's equivalent to the gunner's Boone and Crockett Club record book).

Here is Pope, writing of Ishi's last hours following his hemorrhage:

> I was with him at the time, directed his medication, and gently stroked his hand as a small sign of fellowship and sympathy. He did not care for marked demonstrations of any sort.
>
> He was a stoic, unafraid, and died in the faith of his people. As an Indian should go, so we sent him on his long journey to the land of the shadows. By his side we placed his fire sticks, ten pieces of dentalia, or Indian money, a small bag of acorn meal, a bit of dried venison, some tobacco, and his bow and arrows.

These objects were cremated with Ishi, and the ashes placed in an earthen jar inscribed with these six words: ISHI, THE LAST YANA INDIAN, 1916.

I was not prepared to go bow hunting in the afternoon in just a loincloth, so I got ready with the aid of a neutral detergent incorporating an ultraviolet light reducer. Most detergents contain whitening agents that release their energy in short blue wavelengths, to which deer—unlike humans—are highly sensitive. What we see as screaming blaze-orange, a deer probably sees as muted gray. If you wash that slick camo garment in conventional detergent, it will glow in the woods like a neon sign.

Before I left, I flipped around my wife's makeup mirror and idly daubed streaks of black, green, and brown grease paint on my face. On my way out, I grabbed a newly arrived package of "scent sticks"—just another product I couldn't resist blowing money on in the desperate days of August, when the "special deer-hunting issue" catalogs start hitting the house like hail on a tin roof. If these incense sticks worked as advertised, bucks would come galloping from far and wide, lured by the windborne scent of apples or wild plums. Maybe this would be the ticket to the giant buck I hoped to kill.

In the United States, you don't have to be a ranch-owning dot-com billionaire to hunt right outside your back door; millions of ordinary American citizens do it, all the time. I was lucky; I could step out the door and go hunting anywhere I wanted.

Outside, a puff of breeze raced through the meadow behind my house, rippling the grass; the tawny field was alternately bathed in light and darkness as banks of clouds drifted over from Wolf Hollow. It would soon be moving and feeding time for the deer.

I decided to hunt half a mile from the house, just over the hill from my bluestone quarry, where the dirt road dwindled to little more than a wagon track—a straight, tree-lined bobsled run flanked by big hayfields almost all the way down to the two-lane blacktop about a mile away. I had two ladder stands in one of the upper fields on a neighbor's land where I could also watch the field across the road.

I found plenty of deer sign in the fields—beds, scat, and rubbed trees along the wooded border. Although we were still in the summer cycle, subtle changes were taking place, and they would affect the feeding and travel patterns of the deer. For one thing, all those protein-rich acorns were finally dropping. And each day, the rut drew closer. Whitetail deer are surprisingly social and as breeding season approaches they engage in various meet-and-greet rituals out in the fields. These mixers allow deer to identify and take stock of potential mates, or rivals for mates, both of which include family members.

In the weeks preceding the rut, bucks are still inclined to gather in bachelor groups, like so many boys fidgeting and scowling as they sit along the wall at a school dance. They may be buddies, but each of them is sizing up his imminent rivals— as well as the does they encounter while feeding, traveling, and socializing. The does pay the young bucks no mind, but they're doing research as well, some of it centered on each other in a way that would tease a smile of understanding out of any woman.

These rituals establish a breeding hierarchy for when that big hit song finally brings everyone out on the dance floor to do the rut. Once the hormones really kick in, it's every deer for him- or herself. Generally, deer of either sex will not stray very far from the one to two square miles that constitute their habitat. They get to know each other pretty well. But once the rut kicks in, bucks may roam as far as eight or ten miles in pursuit of does.

Early season October hunting is often about figuring out the travel and feeding habits of deer, and wherever you choose to hunt—along a travel route or a feeding area—you must keep in mind the First Commandment of deer hunting: *Stay downwind.* I decided to sit midway down the length of the field, where I had a good view of a stand of beech trees with a heavily used deer trail leading to the field.

The wind direction wasn't optimal for my setup, but the promotional material for the scent sticks boasted that in addition to reeling in deer, the lure is a formidable masking agent for human scent. We would see about that.

Before I climbed the stand—a twelve-foot-tall steel ladder in four sections, with a seat and footrest at the top—I pulled out two of the scent sticks. I poked the ends into the ground, lit the tops, and, following the instructions, covered the sticks with a three-gallon bucket with holes drilled in the top and sides. Smoke quickly began to curl from the holes. It had the same blue density as the billowing incense I remembered from my days as a Catholic-school altar boy.

I scooted up the stand and buckled up my safety belt. The smoke, and plenty of it, looked nice and blue as it drifted off through the trees. But the breeze shifted, and the rising smoke began to blow into my face—at which point I noticed that it smelled nothing like apples, plums, or any other plant or vegetable I knew. It seemed impossible at first, but I realized with growing horror that the stuff smelled like . . . patchouli oil, that syrupy-sweet ablution that was the standard marinade for every hippie chick of my generation.

The incense smelled so awful that it *had* to be a good masking agent—that part of the maker's claim certainly seemed accurate. But I was enveloped in a miasma; I could barely breathe and my eyes were watering. I saw the beeches through a kaleidoscope. Feeling nauseous, I realized that if I toppled off my perch, I'd be left hanging like a ham in an Italian butcher shop.

Enough! On top of everything else, I hadn't seen a deer. But I still had a good ninety minutes of daylight. I tore off my safety belt and scampered down the ladder. I stomped out the miserable incense and, leaving the bucket behind, hightailed it a hundred and fifty yards to my other stand, near the uppermost corner of the field.

• • •

Ladder tree stands are usually sectional and somewhat portable.

The exertion cleared my head. I was soon settled in again, this time in a ladder stand set just back from the meadow among a good cover of spruce trees, with a good view up and down the field. Deer sometimes gathered in the pines before slipping into the field at dusk.

The remains of the day slid away under a marbled gray sky, the color evaporating in the blazing hardwoods lining either side of the wagon road. The evening thermals carried the cooler air—along with my patchouli-soaked scent—downhill. I noticed two deer feeding high in the field across the road, about half a mile away. They were tiny black stick figures, neither a rack buck.

I looked toward the uphill corner of the meadow, about seventy yards above me, and was surprised to see a doe. She stood stock-still, newly arrived and checking out the field to make sure it was all clear. Shortly, three other deer—a doe and two yearlings—scampered from the woods into the meadow and immediately began feeding. The sentry doe finally relaxed and began to graze.

I weighed the situation. This probably was another family of three, accompanied by an auntie—the largest, most cautious doe in the group. The deer moved farther out into the field, instead of down along the edge and within range. I watched the fawns gobbling grass. Occasionally, one or the other kicked up its little heels and in unison the twins scampered off to a new, random location to resume eating. The adults, though, were skittish. They looked toward me often, and I quickly worked out why: while I enjoyed the show the fawns put on, two other deer had drifted into the lower part of the field, and both of them were bucks—a five- or six-pointer, and a four-point forkhorn.

I could kill one of the bucks for the freezer and continue my quest for a big buck, even in my home state. A general resident big-game hunting license in New York state costs about sixty bucks, and it comes with a single buck tag that you're legally obliged to fill out and attach to the deer as soon as you shoot it (this system is used throughout the nation, although the number of tags you can obtain for deer of either sex varies from state to state).

If you want to hunt with a bow during the three or four weeks before gun season, you have to buy a special bow permit (for a small fee) in addition to your regular license. And you get an either-sex tag with that permit. So if you hunt with the bow and get a buck, you can continue to hunt during gun season. By contrast, the rifle hunter who shoots a buck on opening day (when his chances are best) basically has a one-day hunting season.

I was in no great hurry to get an ordinary buck or doe. I would be traveling to hunt quite a bit in the ensuing weeks, with trips planned to Montana, Texas, and Pennsylvania—places where I had a much better chance of encountering that elusive monster buck. But it was tempting to take what I could at home. And for most people, killing any buck with branched antlers with a bow is considered an accomplishment of a higher order than shooting a doe. It isn't just the mystique of antlers. Psychology and mythology aside, the disparity in the buck-to-doe ratio (as high as 1:15 in some places) defines the buck as a greater prize.

Excited, I studied the two bucks closely. They appeared indifferent to the does farther up the meadow. They moseyed along, side by side, advancing toward me. When they were forty-five yards out, I clipped my release onto the bowstring.

It's hard to keep your mind from racing ahead and becoming overheated as deer move closer and look larger—much larger than you expect, thanks to your nervous state. Either buck would go a good 140 pounds, but they looked bigger—massive, compared to the does and fawns I'd been watching. My stomach flipped, and I worried that my hands would start shaking.

I knew that if I killed one of those deer, I'd feel euphoric and relaxed for hours; colors would seem more vivid, my mind calmer. I would connect and feel in tune with the natural world at a visceral level, more than at any other time in my life. I visualized a buck hanging high by its hind legs in the maple tree, his belly slit open and emptied of guts and organs, ready for butchering. What a gift, in a world where long-faced shoppers in supermarkets bought inferior meat wrapped in plastic in pound-sized, expensive portions.

And still the bucks kept coming.

Which one should I shoot, I wondered. A healthy, well-fed, eighteen-month-old buck can have a handsome if not enormous set of antlers, with three or more tines, or points, on either side; neither of these bucks, while fully grown, fell into that category.

But they weren't spike bucks either, with nothing more than a single eight- or ten-inch tine on either side. For a long time, many hunters (myself included) embraced the myth that every spike ought to be removed from the herd, because it was a genetically inferior deer—theory being that spike bucks never developed multitined antlers, no matter how old they became. But a number of studies destroyed that myth. While genetics plays an important role, the most significant component in antler size and configuration is nutrition.

It was possible that these bucks were eighteen-month-old twins that despite their impressive size and physical condition lacked the good forage and minerals required to grow the optimal antlers hidden in their DNA. Given a choice, why not kill the buck with the larger antlers? The deer were within thirty yards now, shooting range. But they were partially screened by the limb of a maple tree protruding out over the field.

And still they kept coming.

I heard the deer ripping loose mouthfuls of clover. I studied

A spike buck, often but not always the sign of an eighteen-month-old deer.

their skeletal antlers and almost laughed out loud as I thought of the western ballad made famous by Willie Nelson and Merle Haggard, "Pancho and Lefty." I decided that Pancho was the five-pointer.

The deer moved toward a gap through which I could send an arrow. My heart was racing; I could do nothing to stop it. They were at twenty yards when, suddenly, in unison they stopped feeding. Pancho, the five-pointer, began to groom the forkhorn, Lefty. He licked his buddy's face and nipped at his gray muzzle and olive-tan neck. Lefty shivered with obvious pleasure. The bucks separated momentarily, and it appeared that the fork-horn was going to groom Pancho. Instead, the two bucks slowly squared off, lowered their heads, and began to spar.

Antlers engaged, they twisted and pushed. Although their antlers lacked mass, they made quite a racket, clicking and clashing repeatedly. The bucks churned their heads this way and that, but it was all a carefully orchestrated drill, a combination of play and practice for the more deadly engagements that would come when the rut got underway. They briefly separated, then went at it again.

The deer set their front legs and pushed, forehead to forehead. Lefty gave a little ground, then won it back. They parted and stood facing each other, their necks almost touching, faces side by side, each deer motionless, looking into the distance beyond the other's back.

When they stepped away from each other, Pancho was in my shooting window. I took a deep breath as I drew the bowstring; neither deer heard the cables turn the cam, or the carbon arrow slide smoothly back along the arrow rest. I slowly exhaled, settling the green pin just behind the top joint of Pancho's left front leg.

I held and . . . I held. My arm began to tremble. As I tried to ease the string back to its original position, lowering the bow, I banged the riser against the edge of the steel stand. The bucks froze at the loud clink, then quickly bolted, their tails erect, white flags vanishing into the lavender tones of the dissolving day.

Back at the house, chilled through from the ride down the hill on the ATV in the cold autumn evening, I put a few logs in the wood stove, poured myself a Scotch on the rocks, and flopped down on the sofa, wearing just my long johns. Our cat Biscuit hopped onto the opposite armrest and looked at me: *Dude, where's the deer?*

I said: "Sorry, but no heart or liver for you today, buddy."

I had no regrets about letting Pancho slip away. It wasn't that I lost my nerve, nor that the empathy and compassion I feel with deer got the better of me, as has sometimes been the case.

Pancho and Lefty were a pair of decent bucks; next year, they might both be *very* nice bucks—about the best you can expect in a rural area where deer are not nearly as abundant as in semideveloped places where the living is easy, with milder winter weather, better forage, and fewer free-roaming coyotes—and hunters—to suppress the population. My land was good, if not especially rich, and the most basic forage, clover and other grasses, was abundant. We could grow trophy bucks; it just called for a little restraint, combined with better land stewardship.

Next year, I told myself, I was going to put in a few food plots and experiment with mineral licks and other supplements. The only question was whether Pancho and Lefty would make it through the gun season and another of our harsh winters. Besides, this year I wasn't going to take my eye off the ball; I was focused on getting a big buck. Killing a nice deer always takes the edge off, and I needed to keep that tension high.

I know some guys, trophy hunters, who stoically went for years without shooting anything, because they wanted to develop the right mindset, habits, and strategies for killing the once-in-a-lifetime buck. If I wanted to be like them, I had to wear the same hair shirt. If I wanted meat—and I did—I ought to do the right thing: kill a doe.

I realized that despite my lame attempt to accomplish that at Tom's place, I wasn't especially keen on the idea. It's a common dilemma, because it somehow seems ignoble to kill a doe. For one thing, she's a female; for another, she doesn't have antlers, so she seems somehow defenseless. And for generations, the prohibition on killing does was driven by the self-evident theory that does make bucks. Therefore, if you wanted to have enough bucks to shoot, make sure there were enough does. It improved your chances of killing a buck.

But it's since been proven that the way to improve the quality of the bucks (as well as to reduce the herd, where that's a consideration) is to kill does. A healthy herd ought to have a nearly equal buck-to-doe ratio, to ensure that the competition for does enables superior, dominant bucks to do most of the breeding. In the northeast, about 85 percent of all the eighteen-month-old bucks are killed annually, which is why the buck-to-doe ratio is usually so out of whack. Bucks fight over the right to breed, so a shortage of fit, superior bucks enables inferior specimens to do a lot of the breeding, which leads to an overall decline in the quality of the herd.

Maybe neither Pancho nor Lefty had the genes to amount to much; maybe they were examples of how far our local herd had degenerated, after so many decades of indiscriminate buck hunting. I would give them a chance, though. Maybe the future held something better in store, starting with an additional year of life. *You want to kill a big buck,* I thought, *you need to walk the walk.*

It would have been nice to eat grilled venison tenderloin for dinner, but beans and franks would have to do. Again.

PART II

5

Gravity Is a Buzzkill

ANDES, NEW YORK, OCTOBER 22

I WAS RELUCTANT to leave Andes with the deer rut coming on fast, but I had plans to hunt the opening week of Montana's gun season at the Milk River Ranch, which is owned by my friends the Aageson brothers, David and Verges. They're dyed-in-the-wool Montanans whose forbears started putting together their present twenty-thousand-acre spread on the Alberta border thanks to the Homestead Act of 1862.

But first I'd be going to Cabela's big-box store in Hamburg, Pennsylvania, to pick up my Pennsylvania nonresident hunting license, some new cold-weather clothing, and ammo for my new rifle, a .257 Weatherby Magnum.

Cabela's is a remarkably successful retailer that started out as (and remains) an outfit dedicated to fishing and hunting clothing and gear. The company produces nearly a hundred different catalogs a year, dedicated to every niche, including camping, shooting, water fowling, bow hunting, and ladies' clothing, as well as spring and fall master catalogs as thick as the New York city telephone directory, but bound in hard covers. The outdoor writer Bill Heavey has described it, fittingly, as *The Book of John*. Just thinking of the paper wasted on those catalogs makes me want to run out and hug the first tree I see. The company is to the outdoors retail business what Microsoft is to software.

Dick Cabela, a Nebraska salesman, started the outfit in 1961. While at a furniture show in Chicago, Cabela bought some fishing flies. He put a classified ad in a Casper, Wyoming, newspaper, offering a dozen hand-tied flies for a buck, and had exactly one response. He realized he was priced above the market, so he revised his sales pitch: *Free introductory offer! 5 hand-tied flies . . . 25 cents postage and handling*. It was a stroke of genius unlikely to be taught at Harvard's business school.

Cabela placed that ad in national outdoor magazines, and soon the orders began pouring in; he sent the goods out with a modest catalog run off on an old mimeograph machine. Dick, with help from his wife, ran the show out of the kitchen of their home in Chappell, Nebraska.

Dick Cabela's brother left his job soon thereafter and joined the company, and the business exploded. By 2001, Cabela's ranked as the fifth most popular catalog in the nation, and the company was already vested in e-commerce. Cabela's eventually went public and launched a brick-and-mortar division with a novel approach: Cabela's retail stores were to be of epic size and strategically located as regional centers, with features that made them tourist destinations. This is one of those cases where it's not about the journey, it's all about the destination, and Cabela's stores drew pilgrims in camo as powerfully as the fountain of Lourdes draws the miracle-seeking infirm.

Cabela's in Hamburg, for example, has the "indoor mountain," which features full-sized mounts of creatures ranging from tiny gophers to skunks to coyotes to deer, elk, grizzly bear, and, of course, mountain goats and sheep grazing in the rarefied air high above the sales floor, right under the fluorescent lights and aluminum air-conditioning ducts.

In fact, the 250,000-square-foot establishment in Hamburg is officially called (if only in Cabela-ese) a "habitat-recreation retail store." In addition to an abundance of products, mounts, and displays, the store has a restaurant, outdoor kennel, horse corral, and RV dump station. As far as I know, it doesn't yet have a flight simulator.

Like many hunters, I'm repelled by the degree of commercialism in our pastime, but I'm also a red-blooded, all-American consumer who never met a new camo pattern, clip-on flashlight, or grunt-wheeze call that I don't immediately want. I don't even feel guilty about it anymore. And a lot of the stuff is the equivalent, price-wise, of penny candy—or it is until you go to buy a new set of long johns and find yourself back in the parking lot toting an Italian-made shotgun bought with what was supposed to have been the tuition for your kid's freshman year in college.

I had to smile when I entered the store after a long drive and saw that the sales staff—they looked like dwarfs, given the scale of the place—were all nametagged and wearing shooting vests.

I picked up my license and ammo and wandered over to the vast men's clothing section, where I picked up a hooded pullover jacket for ninety bucks, in a nice Seclusion 3-D camo.

I went on through aisle upon aisle of shooting, fishing, and hunting gear, where I perused items like a belt-clip "auto-hoist" device, for the hunter who's unhappy with the primitive means of hauling his bow up to his tree-stand seat (a length of rope, tied to the seat at the top). I examined a "Bear Bladder," a scent-free, biodegradable urination pouch that takes my old-fashioned, screw-cap plastic pee bottle to another level. Unlike the original, though, it isn't available with a "female adapter"

(I wouldn't kid you about that). I came across the original and still one-and-only "Silencer," a tube that suppresses the sound of a cough. I examined a remotely activated flashing beacon that makes it easier to find your tree stand in the dark.

Various scent and other lures ("Pro-Lasses," billed as "molasses for deer") in liquid, gel, incense stick, and even aerosol-can bomb versions occupied an entire aisle at Cabela's, and I found some dryer sheets (similar to the fabric-softening sheets marketed by Bounce) in "fresh earth" aroma, along with Scent-Away deodorant, bath towels, and a special line of Huntress shampoo, moisturizer, conditioner, and lip balm, in pretty pink packaging, for female hunters.

Trail cams—motion-activated, weatherproof, full-flash digital cameras that attach to a tree or fence post and prove to even the greatest of skeptics that there are, in fact, trophy bucks running around almost everywhere—are a hot item these days. So is scent-suppressing clothing, most of which relies on a fine membrane of carbon (coal, more or less) in the fabric to capture and absorb human scent before it escapes to the air.

Two aisles over, I contemplated buying a "Jerky Blaster," which looks like (and probably was, early in its life) a good old-fashioned grease gun. But instead of laying out a bead of lubricant, it makes strips of jerky or sausage. The "Porta-Butcher" is a complete portable butchering kit (including cleaver and rough-tooth saw, for bone work) in a plastic briefcase. And what outdoorsman doesn't lust after a ten-million-candle-power spotlight (with an adapter that plugs into your vehicle's cigarette lighter)? You never know when you might need to help out a friend who's opening a new car dealership.

My travels eventually took me to the dominant feature at the habitat-recreation store, the "Big Mountain." To get to it from the Jerky Blaster and spotlight department, I had to cross a wooden bridge over a little lake filled with live trout—golden and brook trout, which swam indolently through the legs of a magnificent, full-sized bull moose mount. In addition to hosting dramatic mounts of just about every critter native to North America on its slopes, Big Mountain features the eleventh-largest polar bear ever taken by a hunter.

I bushwhacked overland for a bit, ignoring the shoe-and-boot department to get to Deer Country, a special wing of the store dedicated to cervids. It's a museumlike space with artfully done lighting and beautiful, ecologically correct dioramas featuring magnificent taxidermy and educational components that include plaques devoted to whitetail biology and hunting history.

I read that by 1900, the deer was going the way of the carrier pigeon. The estimated nationwide population had fallen to around 500,000; New York state had fewer than 7,000 whitetail. There was no season or bag limit on deer. But the ethic—and legislation—implanted by Teddy Roosevelt and his conservation-minded friends proved effective as well as noble; by the middle of the twentieth century, the deer population was rebounding vigorously, and today's estimated population of fourteen to twenty million whitetail is a good half of what biologists believe was the precolonization population. That's an impressive number, given how much habitat has been lost to human expansion.

Deer Country also features an extraordinary Wall of Fame lined with head mounts of some of the greatest deer ever shot, complete with printed descriptions of how and where the deer were taken, and by whom. This bestows upon deer hunting something that all worthy undertakings have: a history and a mythology. It elevates the enterprise and turns both the unfortunate buck and lucky hunter into creatures worth commemorating, even if some of the narratives swing more toward the farcical than the heroic.

The current world-record typical whitetail was shot in 1993 by Milo Hansen, a Saskatchewan grain and cattle farmer from the town of Biggar, almost a year after the deer that came to be known as the "Hansen buck" was first officially spotted by the local school bus driver. Various residents of Biggar saw the buck over the ensuing eleven months, and scores of hunters hoped to get it in the cross hairs during the 1993 season.

A number of people caught a glimpse of the buck but were unable to get a shot, once the season opened. Then, on the morning of November 23, following a fresh snowfall, Hansen organized a hunt with friends. Two companions spotted the buck on Hansen's land, slipping into a willow run. A group of men surrounded the cover, but the buck stole out. Hansen and a buddy fired Hail Marys, but missed. Hansen was using an old-school deer gun: a lever-action .308 equipped with a simple four-power scope.

The hunters tracked the buck again and were about to quit when the trail went cold—only to see the buck run into a different piece of cover on Hansen's land. This time, they surrounded and flushed out the buck. Hansen and a friend had a decent shot at a hundred and fifty yards but, as Hansen later admitted, both men succumbed to buck fever and fired a few wild shots that missed.

The buck was in the willows again, and this time when he was pushed out, Hansen had a head-on shot. He made it count, although the buck ran off, and Hansen had to track it down and administer the finishing shot in an aspen bluff.

Hansen knew he'd shot the biggest deer anyone around Biggar had ever seen. He felt good: he was pretty confident he would win the trophy at the annual Big Buck Night banquet in the nearby town of Sonningdale. He reckoned that he might even have a shot at winning the trophy in the contest sponsored by his local wildlife federation.

On November 29, a neighbor came over and "green-scored" the rack according to the official Boone and Crockett scoring system. When he finished, according to Hansen, the scorer asked him to review the numbers because there had to be some kind of mistake. By the scorer's calculation, the antlers totaled 213⅝ inches, which would be the new world record.

A few days later, an official Boone and Crockett Club official confirmed the score, and overnight Milo Hansen became an international celebrity, besieged by journalists, hunting-gear manufacturers, and fellow hunters from all over the world. The Hansen buck is a magnificent specimen; its rack is classic (typical), with six of the ten symmetrical tines extending off the main beams exceeding eleven inches in length.

As far as hunting stories go, Hansen's is timeless fare: a group of dedicated hunters locate a monster whitetail, form a posse, plan a smart hunt under ideal conditions, and finally corner and kill the critter. Any number of the men involved might have shot that deer, and you get the feeling from the story that Hansen had first dibs (after all, it was his land where the final hunt took place). Other stories are less conventional.

Take the Bullwinkle buck, a nontypical whitetail so-named because of its heavily palmated antlers and striking pair of drop tines (tines that grow down from the main beam, instead of up, affording the buck with extra neck protection in combat).

In 1987, two men from Kentucky traveled to Jackson County, Ohio, and shot Bullwinkle. Back at home, one of the men caught his wife in bed with his hunting partner. For revenge, the cuckold called the authorities and told them that his friend had killed the Bullwinkle buck without having bought a non-resident license. As a result, the Ohio Department of Natural Resources officials confiscated the antlers and kept the rack for public display.

The Jim Jordan buck was shot not long after World War I by

a man of that name near Danbury, Wisconsin. He was hunting along some railroad tracks when an approaching train spooked several deer. Jordan got off a shot at a good buck, and it appeared to be mortally wounded. But it was strong enough to cross a river before it expired on the far bank. Jordan was about to go after it when he realized he'd left his knife back at his carriage. By the time he fetched the knife and returned, the deer was gone—swept away by the river.

Jordan headed downstream, scouring the bank, and after a long search he finally found the buck. He recruited help to drag it out, because the buck weighed over four hundred pounds. Jordan took the buck to a taxidermist about ten miles south of where it was shot and left it for mounting. But he didn't return for the mount for about a year, by which time the taxidermist—and the mount—had skipped town.

The Jordan buck disappeared for about fifty years, but resurfaced near Hinckley, Minnesota, where a man named Robert Ludwig allegedly bought it at a yard sale for three bucks. It turned out that Ludwig, improbably, was a relative of Jordan, and knew that Jordan owned a bar where he displayed antlers. The men got together and figured out the origin of the deer. An official B&C scorer tallied up the deer at 206-plus—a new world-record typical. But because of its sketchy history, Jordan wasn't acknowledged as the buck's hunter of record until one month after he died in 1978.

The most famous of all the nontypicals may be the Hole in the Horn buck, from Ohio. It was found dead in 1940 between railroad tracks and a chain-link fence on the perimeter of an arsenal, and for many years it hung without fanfare in the Kent Canadian Club of Ohio. Its name is derived from the hole in one of its drop tines, which was first thought to be a bullet hole, but was later determined to have been made by a protruding wire from the fence.

The mount might still be displayed in relative obscurity were it not for Fred Goodwin. An antler collector from Maine, Goodwin was showing photos around while working on the Al-Can Highway when one of his coworkers said he knew of a deer with antlers that dwarfed most of the ones Goodwin was bragging about. Goodwin said he'd give the guy ten bucks if he could produce a picture of a bigger deer. When the photo from Ohio arrived, Goodwin couldn't believe his eyes.

When the Alaska highway project was finished, Goodwin passed through Ohio, found the Hole in the Horn deer, and tried to buy the rack. The asking price was five hundred dollars. Goodwin said he never paid more than twenty-five bucks for a rack—and thereby lost his chance to own the highest scoring (B&C score: 328) of any whitetail rack.

Reading tales of the great deer set my heart racing and my pulse pounding. My head filled with visions; there I was at dusk, dragging a monster whitetail across hard-packed snow by an antler, a dark line of woods in the background. I could almost smell the pine trees and feel the sharp air in my lungs.

There I was in Deer Country! Alas, it was *Cabela's* virtual Deer Country, and as I left the museumlike annex and returned to the main store, my hero fantasies melted away like so much snow in April. I was in a state of something like the shock you feel walking out of a movie theater into broad daylight. I'd spent a good part of the day in the store, including two hours in Deer Country. And I was ravenously hungry.

Cabela's has a special elevator designed to accommodate shopping carts, so I pushed mine into it and went up a flight. I made my way through the furniture and housewares department, where the stock included camo bedspreads, deer clocks, chandeliers, table lamps, and drawer pulls made of antlers—as well as a children's department featuring a board game called

Whitetailopoly, deer hunting coloring books, and a jigsaw puzzle of two old guys sitting in a truck, eating lunch, caught off-guard by a big buck leaping across the road in front of them.

I ate a buffalo burger in silence, suffering from something I never really experienced in the woods: whitetail overload. I was exhausted by it. When I left, a couple pushing a cart laden with hunting articles got into the elevator with me. The guy was wearing an authentic shit-eating grin. His wife stood beside him, smirking. I said hi and smiled at the couple. She finally blurted: "This place is too much. It's the only place I know where you can see guys pushing around shopping carts like they're actually enjoying it."

As I pushed my own cart across the bleak charcoal-colored plain of the parking lot, I felt depressed. Was I leaving a bordello, a church, a dream factory, or a pharmacy churning out medications that only made the afflicted sicker?

Out across I-75, the mountainside was cloaked in dark green forest, with thin, horizontal bands of fog clinging to its side. Somewhere up there, whitetail deer were stepping lightly along a trail, and I wondered if they even took notice of the harsh white lights in the valley below, or the steady stream of headlights on the highway, headed for Cabela's.

On my pending trip to Montana, I would be going from the dense, moist northeastern forests, hollows, and hills to the semiarid northwestern reach of the Great Plains—from hunting whitetail with a bow in tight cover on wooded farmland to ranging, rifle in hand, over the open Northern Plains, although river-bottom hunting in cover was also in the mix.

Good eyes and strong legs are the most valuable assets for a hunter on the plains, for it's a place that challenges an easterner's concept of distances and teaches you the true meaning of the oxymoron, "Hiding right out in the open."

It's counterintuitive, but while bow hunting represents a desire to make contact with tradition and what you might call the "old ways," there's a comparable purity about rifle hunting in open country. Factors like human scent, noise control, and even wind direction take a back seat to your eyesight, knowledge of the terrain, and familiarity with your weapon. The only two critical items of gear for spot-and-stalk-type hunting are a pair of binoculars and a rifle that shoots straight and far. You just put on a good pair of boots, grab field glasses, a rifle, and a handful of shells—and off you go.

Out there, I might be called upon to shoot comfortably and confidently at long distances—two hundred yards and beyond, maybe twice that far. And the last thing I wanted to do was miss my chance to kill a great big buck because I wasn't completely familiar with my gun, the scope wasn't properly sighted in, or I had second thoughts when I saw how small that buck looked in the cross hairs at two hundred fifty yards.

The rifle is a less complicated and far more potent tool than the bow, and a main source of the allure of gun hunting. I'm not a gun nut; I'm basically too lazy, impatient, and unwilling to be fettered to objects to be an "anything" nut. But I love rifles. I love to feel their heft; I love the way a bolt slides into place in the receiver and locks down with a deep, satisfying click.

At a gathering of friends at some Manhattan bar many years ago, an attractive girl I didn't previously know struck up a conversation with me. The talk turned to hobbies, and when I mentioned hunting, she frowned and said, "You mean you have *guns?* When are men going to get over this obsessive fascination they have with phallic symbols?"

"Probably never," I said, smiling. "Can I get you another drink?"

I love the sculpted, elegant lines of a rifle's stock, the fine scimitar that is the trigger, and the piercing suggestion of purpose in the thin barrel, which is married to the stock in such a way that the complete package suggests ultimate stability as well as at-hand volatility. How many other objects so successfully combine utility and beauty of design?

The late Colonel Jeff Cooper, long a guru of marksmen everywhere, had a marvelous ability to cut to the chase on the essence of guns. As he wrote in his slim but essential work, *The Art of the Rifle:*

> The rifle is a tool of power. A good rifleman can bring kinetic power to bear on his environment. He can reach out and cause things to happen decisively and selectively at a distance. With a good rifle in his hand, and the skill to use it well, he becomes, in a sense, a godlike figure. He may not need to use this power, but he commands it, and this is inexpressibly gratifying. This will to power is viewed askance by many who may be described as over-civilized. They hold that a man should not wish to command power, but whether he should or not is irrelevant, since he does.

America loves guns; I'm surprised we don't actually have a chain of stores called "Guns R Us." In fact, America was founded, tamed, kept whole, and defended by guns—specifically, rifles—in the most fundamental of ways. Lewis and Clark's diaries are chock-full of hunting references and stories, and scores of the men (including the well-educated, scientific-minded Meriwether Lewis) took obvious *pleasure* from hunting.

In that, they were both practicing and advancing a tradition that is still embraced by a wide swath of mostly male Americans. But they are also, as Cooper implies, our last link to what you might call "intimate" or perhaps even "just" warfare.

Guns are far more lethal than the lance, bow, or bayonet, yet they're not random, wholesale, or indiscriminate takers of life. The next step beyond the rifle is cannon and artillery, then the missile, followed by the bomb (or throw in a hijacked airliner, full of the innocent and terrified). All of them are designed to distribute death on a vastly less selective and more profligate scale than the gun.

We've gone a long way down the road toward making warfare a ghastly abstraction shimmering in a veil of radioactive dust. But the rifle remains not just the most basic weapon of war, it's the one that keeps intact the vital link between the warrior and his actions, decisions, and responsibilities. At one end of every gun is the shooter, making a decision about whether or not to shoot whatever he sees at the other end. In the wrong hands, the gun is a terrible instrument of destruction, but that's the tradeoff.

This kind of talk creeps out some people, but it's a fact of life and nothing to fear. Guns have been reduced to abstractions by many at both ends of the approval spectrum, representing anything from sacred liberty to the specter of violent crime or large-scale oppression. But it's helpful to remember these words of Cooper's:

> The rifle itself has no moral stature, since it has no will of its own. Naturally, it may be used by evil men for evil purposes, but there are more good men than evil, and while the latter cannot be persuaded to the path of righteousness by propaganda, they can certainly be corrected by good men with rifles.

Amen.

This next bit from Cooper's book has to be taken into account, and taken seriously, by anyone hoping to understand the entrenched position of gun rights and Second Amendment advocates in the United States:

> [The rifle] is a tool of power and thus dependent completely on the moral stature of its user. It is equally useful for securing meat for the table, destroying group enemies on the battle-

field, and resisting tyranny. In fact, it is the only means of resisting tyranny, because a citizenry armed with rifles cannot be
tyrannized.

I've often wondered if some of the genocides we've witnessed
even in our time (those in Rwanda and Bosnia among them)
would have been possible if those societies had evolved with
something comparable to our own Second Amendment rights.

Lord knows, most people love their BlackBerrys and iPods
these days, and while they understand what they do, they know
little about how they work, or how to keep them functional.
You want to walk me through the scary miniature electronic
village that is the motherboard of your cell phone, with its wire
streets and tiny buildings, or explain exactly how my voice gets
digitalized, beamed into space, and comes out loud and clear
when I'm screaming at some poor schmo in Mumbai about my
credit card bill?

The wonderful thing about the rifle is that it's essentially
no different than it ever was; today's sophisticated rifles are
still far more similar to the flintlocks used in the Revolution-
ary War than a computer is to pen and ink, even though both
of them are tools used for correspondence. In an age that values "transparency," even an idiot—maybe even an Ivy League
college professor—can easily understand how and why a gun
works. A few years ago, the *Sports Afield* writer Tom McIntyre
connected some dots and essentially came up with this time-
line for the evolution that gave us firearms:

> 40,000 B.C.—Flaked-stone spear points are hafted to
> wooden handles on a widespread basis, and the spear
> thrower, or *atlatl*, is devised, creating the first force-at-a-
> distance weapon.

30,000–15,000 B.C.—The bow originates in North Africa. At the same time, nomadic Asian hunters trail caribou herds east across the land bridge of Beringia and enter a land inhabited entirely by wildlife.

A.D. 900—Chinese use black powder to make fireworks, although the first formula isn't recorded by the English friar Roger Bacon until 1248.

A.D. 1304—Arabs use black powder in iron-and-bamboo guns to shoot arrows.

A.D. 1600—The gunsmith Marin le Bourgeoys perfects the flintlock, incorporating the frizzen and pan cover in a single piece of steel—to keep priming powder dry—and internalizing the lock's works.

That last item may be a bit puzzling, but it basically means that le Bourgeoys figured out the basics of how a hammer activated by a trigger can fall, create a spark, and ignite gunpowder. When the energy and gasses created by this small explosion are forced to travel through a tube (the rifle's barrel) that contains a lead ball (or bullet), the latter is forcibly ejected and becomes a deadly projectile.

The projectile penetrates as effectively as the laws of physics and certain variables (like the weight of the bullet, or amount of gunpowder used) allow. The bullet is still just a more efficient, miniaturized spear. In fact, "primitive" weapons, like the flintlock and black powder muzzleloader, are in a renaissance (often with considerable refinement), driven by nostalgia and the willingness of many gun hunters to limit the advantage given them by the precision and all-around superiority of regular rifles.

This curious counterrevolution underscores the mind-boggling performance of the modern rifle. An old-time black powder rifle might not fire at all, or it might fire and blow up, taking the top of your skull with it, and it was most accurate when the target was a barn door (or something larger). But the modern rifle is so reliable and accurate that if you didn't know better, you'd guess there was a computer hidden in it.

With today's off-the-shelf hunting rifle and barrel-mounted telescopic sight, the average deer hunter can easily put three bullets into a pie plate at 100 yards. Someone who puts in a little practice time can hit a half-gallon milk jug at 200 yards. A serious marksman can explode a watermelon at 300 yards and beyond, and a trained military sniper can kill a man at well over 1,000 yards—or over half a mile. It's like magic; you make this little explosion in a tube and a millisecond later, 250 yards away, a huge deer—or enemy combatant—falls over, stone-cold dead. Because of the variables, though, it's rarely that easy— especially at greater distances.

The biggest change in the way a rifle works occurred over a hundred years ago, when engineers and machinists figured out how to eliminate the powder and ball by coming up with the cartridge, a brass casing containing a primer that would ignite when struck by a hammer, enough powder to create an explosion, and a bullet tightly fitted into the top of the casing. The venerable but still useful .30-30 cartridge is shaped roughly like a lipstick; the cartridge for a .257 Weatherby Magnum looks like a missile with a deadly nose cone, and it has a tiny, sharp, red polymer tip.

The launching principle has remained unchanged. After you place the cartridge in the receiver (the area just above the trigger that marries with the near end of the barrel) of a bolt-action rifle, you lock it into place with the bolt, which also cocks the trigger. When you pull the trigger, a spring drives the firing pin— which is part of the bolt—forward, and it strikes the primer in the center of the base of the cartridge. The primer "sparks" the gunpowder, and the fierce energy of the subsequent controlled

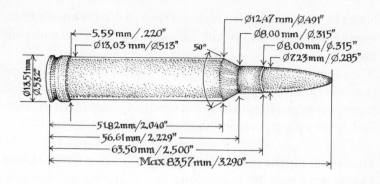

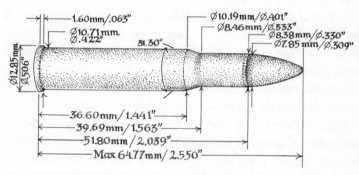

A 7 mm. Remington Magnum cartridge (top) and a .30-30 Winchester (bottom);
both are popular rounds for deer.

explosion contained within the small cartridge forces the bullet
out of the cartridge and barrel: *Ka-boom!*

This was all good fun and pretty straightforward stuff. But
things got considerably more complicated when folks realized
that you could make cartridges in any dimensions you wanted,
as long as you also machined a receiver, chamber, and barrel to
match it. The diameter of the bullet (not the brass cartridge)
at its fattest part (the base) is the basis of the caliber. And guns
are made in a dizzying array of calibers, to address a breadth
of real or imagined needs. Thus, a .270-caliber deer rifle fires a

bullet of that diameter, in inches. Try to stick a different caliber cartridge in there and it will ruin your day, your rifle, or your life.

It's easy to mass-produce cartridges of any size and shape, so gun-nut engineers, pro and amateur, began a race that is still being run to produce the ideal cartridge for any given application, from squirrel hunting to the needs of a nation's army.

The search for the perfect bullet proceeded in a helter-skelter way, leaving us with a confusing set of standards. The most important component in bullet configuration is caliber, so let's compare two of the top three deer hunting cartridges, the .30-30 and the .30/06. The important number in the former is the first thirty; the decimal point tells you the basic diameter of the bullet (to be precise, the .30-30 is .308-inch), hence, it's a thirty caliber. In this case, the second thirty stands for the amount of powder in the cartridge—thirty grains.

The .30/06 is a distant relative of the original .30-30, created when a designer brilliantly figured out that you could reduce or "neck down" the top of a casing, so you could use a relatively large casing to fire a smaller-sized bullet than a comparable old-fashioned cartridge. The .30/06 launched a .30-caliber bullet farther, faster, and with more energy than its forbear, but it was important to distinguish the various .30-caliber rounds from each other, because the much larger casing of the newer cartridge won't fit in the chamber of a gun in standard .30-30. The "06" was added to denote the difference; it stands for the year (1906) the "aught-six" was created.

Most U.S. cartridges go by the simple caliber designation: .243, .270, .308, and almost all modern cartridges are necked down. But even bullets of the same diameter can be larger or smaller, and can be launched by different amounts of powder. Hence, you're not just shooting a .30/06, but one with a 150-

grain bullet, powered by 51.8 grains of powder. Those three critical statistics are printed on every box of shells.

Calibers are sexed up with hyphens in random fashion, although they represent most important distinctions in design and/or materials. Sometimes, a guy who develops a bullet likes the idea of attaching his name to it, as in the case of the .257 Roberts or the .257 Weatherby Magnum (for fame-whores Ned Roberts and Roy Weatherby, respectively). Weatherby was instrumental in taking cartridge design and ballistics to the potent, magnum level. Stay tuned.

One obvious question pops up: *So why isn't the .270 simply rounded down and called a .27 caliber, as in the .30-caliber guns?* Well, it's done that way to eliminate fractional confusion. In order to be accurate and functional, the barrel that shoots the round must precisely match the caliber. Over time, the increasing sophistication of manufacturing techniques opened the floodgates. The real-world difference between a .223 Remington and a .243 Winchester is minimal but significant. And since gun makers are also ammo manufacturers (hence distinguishing a caliber by adding the name "Remington"), they love to double dip with proprietary calibers. Cartridge design has evolved with little rhyme or reason, and a striking lack of standardization.

Despite the plethora of calibers available for deer hunting, almost all of the commonly used ones range between .223 and .308. When it comes to hunting whitetail, a lot of people have spent a lot of time monkeying around with a difference of *less than* eighty-five thousandths of an inch. There are at least seventeen cartridges in what is roughly known as the .30-caliber (or 7.62 mm., in the European system) division *alone,* and fifteen in the .270 (7 mm.) category.

The final, great leap forward for gun-toting mankind was the birth of the magnum calibers. Basically, a magnum is a regular cartridge on steroids, developed by tinkerers (including the prominent American gun nut Roy Weatherby) who figured out that you could fit a mighty small bullet into a mighty big casing containing a crazy amount of gunpowder by dramatically necking down the casing at the top.

Ka-boom! suddenly grew up and became *KA-BOOM!*

The needle of the macho-meter leaps into the red with the magnums, because they can deliver tremendous killing power —and make a gun kick like the proverbial mule. This development ramped up interest in the science of ballistics, which is the study of the flight and properties of projectiles. It did wonders for chiropractors, too.

A heavy, blunt bullet powered by a relatively modest amount of powder (like the .30-30) loses energy quickly in the face of gravity. It travels in a mild parabola, because gravity is a buzzkill. In the case of the .30-30, the bullet begins to drop soon after it's traveled the length of a football field. But an aerodynamic bullet, powered by a hefty load of powder, retains its energy far longer, so it doesn't begin to drop until later—much later, giving rise to the term "flat-shooting load."

I bought a .257 Weatherby Magnum for my Montana trip, as backup for my go-to gun, a Howa 7 mm. Remington Magnum. The Weatherby shoots a considerably smaller, lighter bullet, but at a slightly faster speed than the larger caliber. But both loads outperform the old standbys. While a round-nosed, 100-grain bullet for a .30-30 leaves the barrel at 2,684 fps (feet per second), a spire-point bullet of the same weight leaves the Weatherby at a scorching 3,602 fps. This means that if you were to fire the Weatherby from your bedroom window at the moon (we've all been there, right?), it would travel the 238,857 miles and hit the cheese in just about 66 seconds, give or take a millisecond.

Yee-haw.

Of course, no bullet retains its energy long enough to travel such a great distance, because gravity eventually pulls it down. Still, the .257 Weatherby hits about two and a half inches *above* point-of-aim (POA) at a hundred yards, because the bullet is still rising; at two hundred yards, it's about three inches high— and at the peak of its parabolic journey. Then it begins to drop relatively swiftly. It hits POA dead on at three hundred yards, but it hits more than seven inches low at four hundred yards. By contrast, at three hundred yards the .30-30 is practically bouncing end over end along the ground.

The various calibers appropriate for deer hunting all have staunch devotees. Chuck Hawks, a gun nut and operator of the valuable *Guns and Shooting* website, lists the ten most popular deer cartridges, with the .223 more or less tied with the .30/06 for the top spot. This is a bit puzzling, as the .223 is generally considered a military or varmint cartridge barely suitable for big game. The leaders are followed closely by the .270 Winchester and that ultimate survivor, the .30-30. I like the 7 mm. Remington Magnum because it shoots flat but still features a bullet with more mass than some of the other hot loads, like the .257 Weatherby.

I bought the Weatherby .257 Mag Mark V for the same reason some middle-aged men buy a canary yellow Corvette convertible. Because it's sexy, and I'm not. The Weatherby is the prettiest, most expensive gun I've ever owned, even though I opted for a tan synthetic stock over natural wood. Synthetic stocks are less affected by weather, they're lighter, and you don't worry as much about scratches or dings. The gun is almost dainty, with a fluted barrel and other weight-saving touches that make it easier to carry around on long hikes. It has that "updated classic" look, and for a while I was happy just to look at it.

I put off adjusting the scope of, or sighting-in, the new rifle until an unseasonably mild and humid day shortly before I left for Montana. Tony Perosi, my local gunsmith, had fitted the gun with a Bushnell scope. Tony is a part-time Christmas tree farmer, which explains the sign in front of his combination home and shop: *Perosi's Guns and Trees*. Just like that, as if it were, say, *Pantyhose and Auto Parts*.

These days, sighting-in can be a snap, thanks to "bore sighting" (which has nothing to do with spotting Al Gore picking up a bean taco). By inserting a nifty little device with a laser into the chamber of the rifle barrel, a scope can usually be adjusted to hit somewhere on an eighteen-inch-square paper target at fifty yards. Once you're on paper (where you can tell how far off point-of-aim you are), the rest is easy. The scope has two covered adjustment dials, one that moves the cross hairs up or down (for elevation), the other, left to right, for "windage." (This has nothing to do with Al Gore's physical reaction to said bean taco.)

I expected sighting-in, also known as zeroing, to be easy. I stapled a new paper target to a two-foot-square piece of plywood and hung it in a frame made from PVC pipe. I set up the target in a hay meadow, with the berm of my pond for a backstop. I positioned the Deermobile to serve as my shooting bench, resting my rifle on a pillow on the hood to provide a steady rest.

The critical component in zeroing is potential human error —hitting far off POA not because the scope needs adjusting, but because you're incompetent, unable to keep the cross hairs on target when you squeeze off the shot. Therefore, you shoot three

A high-powered rifle scope.

or four bullets at a time, starting at fairly close range (sixty or seventy yards). If the bullets are clustered close together, within a two- or three-inch diameter, the gun is shooting fine. It doesn't matter how far off the bull's-eye (your POA) they are; if the bullets are grouped together, the gun is fine. You just need to adjust the scope to move the point-of-impact into the bull's-eye.

After that, you check your group at the baseline range of a hundred yards. For flat-shooting guns, you zero in slightly high on purpose. For the .257 Mag, I wanted to be two and a half inches above POA at a hundred yards. That's still well within the kill zone, and puts me dead on the bull's-eye at three hundred yards under ideal conditions.

You can often tell the quality of your shot the moment the gun goes off, just like a golfer or tennis player automatically feels how well he or she hit a ball even before it lands. Serious marksmen spend a lot of time building or customizing bench rests to stabilize and hold a rifle in a viselike grip, and they use aids like leather bags filled with sand, all in the effort to reduce the possibility of human error. I wasn't worried about that, though, as I prepared to sight-in the .257. I told myself, "Should be a piece of cake."

In fact, I set up the target at a hundred yards and rushed back to shoot. I had to run back to the house to get my ammo and ear protection; I was still breathing heavily as I worked the bolt to chamber a round. It seemed a bit sticky, and I had trouble positioning the cartridge in the chamber for proper feeding when I closed the bolt. It takes time to get accustomed to a new rifle, especially if you don't handle it daily.

I leaned against the side of the truck, settled the rifle on the pillow, and wriggled into a comfortable position looking out over the hood. I set the cross hairs on the target and squeezed the trigger. I squeezed it tighter. It felt a bit stiff but suddenly the gun went off: *Ka-boom!* I was surprised by the attending kick; clearly it was the tradeoff for the light weight of the pretty gun. But the shot still felt okay.

I fairly sprinted out into the meadow to see if by some miracle I hit dead on. The target was pristine. Tony said he'd bore-sighted the gun, which ought to have put the bullet *somewhere* on the target. Could I have made such a poor shot?

As I hurried back, I thought, *Okay. Let's take it easy here.* I fired that first shot nervously, in haste; now it was time to get serious. I fumbled another cartridge into the receiver.

I wriggled around, trying to seat the stock firmly in the pocket of my shoulder. It didn't feel quite right. The rifle has a handsome "Monte Carlo" style stock, which looks good and always felt fine when I shouldered it for fun. But shooting a rifle is different from playing around with it, and it's hard to shoot confidently if you're not entirely comfortable.

I was so busy thinking about all this that I forgot to replace my ear protection before my next shot. I realized my mistake on the report, which reverberated in the shallow natural bowl of my meadow. Dang it! I grabbed my headphones, fed another cartridge into the chamber, hunkered down, and touched off my third round.

As soon as the gun barked, everything went dark and my head flew back. A moment later, eyes wide open, I felt warm blood trickling down the bridge of my nose, mingling with the perspiration that was now streaming down my face. In my haste, I'd crowded the scope, and on report it kicked back and slammed my forehead. The popular name for this embarrassing and painful duffer's mistake is "scope eye."

I trudged down to the target, wishing I could just take back the past thirty minutes of my life and start all over. The blood was drying on the side of my nose. I braced for the worst. I was still off the paper, all right, but I also noticed three tiny holes at the lower right-hand corner of the plywood backing. It was less like a group than a loose association.

Let's be smart about this, I told myself. I vowed to take things one step at a time. I brought the target in by half the distance, to fifty yards, and returned to the rifle. I unscrewed the elevation and windage caps and rotated the bezels thirty-two audible clicks in the "up" direction (each click represents a quarter of an inch), and then dialed eight clicks left on the windage dial. That ought to bring me way up, and toward the center of the target.

I had a good additional reason for getting it right: a box of cartridges for my cute new gun goes for about sixty bucks, or three bucks a bullet. This rifle had its work cut out if it was going to provide more bang for the buck. I loaded another cartridge, took my time, and touched it off. I expected to see a hole with my naked eye at fifty yards, but the paper looked clean.

How could I not even be close after that adjustment, especially at a mere fifty yards? Maybe that sexy little bullet traveled through the plywood so fast that it left a really inconspicuous hole right in the bull's-eye. I resisted dashing out to take a look. I forced myself to shoot two more bullets. When I checked the target, it was clean.

I was on the verge of real panic. I had just bought a handsome, expensive, state-of-the-art, flat-shooting rifle—a gun nut's version of that yellow Corvette. And it was like I couldn't find reverse to back the car out of the driveway. In the right hands, the rifle could explode a liter bottle of water at four hundred yards. I couldn't hit a two-foot-square sheet of plywood at a whopping hundred and fifty feet.

Hell, I could probably hit the bull's-eye throwing a freaking rock—and don't think I wasn't tempted.

I stared at the stupid, clean target—unsullied but for the three small, original holes in the plywood. My confidence was shot, I was hot, and the wound on the bridge of my nose had opened up again. Blood trickled down the side of my nose.

I studied the target some more. Was there any chance that

in my distracted state, I'd adjusted the elevation and windage dials in the wrong direction? It's been known to happen. And then I remembered something else: a few months earlier, I had fooled around some with my .22-caliber rifle. Was that the source of those three holes?

It was time to return to square one. I dialed the scope back to its original bore-sighted position. I resolved to shoot three more rounds at fifty yards and, if I saw no improvement, I'd go back to Tony and stare at my shoes as I tried to explain. Or I'd just throw the gun into the deep end of the pond.

I shot the next three rounds feeling calm resignation. So what if I never got over being a nimrod, there was more to life than giant whitetail bucks, right? As if to punctuate the thought, I flinched on the final shot; it would certainly be a flier.

I was shocked when I examined the target. The three holes formed a perfect triangle, with two of the holes a respectable inch apart. The group was about six inches high and about three inches to the right. That wasn't very far off at all.

My confidence was returning. I moved the target back out to a hundred yards. This time, I was extra careful to crank the dials in the correct direction, down and to the left. I fired three more shots that produced a good group that I could almost cover with a quarter, about an inch and a half high and an inch to the right. I brought the windage four clicks left, and the elevation four clicks up. I shot a single bullet and hit dead on and four inches high. I brought the cross hairs down by two clicks and called it good.

I would double-check and fine-tune the scope later in the afternoon, because I certainly needed to spend more time with the gun. Bloody, bathed in sweat, I trudged back toward the house to celebrate with a beer. It wasn't such a bad gun after all. And it sure was pretty.

6

The Whitetail Express

GREAT FALLS, MONTANA, OCTOBER 24-28

ON THE PLANE from Newark, New Jersey, to Salt Lake City, I sat on the aisle next to a bland-looking man in a pale blue polo shirt and gray slacks. He was traveling with his girlfriend or wife, an attractive woman of Chinese extraction who knew her designer labels. They were heading for a long weekend in Las Vegas. The row behind us was filled—and I use the word literally—by a pair of hunting buddies from New Jersey and a man in a suit heading for a wedding in Salt Lake City. The guy in the suit volunteered that he too was a hunter, but doomed to spend the weekend at a wedding.

I was on the whitetail express, surrounded for once by like-minded deer hunters rather than anonymous strangers. Most of us were heading for points west for the opening of big-game season. Somewhere out there, I hoped, my monster buck waited.

My fellow pilgrims leaned toward facial hair and were dressed in workingman's designer labels by the New York Giants (Windbreakers) or Carhartt. They wore camo or blaze-orange trucker caps and traveled in small groups of three or four, each guy a camo fanny-pack-toting genetic masterpiece of blended muscle and fat adding up to one tough hombre. They were men who went to work in cushioned white socks and tan boots. Men with reserves, who would endure and survive.

They weren't so different, I mused, from the hardy souls who originally went west to try their hand at trapping beaver or prospecting for minerals—a gamey lot, meant for a rough life that has vanished, but echoes of which might still be evoked when the wind whispered in the pines somewhere up in the Crazy Mountains, or elk bugled yonder in the Bitterroots.

Mixed in among them were softer men who were also, clearly, going hunting. Accountants and lawyers and salesmen, I imagined, in their khaki slacks, white Reebok sneakers, and Zuni-patterned chamois shirts. Some wore jaunty cowboy hats of woven straw. Live the life, speak the language; I felt I was among friends.

The boys from New Jersey were pretty jacked up, and before the flight attendants even started serving their Jack Daniel's and Cokes, they were telling hunting stories peppered with observations heard around campfires and in honky-tonks since forever: *And wouldn't you know it—there stands the buck! . . . That didn't work out so bad . . .* Or, *I wouldn't've believed it, but I seen it with my own eyes . . . So I wondered, "What's the worst that could happen?"*

I wondered if the nicely dressed couple in my row were listening, aghast. But they were absorbed in a close examination of the man's brand-new iPhone. When we emerged from the clouds above Salt Lake City, not high above the surrounding, rugged peaks, the woman briefly forgot the phone and her plan of attack for the baccarat table in Las Vegas and gasped: "Oh my God, look, snow!"

During a brief layover in Salt Lake City, I joined the reprobates in the smoking lounge, a Skinneresque glass box where disapproving passersby peered at the grim, guilty-looking addicts sucking down their Marlboros and Newports in a dense fog of blue tobacco smoke. I bummed a cigarette and sat down between a well-groomed woman traveling for business and a college-aged kid in a black Pearl Jam T-shirt and the obligatory ski cap.

Across the aisle, two well-heeled good ole boys from the south were volubly discussing the food plots they had created in order to improve the antler quality of the deer on their hunting property. One of them launched into a graphic tale of how his young son mangled the job of gutting the first deer he'd ever shot. As the talk drifted to the gory details, some of my fellow smokers cringed and looked the other way.

The lobby of the airport in Great Falls features a towering stuffed grizzly bear, paws aloft, and a lovely bronze sculpture of Sacagawea. I stopped to pay my respects at both before I picked up the rental car and crossed the river of ultimate romance, the Missouri. The wind, gusting up to fifty miles per hour, whipped the gray-green surface to a froth under a gray sky. On the horizon the backlit clouds looked like snowcapped mountains.

Great Falls was named for the portion of the Missouri River where the Lewis and Clark expedition experienced some of its most debilitating hardships. The five distinct "falls" were rapids that now lie buried under a reservoir, but it took the Corps of Discovery a full month to portage the party's five gigantic dugout canoes, and tons of gear, eighteen miles around the falls— and they were tormented by hailstorms, grizzly bears, and the prickly pear cactus growing underfoot nearly every step of the way.

Great Falls, southwest of the original falls, is at the eastern edge of the Rocky Mountain front, and while the city takes great pride in its history (the Lewis and Clark Museum, located in the heart of a sleepy, neat neighborhood of modest one-family houses, is a treasure), it remains very much a working—and a workingman's—town. It looks forward in time rather than back.

The town is chock-a-block with mills, silos, storage facilities, and functional gray cinder-block or steel-and-aluminum buildings and sheds, built on a scale to accommodate heavy machinery and railcars. Great Falls grew up around the railroad, which still weaves its tentacles in the form of branch lines and sidings right through the heart of town. Great Falls developed much like the nation itself, outwardly and horizontally from a small, nuclear center, along arteries of commerce where the trails were most easily beaten into roads, or happened to go in expedient directions for either commerce or the steady westward march of settlement.

Those original arteries now are lined with car and truck dealerships, mini-malls, big-box stores, and chain motels and restaurants. Say what you will about American food, nutrition-wise, there's nothing quite as friendly and inviting as your typical, brightly lit, mostly glass restaurant that features menus laminated in plastic, booths upholstered in Naugahyde, and waitresses wearing nametags.

Gusts of wind buffeted the car; the skies were turbulent and dry. I dialed in the local country station and caught a blizzard of advertisements for Big Bear sporting goods; if you read the local papers, listened to the radio, or watched television pretty much anywhere in Montana, it was impossible *not* to know that the big-game season would open in less than forty-eight hours, and that was a far cry from the situation in New York. Hunting in the Rocky Mountain region carries no stigma; it's an organic, free-range enterprise.

The radio pitchman for Big Bear gently reminded listeners: "We are here for guns and ammunition—things that have been on your mind for quite a while." At 7:00 P.M., Big Bear would be giving away an all-terrain vehicle—the lucky winner's name would be drawn in public, out in the parking lot. I couldn't stay that long, but I did stop to do my part for the local economy and take in the atmosphere.

Big Bear was doing a bang-up business, with children—mostly, but not all, boys—bewitched by the plethora of guns, knives, fishing rods, and camping gear. I watched one agitated eleven-year-old plead with his father for a new fishing rod and reel combo that cost twenty-five bucks. But his dad, a man with sandy hair and the ruddy complexion of someone who spends more time outdoors than in, told him: "No, son, we ain't got enough money for that."

These appeared to be people who worked hard for the little they had, and took pride in their ability to make do. Some of them bore earmarks of a punishing life, in the form of missing digits, a limp, or a hacking cough. I wondered how many could trace their roots back to the original mountain men who first explored this country in the early nineteenth century. For they, too, were a lot to whom physical brokenness was a sign of having lived hard, which was synonymous with having lived well and true.

Every summer during the peak of the fur-trapping era, those prototypical frontiersmen would gather in some high Wyoming or Idaho mountain valley for what came to be known as "rendezvous." It was a carnival of traders, trappers, Indians, charlatans, scouts, snake-oil salesmen, explorers, whiskey runners, and whores from near and far. Many were Frenchmen, a fact so surprising that upon hearing it a self-styled red-blooded American might drop his freedom fries.

The mountain men convened to barter, buy, drink, screw,

gamble, race their horses, and shoot—often, at each other, because that was back when a drunk was a drunk. They found squaws to marry and new pardners with whom to go yondering. By the end of rendezvous, many of the men had pissed away the value of their entire winter's worth of hard-earned beaver pelts; others had pissed away their lives.

One of the few common threads connecting their life to ours, despite the enormous changes wrought by modern life, is hunting—particularly ungulate hunting. Men still have a hankering to go off into the mountains to pursue deer and elk; they still feed their families venison they're proud to have been crafty, skilled, or lucky enough to pursue and slaughter. And they still use these ritual activities to forge or strengthen transcendent bonds with other men and family members—ties that last longer than twenty-five-dollar fishing outfits.

I also stopped at the local Albertsons supermarket, where kids with mullets called me "sir" and helped me find anything I needed. I chanced upon a few Hutterites, members of a sect with Anabaptist roots who live a communal life on expansive and often isolated land holdings throughout the West. The men were wind-burned and bearded, dressed in cowboy hats and black frock coats over white shirts, like bounty hunters in an old Western movie. One of their colonies, Guilford, is very close to the ranch where I would be hunting with my friends, David and Julie Aageson.

Out in the Albertsons parking lot, a fierce puff of wind ripped the ten-gallon hat off a three-hundred-pound male specimen in a skimpy navy tank top; after an impressive display of broken-field running, he just gave up, and I commiserated with him as we watched his smart hat tumbleweed out onto the highway. He just stood there, hands on his hips, cursing the wind pouring in off the great Northern Plains.

I picked up some fresh flowers for David's wife, Julie, and

pointed the car northeast, into the plains, heading for Fort Benton and, ultimately, the Aagesons' Milk River Ranch. The town nearest their ranch is Rudyard, which is little more than a rail siding (for shipping grain) with a gas pump, the shuttered Hi-Line movie theater, and a bar.

The sign welcoming me to Rudyard on Route 2 said: WELCOME TO RUDYARD, 596 NICE PEOPLE AND ONE OLD SOREHEAD . . .

Julie, an attractive blue-eyed blond, waved from the window of the Aagesons' cozy one-story home as I pulled into the gravel drive at the ranch. David and Julie live within a stone's throw of David's brother, Verges, and his wife, Noreen, in a ranching family compound—a cluster of machinery sheds, barns, and grain-storage facilities, among which the actual homes are the smallest buildings.

Julie greeted me warmly and told me that David and Verges were off somewhere on ranch business. Beyond the lone pine tree in front of the house, a sea of uninterrupted prairie stretched in every direction. To the northeast, the canyon of the Milk River was discernible, the bluffs beyond it evening plum tinged with orange. That was where the whitetail would be, down by the river, the de facto lifeline of the Aagesons' sprawling ranch.

Over coffee, Julie told me that the small Hill County herd of elk had been spotted seeking shade and lollygagging down by the river in recent days. But prairie elk are wizened survivors, with a remarkable capacity for melting into the country. The big-game staples are deer (whitetail and mule) and antelope. The latter run free across the endless prairie, impudently flashing their bright white asses like smiling ham actors at one and all, always just out of range, but always curious—and always ready to lope off and put another half a mile between you and them, seemingly just because they can. Then they stop and look back over their shoulders, too far away to tell if they're actually sticking out their tongues.

The mule deer, by contrast, stay close to the Paleolithic breaks and coulees—deep, violent gashes filled with prehistoric rubble and a surprising amount of flora and fauna. These ravines were ancient watercourses, carved in the earth by torrents of commingled fresh and salt water in what was once a steaming and fetid wetland thick with dinosaurs. David and Julie named their daughter "Maia," after the maiasaur, a dinosaur once so abundant in the Milk River country that each time a bank crumbles on the ranch, David is apt to stumble upon a fossilized bone or two. Although the country is high prairie and notionally flat, from a few thousand feet up it would look more like an intricate lace doily, with the coulees representing the empty spaces in the fabric of the prairie.

Over the coming days, we would hunt both of the deer species as well as elk, because the Aagesons had all the required permits and tags. As a nonresident "landowner-sponsored" hunter, my four-hundred-dollar license and single tag entitled me to shoot one buck, either mule deer or whitetail, and I also was entitled to fish and hunt small game, including the highly desirable local game birds—Hungarian partridge, sharp-tail grouse, or pheasants. While the prime river-bottom whitetail habitat at David's ranch is limited and would have to be hunted lightly and carefully, the mule deer range is practically endless —and the elk could show up anywhere.

"I'm about to go down to feed the horses," Julie said. "Want to help load some hay while I mix up a tub of beetroot?"

We loaded up the truck and drove the four miles down to the river and corral. The Milk River was named by Captain Meriwether Lewis during the Journey of Discovery. As he wrote in his famous journal: "The water of this river possesses a peculiar whiteness, being about the color of a cup of tea with the admixture of a tablespoonful of milk. From the color of its water we called it Milk River."

That milky tint is caused by suspended particles of rock flour—a fine sediment created by glacial erosion at the Milk's headwaters in the Rockies. In the reaches where I know it, the Milk is merely a slate gray shadow of its former self, because enormous amounts of water are drawn off for irrigation. The portion that runs through the ranch is a shallow, opaque artery that barely appears to move between wide mud flats and steep clay banks. The Milk is rarely more than sixty feet wide, and mostly knee-deep, easily forded by horse or even truck at any crossing where the bottom is sufficiently solid.

You'd pretty much have to pass out drunk and fall on your face in the Milk in order to drown, and that's been done, more than once. The Milk is a frayed, taut river, but still a remarkable lifeline in a hard country given to extremes—searing heat, strong, unrelenting winds, bitter cold. It isn't that far from Rudyard to Browning, the Montana town that holds the distinction of having experienced the greatest twenty-four-hour swing of temperature ever recorded. In that period on January 23, 1916, the temperature fell an even hundred degrees—from 44 above to 56 degrees below (Fahrenheit).

In addition to running cattle and growing wheat, the Aagesons have experimented with coriander, chickpeas, and red beans. They also have some land in the Conservation Reserve Program—a government initiative that some might offhandedly ridicule as an example of taxpayers paying farmers not to grow crops.

But the reality is more complicated. A cultivated field is, for long portions of the year, a barren wasteland that offers neither food nor cover for wildlife. The CRP compensates farmers for allowing parts of their land to revert to natural grasses and shrubs, which are of enormous value as wildlife habitat and forage. And rested CRP lands can make for better crop fields when they're put back into rotation.

David and Julie still work their cattle with horses. It sounds preposterous in this day and age, but just a few years ago David got into deep trouble while driving cattle in the backcountry because his horse, Winks, got into some quicksand. In the ensuing panic and thrashing around, Winks broke David's ankle and expended so much energy trying to extricate himself that he had to be put up in the corral for months to recuperate.

Julie, though, is the official family cowpuncher. She's a former barrel racer, and as we fed the horses she told me about the time she and two lady friends had to wrangle a cow in order to treat it for pinkeye, a more menacing disease in cattle than in humans, partly because it's a lot harder to put eye drops into a cow on the range than a child sitting on the edge of a bed.

"We couldn't get to this particular cow with the truck, and with pinkeye, every hour counts. So my friend Claudie came up with a plan. She said, 'Let's us just go and rope her.' So I figured, Why not?

"The plan was for Claudie's daughter, Blue, to head her [throw a loop around the cow's neck] and Claudie to heel her [lasso the hind legs]. Once they had the cow stretched out, I'd jump down and inject the medication—it has to be injected with this big steel hypodermic needle, right into the inner eyelid.

"Oh, you should have seen us! Them with their lassos and me carrying this great big hypodermic needle, all loaded up, as we went barreling after that cow across this flat. The horses were jumping left and right, trying to avoid the sagebrush, the cow was giving us a run for our money. But we finally caught up with that ornery cow and we got the job done. Mylanta, but it was some show."

"Mylanta?" That's just a Julie-ism.

David could be forgiven for feeling less passionate about cowboy ways. His father, Arvin, had two brothers, Wallace and Eugene. One day when Eugene was eight, he and Wallace were playing cowboy, roping each other for fun. Wallace threw a loop and caught Eugene. For some reason Wallace's horse unexpectedly spooked, bucked him off, and lit out. The rope—with Eugene at the other end—was looped around the pommel, and the boy was dragged to death as his father looked on helplessly from nearby, on the seat of his tractor.

Until the day he died, Arvin warned his own boys, David and Verges, each time either of them climbed on a horse. It was often a hard life on the Milk River Ranch, but also a vigorous one. It still is.

The brothers Aageson were back at the ranch in time for supper. David is two years older than Verges and unlike his brother in almost every way. Where Verges is heavyset with a great shock of white hair and possessed of many strong opinions that he's willing to share, wantonly but always in a spirit of bonhomie, David is prudent and soft-spoken, carefully measuring his words before he speaks.

Lean and sinewy, David has a well-trimmed mustache and wears photochromatic eyeglasses. He's bowlegged, like a movie cowboy, but neither he nor Verges has ever affected a cowboy hat (as Verges told me, "It's just too damned windy out here to keep one on"). David wears Roper boots, drives a Dodge truck, and dips Copenhagen snuff. As a child on the ranch, he suffered so severely from hay allergies that during harvest, he was often forced to sit in the truck, windows rolled up, perspiration rolling down his face in 110-degree heat. "But," he told me, "I wouldn't have missed harvest for the world. Even if I just watched, boiling in the truck."

David graduated (as did Verges) from St. Olaf's College, and also studied in England at Cambridge, where he experienced "culture shock" upon learning that you couldn't get Copenhagen snuff in London.

Shortly after David returned to the ranch in 1971, ready to help Verges and Arvin, he was recruited to fill a vacant seat in the Montana State Legislature. He subsequently ran for reelection (at age twenty-three), and—much to his surprise—won. He served in the legislature until he and Verges bought the ranch from their parents, in April 1978.

David first met Julie (née Billings) when she was a thirteen-year-old page at the statehouse, brought there by her grandmother, who also served in the assembly and sat in the row immediately in front of Representative David Aageson. Julie did not go unnoticed by David, and in such a sparsely populated state, it was inevitable that they would keep tabs on each other. But they didn't officially begin dating until after David left politics.

The first time David and Julie were to go out was also the first day of operation for the ranch's brand-new irrigation pivot. The device malfunctioned, and repairing it caused David to be a mere four hours late—which isn't too bad, when you consider the distances people have to travel in a large state as sparsely populated as Montana. Shortly thereafter, David took Julie home to the ranch for the obligatory first dinner with his family. During dessert, he suddenly leaned back from the table and spat a stream of tobacco juice right on his mother's carpet. Julie told me, "God, I just about jumped out of my chair and ran out of there for good when I saw that!"

David still can't explain what possessed him to do something so uncharacteristic, for he's a mannerly man. But the courtship survived that incident and, by the fall, David and Julie were married. David frankly admitted: "It was a great relief to the folks all around here when I got married, because by that time they were starting to think I might be gay. But I was just busy with ranch life." Two children (Maia has an older brother, Roald) and many years later, David and Julie still flirt and tease each other like high school sweethearts.

With the Sunday season opener one day away, we had scouting to do. But David and Verges were unable to join me on Saturday. They were meeting with real estate appraisers. Like many ranchers of their generation, the Aagesons face some tough decisions about what to do with the ranch in an era when it's no longer assumed that the kids will either want or be able to carry on farming. They don't want to subdivide, partly because the ranch is an enormous repository of fossils, dating back to the Cretaceous period, and it occupies land that is not just rich in Indian artifacts but still considered sacred ground by a number of tribes. They feel it ought to remain of a piece.

Some natives say that the last buffalo on the plains were shot on the Milk River. On one visit to the ranch, a tribal leader asked Verges Aageson if he could "feel the spirit" of the place. In a signature Verges moment, he replied, "Quite frankly, I can't. I guess I'm too used to scaring the shit out of myself chasing cows at forty miles an hour along these drop-offs and cliffs."

It was still dark outside when I got up to go scouting on Saturday morning. David was already up, making coffee. "Better layer up," he said. "It'll be pretty chilly until that sun comes up."

The Aagesons' spread hugs the southern and western edges of an intricate network of badlands and coulees created by, among other things, the ever-changing bed of the Milk River and its numerous seasonal or long-vanished tributaries. The flood plain is broad, filled with cottonwoods, sagebrush, and buffalo berry, and framed by vertical cliffs frequently notched by coulees that drift and meander back away from the river, sometimes for miles.

The land is like a photonegative of what most people think of when it comes to landscape. Where most rural land outside the Great Plains is black with trees, this country is blond with grasses; where most flatlanders are accustomed to mountains erupting on the horizon, here the coulees plunge deep into the earth—the passes and switchbacks take you down below the level of the plain, to the river.

In the hour before dawn, the upper atmosphere was a fine silvery blue, with long black streaks of cloud clinging to the horizon. I drove slowly, without lights. On the crest of land near the pivot, I briefly saw the silhouettes of half a dozen deer, including one with a great rack of antlers etched into a background of fading stars. I was almost sure they were whitetail in the irrigated field, because they have an affinity for man's crops and know how to find them, machinery or human activity be damned.

I rolled slowly through the first choke between two steep hills and began a gentle, winding descent to the river. Leaving the truck by the corral, I visited with the horses until there was adequate daylight to walk the wagon track along the river, scanning with binoculars. I studied the overgrown islands in the braided-up section of the river; in one place, the river makes an enormous oxbow, and only an eight- or ten-foot wall of earth lies between the currents going in different directions. Within a year or two, when the wall fails, an entire half-mile of river will simply vanish and become part of the rich flood plain.

Whitetail love brushy cover, and the reeds, grasses, and dense stands of buffalo berry and chokecherry growing amid the groves of cottonwood and autumn olive trees provide plenty of it. As careful as I was, I was busted by a pair of deer bedded near the edge of an island. I saw only their white flags as they bounded off. By then, light was breaking over the bluffs to the east. A pheasant cackled, welcoming the new day.

I was disappointed not to see more deer, but the cover was excellent and the local whitetail population was still on the rebound from a recent outbreak of "blue tongue," a fatal virus that affects livestock and deer. David had seen some nice whitetail bucks here and there all summer, but they were scattered, and the rut was not yet upon them. As sunlight began to creep across the floor of the flood plain, I returned to the truck; I wanted to glass the upper valley with binoculars from some high bluffs before the heat of the day drove the deer into the brush or coulees.

As I rolled down over the rise at Gunsight Pass, I spotted a three-by-three buck mule deer (out West, they favor that description to "six-point") about a hundred yards off and to the left. I killed the engine and picked up my field glasses. The buck was heading my way, following a shallow wash that crossed the road up ahead.

Mule deer are the product of a curious string of incestuous couplings. The blacktail deer, the third major deer subspecies, is thought to have evolved from the original whitetail. As both species flourished, these distant relations met again at the margins of the prairie and interbred, their descendants evolving into the lord of the plains, the mule deer.

Much like the whitetail, the mule deer derived its name from a distinguishing physical characteristic. Having great ears instead of a highly visible tail that can be seen by other deer, even in thick brush, might seem a logical tradeoff for life on the open plains. But the main survival advantage of the mule deer's oversized ears has nothing to do with hearing. Their main value is thermal. Those oversized ears serve as twin head-mounted radiators.

Like most mammals, deer have a limited internal cooling sys-

A mule deer has notably large ears, and its antlers are all forked, with additional forked antlers growing from the original pair.

tem (humans, with their ability to perspire, are a good example of advanced engineering). Blood is, among other things, a liquid coolant that helps keep the core temperature of a deer at an acceptable level. When blood is pumped through the large ears of a mulie, it's distributed by a complex network of veins over a fairly large area very close to the surface of the skin, where it's cooled by the air. This is a critical function in the harsh, often scorching environment of the Great Plains.

Out on the open range, good hearing and scent detection are useful tools, but the eyes take on a dominant role in survival. When a mule deer senses danger, it signals its cohorts in a more unusual way than the whitetail, by "stotting."

Stotting is a kangaroolike hopping on all four legs, as if the deer were on a four-pronged pogo stick. Mule deer can trot and gallop like any whitetail, but often fall back upon this unique gait when mildly alarmed. Stotting also enables mule deer to see over tall brush, and to go over rather than around obstacles.

In contrast to a whitetail's lavish flag, a mule deer's tail is short and stubby, but it recoups a measure of sex appeal with its shapely, tan rump. The antler configuration of America's two major deer is another signature difference. The whitetail has a pair of main beams that basically sweep up and forward from the skull. The additional tines, or points, grow out of the main beams like perpendicular pickets in a fence.

By contrast, a mule deer's antlers always end in forks. The first antlers of a young specimen are like a forward canted letter Y—similar to a forkhorn whitetail. The following year, the buck will grow another Y at about the midpoint of either original antler. Most mature mule deer are four-by-fours; it's the width, height, and mass of the antlers, not the number of points, that separate a trophy from a merely nice buck. Like the whitetail, mule deer often have brow tines—single, short tines growing out of the base of each antler; these protect the eyes and face of the buck, especially when it battles other bucks during the breeding season.

Whitetail hunters for whom the chase is all sometimes scorn the mule deer because it's seemingly less wary than the brush-loving whitetail. Broadly speaking, that's true, but only because the mule deer—like the antelope—evolved in open environments, doesn't need to be quite so wary. It also has far fewer escape and evasion tactics than the forest-dwelling whitetail. Usually it can just outrun trouble. The mule deer is larger and in many ways hardier (the Great Plains are a more severe environment than the temperate northern forests), but the whitetail has a trump card in the quest for survival: a greater capacity for coexisting with and outwitting man.

Whitetail are flourishing, but mule deer and West Coast blacktail have been in decline. Since the late 1950s, the mulie and blacktail herds in California have declined by a staggering 75 percent—from two million animals to just six hundred thousand. The decline is ongoing throughout the mule deer's range; California is a particularly dramatic example because of the state's accelerated rate of development. Some researchers estimate that over two thousand acres of suitable mule deer habitat is lost to development—every day.

But housing developments, parking lots, and shopping malls are only part of the problem; changes in rural habitat are also occurring on an unprecedented scale. Mule deer are browsers—less than 10 percent of their diet comes from the grasses preferred by an ungulate relative, the elk. More than half of the mulie's diet is browsed from shrubs, principally the signature Western shrub, sagebrush.

Unfortunately, cheatgrass—an invasive species from Russia—is a major threat to sagebrush. It not only robs already dry land of precious moisture before other plants can use it, it seeds out early and becomes dry as tinder at just about the time that the wildfire season rolls around on the plains. While fires are extremely beneficial on rangeland, if they occur too frequently the burnt sagebrush doesn't have enough time to recover. Presently, cheatgrass is viewed as a great potential source for biofuel, which could ultimately put millions upon millions of acres of rangeland into cheatgrass production, further reducing the mule deer's primary source of forage.

Also, mule deer are migratory. In many places along the Rocky Mountain front, they have always relied on "winter range"—places like gentle, south-facing slopes, sheltered from the wind, where the effects of a frigid winter are not as severe, and food can be gotten at more easily during the critical late stages of the season. Man also likes those sorts of places, and for the same basic reasons. Development on the desirable winter range, as well as on the ancestral routes mule deer have always traveled to get there, poses formidable obstacles that can keep mule deer mountain-bound and—inevitably—starving.

Where the whitetail and mule deer clash over habitat—say, on the brushy river bottoms that they both use, but the whitetail prefer as permanent living quarters—the whitetail tends to win out. It doesn't seem quite right. But the whitetail has the same characteristics that sometimes are broadly applied to *people* from the east: they're more sophisticated and clever, but also high-strung and delicate, seemingly less fit for the rugged life on the plains. But because they are more aggressive and adaptable, whitetail have been winning the turf wars on shared range.

Whitetail are great colonists and imperialists—doers, bullies, survivors, charlatans. Unlike the whitetail, the mule deer is unsuited for a life spent slipping under fences or surreptitiously nibbling rosebushes out behind a two-car garage in the suburbs. Mule deer are tough. They're as much of an emblem of the Western plains as the buffalo once were, if not nearly as defenseless against hunting as those shaggy brutes that stood, stoic and uncomprehending, as the thundering Hawken rifles mowed them down in horrific numbers.

The mulie I was watching sauntered toward me, slightly knock-kneed in the manner of a mature, well-fed buck. His antlers gleamed in the cool, honeyed morning sunlight. He stopped to browse, jerked up his head to process some sound or scent that didn't seem quite right, and then resumed feeding. With the rut approaching, his stores of testosterone were rising. But for the time being, there was nothing to fight but sagebrush.

The buck eyed up a nice clump nearby, walked over, and went to work. He lowered his head, hooked his antlers into the lower stem and branches and churned this way and that, stripping the pale green leaves and bark. The resistance appeared to give him great pleasure; he amused himself trashing the bush for another ninety seconds, and then lost interest and continued rambling. I watched him cross the road and scamper down into the brush. I started the truck and very slowly went my own way.

Back up on the prairie, I drove out to the rim of a great bluff where I'd have a commanding view of the flood plain. Men who know the country, like David and Verges, can point out vestiges of the wagon tracks left by the settlers who once passed this way. I hoped to scan up the elk that had been spotted a few days earlier, close to the water, because it would be a coup for us to fill one of David's elk tags. But the small herd has an enormous amount of country in which to hole up.

Besides, the northern boundary of David's ranch is the border between the U.S. and the Canadian province of Alberta, whose own big-game season doesn't open until later. Wildlife have a sixth sense about such things, and a betting man would put the elk somewhere safely in the confines of Alberta by dawn of opening day in Montana.

It was developing into a brisk day with hard, clean light, and I saw many deer, all of them mulies, with a number of nice bucks mixed in with the does, fawns, and pickle-fork juveniles. At another high vantage point at the western end of the ranch, I watched a string of mule deer march across the sagebrush flats. I counted fourteen in all, led by a big doe. The only buck in the group was a little guy, content to bounce along like he hadn't a care in the world, the caboose of the herd.

I watched them until they became too small to pick out among the clumps of sagebrush, and when I could no longer see them I reveled in the silence and emptiness.

7

Lord of the Plains

RUDYARD, MONTANA, OCTOBER 26

I STUDIED THE BEAR of a man sitting across the dining room table at David's on the morning of opening day. He sat with his massive head down, methodical and self-absorbed, eating his pancakes.

This was Rex. Rex was my enemy.

Rex, a slow-moving, bearded man who looked to be somewhere between forty and seventy years of age, had come to the ranch on business on Saturday morning, when I was already out scouting. He was some sort of real estate appraiser who just happened to make his appointment on the day before the Montana opener, arriving in a pickup loaded with his rifle and hunting gear. Even for Montana, that's an unusual way for a real estate guy to travel.

When I returned to the ranch house in the afternoon, Rex was holding court in the living room, telling David and Julie about real estate values in Australia, where he'd been some kind of college professor. I listened impatiently; David and I were supposed to take a ride to poke around some parts of the ranch I couldn't drive to on my own.

I didn't have to listen very long to figure out that Rex was one of those superior types who took great pride in what he knew, most of which was stuff we didn't know, mainly because most of us would pass out from boredom before absorbing it all. There's a place for guys like this in the world, but it isn't on a barstool alongside me. People like that have a way of preempting discussion, and that's all right by them, because they're basically talking to themselves and like the sound of what they hear.

After he taught us all about the difference in the economies of Australia and Montana, Rex wanted to shoot his gun to make sure the scope was on target. It dawned on me then: Rex was staying to hunt with us in the morning. I had a premonition that by the end of the following day, I'd have either shot a monster buck or a plodding, long-winded former college professor.

It took Rex about twenty minutes to get his gun and a few rounds out of the truck, after which the three of us piled into David's truck and drove out to a coulee, where I suggested that Rex just pop one off at the ersatz target we'd drawn on a cardboard box at fifty yards. The way the guy lumbered around, I could run a marathon in the time it would take him to set up the target a hundred yards away and take a practice shot. "I prefer to shoot at a hundred yards," he began, "because at that distance I'm an inch high, because . . ."

Yadda, yadda, yadda.

Rex took his shot. He walked back out and studied the target. Who knew a bullet hole could be so interesting?

Over dinner, Rex told us that the American people had to wise up and elect a government that would make us a better, more successful nation, a country more like Germany, or France, maybe even Australia. It never seemed to occur to him that he was expressing opinions; to him, these were self-evident truths that any "smart" person—the only kind that really mattered—understood.

By the time we were ready to turn in, I wanted to strike a match under the guy's gray beard. The last thing I wanted to do was hunt with Mr. Buzzkill.

It was a cold opening morning. A steady breeze whispered across the black sea of prairie, and stars carpeted an indigo sky; a hunter knows that there are as many kinds of dark as there are colors. A fine blue ring surrounded the floodlight at the corner of David's house where the truck sat idling while Julie filled thermoses with coffee inside and I rassled the big cooler containing our drinks and sandwiches into the truck bed.

Ordinarily, I could ignore a guy like Rex. But it was just his kind of brazen, low-key opportunist who might end up shooting the great buck—especially if you were dumb enough to play the nice guy, or even the proper host. *Aw, you're only here this one day, Rex, you go ahead and walk point at this coulee...*

The next thing you know, a monster buck is lying there and you're feeling oddly like you're going to puke.

So, in addition to my own hunt, I took it upon myself to keep Rex from exploiting the Aagesons' good nature. This was war, I decided, and I formulated my strategy and tactics: I would stake out the front seat of the truck; make sure my own rifle was handy at all times (even when I went to relieve myself behind the truck); keep what sense of courtesy I had on a tight leash. No way was I going to invite Rex to take up the best position during a spot-and-stalk maneuver. And I needed to do all that without seeming a lout, in order not to create overt friction that might embarrass my hosts.

Was this plan petty, bordering on childish? You bet. But this was a hunting trip, not ecotourism.

I was happy about one thing, though. David was, wisely, reluctant to hunt the prime whitetail habitat on the western fringe of the ranch; it would be too easy to blow out the cover and drive the whitetail off and into the sights of hunters on adjacent lands. This appeared to frustrate Rex, which increased my own satisfaction. A Montana resident from the progressive college town of Missoula, he had a tag for an antlerless (doe) whitetail in addition to his buck tag. He seemed interested in filling it, even though the whitetail population down Missoula way, which has been spared the blue tongue epidemic, was far more robust.

David also figured that hunting-related activity might lead elk to seek refuge on his ranch, and he had a hunch they would be hunkered down up north, near the Alberta line, near an area we called the Lost River breaks. We'd begin our hunt there.

The elk is the largest member of the four main deer species in the United States, and where it exists—mostly in the Rockies, from Montana down to New Mexico—it's usually the most prized of all the ungulates because of its sheer size, massive antlers, and status as a symbol of the Western backcountry. An elk hunt is usually a rugged undertaking that must be well-planned; nonresident hunters lucky enough to draw a tag in the annual lottery of any Western state usually book one of the outfitters who have dibs on the specified zone.

The odds on drawing a tag in a prime area are ridiculously low—a one-in-ten shot—or worse. In some states, outfitters themselves have access to tags, enabling erstwhile nimrods to just make a phone call and write a check. And it's usually a big check, because an outfitted elk hunt in the backcountry can easily run a thousand bucks a day. If you choose a custom hunt on private land (for many ranchers and other large landowners in the Rocky Mountain states, hunters represent a lucrative side business), it can be significantly more.

Some elk hunts tap fully into the romance of the West. Horseback may be your only mode of travel, with pack mules lugging your gear to a wilderness spike camp in the high country. Ironically, elk are originally plains creatures; they fled to the mountains seeking refuge in the wilderness because it put them farther out of reach of man. Small remnant groups on the plains (like the Hill County herd) survived into the era when the great national conservation ethic emerged and the public endorsed concepts like hunting seasons, bag limits (which spawned the tag system), and sound wildlife management.

The Milk River elk once were abundant, but of lesser interest to the indigenous people than the sea of wooly-headed bison with which they shared the range. David's ranch is within what once was a sacred triangle formed by three isolated mountain formations that erupt out of the Plains: the Cypress Hills (to the northeast in Alberta), the Sweet Grass Hills (west), and the Bear Paw Mountains (south). These nearby mountains, which provided shelter and relief from the extremes of weather found on the open plains, promoted and enhanced the diversity of life on the prairie separating them.

In aboriginal times, the hunting in the sacred triangle was prime, and the land is still supercharged with spiritual value for natives. There are still dozens of tepee rings—distinct circles formed by football-sized stones—on the Milk River Ranch. It's easy to miss them, because the ground everywhere is fairly stony. And in many places, the telltale rocks are almost entirely buried beneath centuries' worth of grit and dirt. There are Indian burial cairns as well: oval piles of stone, some of them overgrown with grasses and prickly pear cactus, that were heaped on the dead to keep the wolves and coyotes from getting at the corpses.

David, a student of history, has an abiding love and respect for native ways, beliefs, and traditions. He takes pains not to disturb these monuments to a nearly extinct culture. He told me that by his informal count, the ranch has over a hundred identifiable tepee rings and roughly half that many burial mounds. A good part of his time these days is spent trying to figure out how to ensure that the unique value of the ranch will be preserved long after the last of the ranching Aagesons pulls up stakes.

David and I were in the front seat of the big Dodge truck, with Julie and Rex in the back. We left the ranch compound, crossed the river, and followed a dirt track until we rolled through a rocky patch with a thin ribbon of water running almost invisibly among and under the rocks. "That's Lost River," David said, and I had to smile at the grand name given to a rivulet.

In such dry country, though, a spring is as good as a river. And in the past it often spelled the difference between life and a miserable death for a lonely, traveling cowpuncher or pioneering family (the Indians, by contrast, knew where every spring and seep was located). Countless families came to a bad end simply because they had no idea of where or how to find water. They sometimes passed within yards of it or overlooked sinkholes where more savvy travelers knew that if you scooped out a few handfuls of sand and had the patience to wait a few hours, the cavity would fill with clean, cold water.

We went through a few cattle gates, and each time the track grew fainter, until it looked like David was just driving through a sea of sagebrush. Rex droned on about real estate tax codes, but at least that had some practical value to David and Julie. I selfishly wanted to talk deer, guns, or elk.

As the daylight developed, we made out the dramatic ridges and promontories of the Lost River breaks. Here, the high plateau of the Canadian prairie simply crumbled and fell apart, due in part to fantastic geological pressures as the Rocky Mountains inexorably gathered and rose on the plains to the west.

At the same time, wind, water, and erosion had their way with the compacted sediments left over from the Cretaceous period, which ended sixty-five million years ago (but had lasted twice that long). Gradually, the sediments were sculpted into badlands—an antique garden of canyons, ridges, preposterous spires, boulders carved like gargoyles, towers of stone, and piles of rubble that look like sheer geological wreckage. In some places, you could scale a Frisbee across a chasm four or five hundred feet deep on either side and land it on top of the next ridge. Yet somehow, you're always aware that you're on the prairie.

This wild land was ideal for spotting and stalking buffalo and other game on the flats below and in the bays of the coulees, and it was also perfect for conducting war over hunting rights. This was Blackfeet country, but it was of interest to all tribes. Some, like the Salish-Kootenai and Pend d'Oreille, were drawn to the sacred triangle from their ancestral homes across the Continental Divide in northwest Montana.

The Blackfeet appear to have treated all the interlopers evenhandedly, slaughtering them with equal vigor. Legend has it that the prominent Salish-Kootenai chief, Michelle, once was overrun and captured by Blackfeet in the sacred triangle, and subsequently was forced to watch his captors cut out the heart of his still-living son. It was a warning against further trespass, but Chief Michelle apparently returned—and was himself captured and put to death.

We slowed to a crawl and began to scan the landscape for elk. It promised to be a clear day; the dried grass, cropped down by cattle and game, was dun-colored in the early morning. When Rex stopped jabbering for a moment or two, I felt I could almost hear the bawling and snorting of "buffler," and the lamentations of native spirits. I idly fantasized about giving Rex the same treatment accorded Michelle's son.

We spent about an hour up near the Alberta line, stopping here and there to walk the lip of a coulee, or to scan a brushy draw.

If the elk were on the ridges and knolls, where we expected to see them, they would have been visible from a mile or more; in other places, they could have been within a hundred yards, but safely hidden behind rocky outcroppings, below benches, or just around the corner from a peninsular cliff jutting into a coulee like the edge of a tomahawk.

Satisfied that the elk were hunkered down somewhere, we left the truck to hunt on foot. Or at least David and I did. Rex had convinced Julie to take him back down to the Milk, where the hiking would be less demanding on the flat ground. I smelled a rat—Rex probably was itching to kill a whitetail. But there was little I could do besides trust his seemingly lazy nature. Rex wasn't much into walking; the truck would alert the deer and keep them safe.

Julie left us at a granite marker alongside the U.S.-Canada border, which is marked by a well-maintained, four-strand fence that runs as far as the eye can see, east to west. Beyond it, in Alberta, lay the largest, uncorrupted, contiguous native prairie left in North America. Much like David's ranch, it hasn't been heavily impacted by cheatgrass or other invasive plant species. It's still almost all buffalo and needle grass, crested and northern wheatgrass, and other native flora.

We walked along the fence and soon came to a steep incline where the fence plunged almost vertically for about three hundred feet and back up again after crossing a flat, thirty-yard choke that marked the head of the massive Lost River coulee system. We glassed the valley to the south and then started down the rugged slope. At the bottom, we stopped to rest and study the cliffs encircling the valley, and began the climb back up along the fenceline.

By the time we got back up on the prairie, we were sweating, even though it was a chilly, glittering day with a stiff breeze and occasional gusts. We drank from our water bottles and worked out our game plan: a hike across a long stretch of isolated, rolling prairie to a set of coulees where we could glass and stalk, and ultimately drop down through a saddle called Dodge Pass to hook up with Julie and Rex down near the Milk.

It was easy walking; the thin grasses barely covered the liver-colored soil and pinkish-tan rocks poking up out of it. Spot and stalk hunting is companionable, and a fine way to spend time with a friend. Eventually, we came to the network of coulees forming a great ragged bowl with Dodge Pass opposite us and a circular flat far below. We began to work our way around, hugging the edge of the precipice, heading into the wind.

In the clear air and open country, it was easy to spot deer as far as half a mile away, but we tried to look farther, stopping at strategic points to sit and carefully glass the endless nooks, crannies, and benches carved out of the walls of the coulees. The deer might be anywhere.

We began to see mule deer; the first group was a herd of six or seven does, most of them trailing yearlings, that we caught crossing the open floor of the valley. With diligent glassing, we managed now and then to pick up a single, small buck or a pair of deer bedded down.

Generally, the bedded deer had the wind behind them to warn of danger from above while they watched the valley or the rugged slopes to either side. In some places, it was hard to imagine how even a creature as agile as the mule deer could pick its way out onto a ledge in what appeared to be the sheer face of a stone or clay cliff. Yet there they were, placidly chewing their cuds while gazing off into the distance, much like their ancestors had done for thousands of years.

For all the talk about mule deer being less wary than whitetails, these prairie deer were alert. The ones we saw most often were already watching us. Some of them scampered off immediately, others just melted back into the maze of brush and rocks that ran the gamut of color, from bright orange to blazing white, but were mostly shades of gray, tan, lavender, and brown.

Occasionally, we picked out a deer before it saw us and studied it at our leisure. We hoped to come upon a good buck from a screened position; the broken terrain lent itself to a long, careful stalk.

David was out in front, glassing, when suddenly he cried, "Shit."

I hurried over and got my field glasses up in time to see two does vanish around the corner of a stone pier thrusting out from the side of the slope, about eight hundred yards away. "That was a big buck," David said. "A monster."

"All I saw was the last two does."

"There were half a dozen, running with the big fella. Geez, he was all silver and gray. Kind of grizzly. His rack was enormous."

"I guess they spotted us first," I muttered. "Maybe we'll catch up with them as we circle the canyon."

If we were careful, we might sneak up on the big buck. He might slip into one of the draws instead of bolting up onto the prairie or across the level floor of the valley below us. But there was one place where the deer had an escape route—a short stretch of prairie that separated us from an entirely different set of coulees that stretched a long way along the north bank of the river. We were three large bays from Dodge Pass; the big buck might be in one of them . . .

"Let's take it slow and give them time to hole up somewhere," David said. "If they make a run for it across the bottom or through the gap at Dodge, we'll see them for sure."

At the first of the two remaining ridges, David and I crept to the edge and looked over into the bay below, just in time to see a pair of two-by-two bucks heave to their feet and stott diagonally downhill. They couldn't have used the terrain any better. I had the gun up, but it was only to practice acquiring a moving target. We weren't hunting pickle forks.

We moved on and glassed the next bay with extra care, but it was empty; one lone coyote caught our wind and, after a dazzling piece of broken-field running through the rubble, sprinted across the valley floor—only to vanish into a low spot in what appeared to be land as flat as a billiard table.

With agonizing care, we worked our way out to the very tip of the last peninsula, belly-crawling the last thirty yards to keep our shadows out of the bay and our silhouettes off the skyline. If there was anything over the lip, on the gentle slope falling away to the pass, it would have been visible to our naked eyes.

Disappointed, sure that the slope was barren, we sat up and resorted to the binoculars, scanning various swales and nooks, searching for a glint of sunlight on the tip of an antler, or a dark shape down in a depression. But we came up empty.

A strong breeze swept the hillside and fluffed the sagebrush down on the flat. It was a long way across the break in the giant bowl. It was unlikely that the deer could have made it unseen. The big buck—we had already dubbed him Grayface—probably had taken his chances sprinting across the prairie to the bluffs near the river.

It was likely that even as we scanned Dodge Pass, Grayface and his harem were far behind us to the east, picking their way through the coulees down by the river.

Then it hit me: *Holy crap . . . Rex!*

I needn't have worried.

It took us about forty-five minutes to hike out through the pass and find the truck, with Julie sitting behind the wheel looking through the spotting scope. She was watching a truck parked at the tip of a towering bluff hell-and-gone across the river. It was conspicuous, though, because of the telltale sun-burst flaring on the windshield. "That stinker," she muttered. "He's up there watching our land. Probably looking for the elk."

This was a sore point with David and Julie, and had been ever since, a few years ago, a group of some twenty-odd hunters on vehicles ranging from pickups and ATVs to dirt bikes, hav-ing illegally employed a spotter plane, cornered part of the elk herd on the ranch and commenced a slaughter.

"It was a regular shit-show," David said. "We figured out what was going on, but we got to the scene too late. There were guys all over the place, and dead elk everywhere. Some of them weren't even dead. They were kicking and bellowing and trying to get up. We were lucky, though, the law got there shortly after we did. They pretty much rounded up the bunch of them."

"Where's Rex?" I asked Julie.

"Over yonder, toward the river."

I picked up the hunter-orange vest of our companion, trudg-ing slump-shouldered toward us. Julie had been chauffeuring him around. Rex would tell her where he wanted to go and where to pick him up when he was done with his brief walk.

Rex was huffing and puffing when he reached us, and for a moment I felt bad for the guy. He looked happy to be back among people; they would give him the opportunity to talk again. I jumped into the bed of the truck and fished out veni-son salami sandwiches, chips, and cold drinks. David politely inquired about Rex's hunt and told of our own as we sat on the tailgate, enjoying the strong October sun at the warmest pe-riod of the day.

Before long, Rex started in on the Iraq War and all the other terrible things the U.S. government had done in Vietnam, Chile, and Guatemala. I listened for a while and then almost lost it, tersely telling him in so many words that I was there to hunt deer and celebrate our amazing native landscape, not piss and moan about what an awful nation and people we were.

For a brief period, the silence was stony. But I sensed that David and Julie were no more interested in Rex's pontifications than was I. We soon packed up and moved on, crossing back over the river to hunt some of the coulees near the western border of the ranch.

The shadows were lengthening by the time we began the familiar routine of driving, followed by walking and glassing. We saw numerous mule deer, including a good number of bucks, but nothing like Grayface. Almost all of them were already showing us their hinds by the time we got the binoculars up for a closer look. We marveled at their sure-footedness as they trotted along wisps of trails, always knowing to avoid the ones that led to dead-end benches or petered out along towering stone formations.

Now and then, as we drove along the upper edge of a coulee, we'd come upon a deer at close range. One of them was a nice, fat little two-by-two mulie, standing on the far side of a shallow wash. David hit the brakes, in case the buck had companions that we couldn't yet see, halting Rex in mid-sentence. "That's a good-sized deer," Rex said. "It's getting late. Maybe I should shoot it. We can always put Julie's tag on it."

I was dumbfounded. Rex was proposing something illegal, although I wasn't going to get all holier-than-thou about it. Many of us hunters have been there. Country people in particular believe that a tag, once purchased, entitled you to a deer; so what if your wife, cousin, or best friend didn't shoot the animal and you did? The tag was paid for; it was fair if not exactly legal to make use of it.

All legal issues aside, the galling part was the way Rex so blithely put Julie in an uncomfortable position. If he used Julie's tag, she'd also have to break the law if she shot anything when David and I took her on a hunt later in the week.

"Oh, I don't think that's a good idea," David said calmly, leaving it at that. Rex lost interest in the deer and slumped back into his seat, sulking.

We parked and walked along the upper edge of a few more coulees, encountering one nice little herd of mulies, including three decent bucks, working their way up from the canyon floor. They lost no time scrambling over the lip of the prairie and galloped off into the smoky evening air, signaling the end of another opening day in Montana.

Rex would be moving on, going back to wherever the hell he'd come from, that evening. It was a relief, because I was in danger of allowing Rex to become my Great White Whale, even though I was supposed to be hunting, not fishing.

8

The Big Empty

O N A GOOD HUNTING trip, your focus on the task at hand and the clearly defined, repetitive routine of walking, stalking, glassing, and talking makes it easy to lose track of time. One evening we quit hunting a little early because Ross and Rhonda Ritter, friends and neighbors of David and Julie, were coming by for dinner.

Before we ate, we all piled into David's truck to check out the irrigated fields. We admired the play of colors on the walls of the coulees and the vast, golden fields of winter wheat. We spotted three whitetail, including a good buck; the deer ran parallel with the truck, about two hundred yards away. It was a good sign, for in the morning we were going on our annual "death march," a long hike through ideal whitetail habitat by the river.

Ross, a hardworking guy, had been dividing his time between the Ritters' nearby ranch and Bozeman, where he builds houses for the flood of newcomers, many of them from the east, who have been flocking to the southwestern corner of Montana. Rhonda is a droll blond with a dark sense of humor. Just days earlier, she'd killed a beautiful antelope, but her avocation is dusting coyotes.

One morning, she told us, she was out of bed at first light, feeling something was wrong. When she looked out the window, she saw a coyote prowling around near the ranch house. "Well," she said. "I wasn't going to put up with that. The window was open, so I just snuck to the closet, grabbed my gun, and fired through the open window. Got 'im, too, but I kind of worked the bolt, by habit. The shell flew out and didn't it land right on Ross's chest? It was still real hot, and he just jumped out of bed, screaming, 'Rhaaaaaanda, what you shoot me for, honey?'"

Ross grinned sheepishly; Rhonda chuckled, shaking her head. This is a woman who can hold her own with the men and doesn't see why they should have all the fun.

She told us how, the previous Christmas, she'd let it be known that the only thing she really wanted from Santa was a neat little Ruger .204 they had down at a local gun shop in the nearest sizable town, Havre. It was the ideal coyote gun. The small caliber had plenty of punch to stop a forty-pound dog, but it was a flat-shooter with very little kick.

Ross went out and bought the gun. Come Christmas Eve, it was safely tucked under the sheets on their bed. When they crawled under the covers late that night, Rhonda felt the cold steel against her bare leg. Ross's eyes lit with pride as he described her reaction: "She threw her arms around me and cooed like a little dove. 'Aw, honey. You shouldn't have . . .' You'd about've thought I gave her a diamond the size of a softball."

The Ritters and Aagesons are friendly with the Hutterites of the nearby Guilford colony, which is a village unto itself—a cluster of neat, well-kept, nearly identical homes laid out with barrackslike symmetry; various hangar-sized aluminum and steel sheds (where the colony has, among other things, an industrial-grade steel workshop and a garage that would be the envy of any auto-repair outfit); and the focal point of the colony, a community hall that must be twenty thousand square feet, and so clean you'd mistake the polished linoleum floors and well-lit hallways for those of a hospital.

The communal kitchen has as many giant stainless-steel fixtures as a suburban banquet hall (at the colony, though, the men and women, including married couples, sit on opposite sides of the dining room). The heating system uses "green" thermally heated water pumped up from hundreds of feet below the ground. These self-sufficient folks make everything they can at the colony, including bread and soap.

Hutterite women wear black stockings and gray frocks with a white blouse; the kerchief is ubiquitous. The men prefer black jeans and cowboy hats, but there isn't really any dress code. Like the Mennonites and Amish, the Hutterites trace their roots to the Anabaptists. Unlike the Amish, the Hutterites aren't bound by antiprogressive strictures on how they live; mostly they remain dedicated to an ideal of sharing their goods and possessions based on the model of Christ and his disciples.

Despite their strong, seemingly antimodern traditions, Hutterites are flexible and surprisingly curious about the "outside world," even as they fight to resist its influence. The men are shrewd and enthusiastic horse traders, and willing to avail themselves of the latest technologies, especially when it comes to their main businesses, agriculture and cattle.

Rhonda frequently hunted with Johnny Stahl, and the Ritters have a soft spot for Johnny's young son, Lucas. One day, Ross took Lucas for a ride on his ATV. Along the way, they spotted a fox about two hundred yards out. Lucas begged Ross to pull over and shoot it; Ross reluctantly obliged—and missed.

"Shit," Lucas said. "I could have made that shot."

At the time, Lucas was five.

Inevitably, the conversation drifted to ranching, and how the year's wheat crop had been surprisingly good—but prices had fallen yet again. It was increasingly tough to stay a step ahead of the creditors. The Ritters left fairly early, because Ross was looking at a long drive to Bozeman early the next morning, where he could at least make some decent money building western McMansions.

Hunting alone reminds you that solitude is a different state of being, in which you have a much denser specific gravity. We're both meant for it and lucky to be rid of it when we return home to see the porch light on, and shadows moving across the curtains beyond the door.

One morning when the Aagesons were otherwise occupied, I took the truck and went to hunt in a coulee that begins as a shallow ditch at the corner of a vast wheat field and ends up widening into a spectacular steep-walled canyon. I was out early and saw a few deer filtering back into the coulee after an evening of feeding on the CRP land above. But it was still too dark to identify them by sex. Once the sun hit the field, I threw a sandwich and a bottle of water into my pack and set out. The sharp breeze made me pull up the hood of my sweatshirt. My ears wouldn't be much use on this hunt anyway.

This draw runs south, with a stock reservoir twice the length of a football field at the upper, north end. Below the reservoir, the coulee gets deep, dramatic, and rugged, with tributary draws. I enjoyed walking and glassing the broken terrain just over the lip of the prairie. Now and then, I'd find a good spot to sit and carefully glass the walls of the coulee and the flat at the bottom. I came across some bitterroot, Montana's lovely state flower, and many patches of my own favorite, the prickly pear cactus. In the fall, the pale green discs of this small cactus are rimmed with delicate shades of orange, red, and blue. It looks more like an exotic fish you might find twenty leagues under the sea than a desert plant.

About half a mile from where I left the truck, another major coulee comes in from the northeast, just below the reservoir. Movement caught my eye; four deer were running down the steep opposite bank. One of them was a fine five-by-five buck, a definite trophy of Boone and Crockett quality.

The deer ran into the big tributary draw, vanishing around the corner of a tawny bluff. I decided to track them, knowing that the draw ended in a cul-de-sac with nothing but prairie above. I started picking my way down the nearly vertical slope.

The bottom of the coulee was a patchwork of bright green grasses and large, multicolored mineral stains. It was still, even though a good breeze rattled the dry wheat stems up on the plains. I sat down on a pleasantly warm rock to drink some water and enjoy the sunshine; moving too fast is usually a greater mistake than proceeding slowly. Suddenly, the back of my neck went prickly. This wasn't mountain lion or bear country, and I was carrying a 7 mm. magnum rifle. I had nothing to fear, but being on the floor of the coulee gave me the willies. The walls towering all around me made me feel as if I were being watched. *This*, I thought, *is how a deer must feel.*

I eventually crossed the flat and found the tracks of the running deer. I easily picked out the ones left by the big buck. They were punched deeper into the sandy soil and nearly twice the size of the others. They were easy to follow until I came to the bluff around which the deer had run. It had a broad skirt of hard, pumicelike stone that wouldn't hold a track. I spent half an hour combing the nearby soil, without luck. Could they have run up the rocky side of the coulee and out on the prairie, hidden from view?

I doubted that, so I pushed on deeper into the draw, searching for signs. I found none. Eventually, I came to an eerie pillar of hardened sediment standing all by itself. It looked like a twelve-foot-tall gray candle draped in a coat of its own hardened drippings, which spread out widely from its base in all directions. Tracks would be easily visible anywhere in it, but there were none, not even those of Salvador Dalí.

Beyond that landmark, a barbed-wire fence ran the width of the narrow coulee floor. I walked the entire strand, carefully looking for hair on the wire or signs on either side of it, where deer might leave an impression before or after jumping. But I found nothing. I saw all the way back to the cul-de-sac and studied every inch of it. But the deer had given me the slip. I reluctantly turned and backtracked.

Later that afternoon, Julie carried her own gun as we explored the massive bluffs on the south bank of the Milk. We side-slipped and climbed hand over hand along the rugged slopes and worked our way east at the base of the cliffs. Sagebrush stretched across the broad level all the way to the river. We found a cave where cliff swallows had cemented dozens of nests on the upper walls, creating an elaborate avian village.

Late in the day, Julie spotted a herd of deer running out of a coulee toward the river. We caught just a glance, so we scaled a pinnacle of crumbling sediment and stone that gave us a commanding view of the flood plain. The two of us barely fit on the tip of the outcropping. We talked and watched small groups of deer, mostly does, filter down toward the river while the bluffs across the river turned gold, then orange, and finally plum blue.

David was worried. The weather had turned against us, with high winds and unseasonably warm temperatures, a terrible combination for hunting. So much so that we decided to postpone our death march through whitetail country. Now we were above the river again, near the Alberta line, waiting for daylight.

We sipped coffee, quietly talking about nothing in particular while the occasional gust of wind gently rocked the vehicle and whistled along its seams. Gradually, a fine orange wire slowly formed out in the blackness, lengthening beyond our peripheral vision on either side to mark the edge of the world.

My imagination ran wild peering into the CRP field lying before us in the dark. I saw moving, dark shapes out there—here, there, everywhere!—but they couldn't have been deer any more than they were wooly mammoths. Actually, chances were better that they *were* wooly mammoths.

The prairie that finally emerged from the night was an angry black sea, as gusts of a south wind rhythmically bent and released the knee-high native grasses, creating the illusion that we were watching waves racing toward the horizon.

Finally, from somewhere at the edge of the world, a deep golden light began to creep toward us. Daylight, the truthbringer, was upon us, and soon we felt like a couple of losers holding worthless lottery tickets. Whitetail and mule deer both were known to use the CRP, but nothing was visible in any direction but undulating grass.

Game would still be moving for a few hours, and we had staked out the plain because it was fairly close to coulees that led back to the safety of the river bottom. We hoped to catch deer coming off their evening feed, heading for the shelter and shade of the cottonwoods and thickets along the river. After thirty minutes, David started the truck and we took the gravel road, scanning the vast CRP field lying to the north.

Even here, on the Great Plains, it's a misnomer to call the prairie flat. It isn't that at all; the land gathers and swells or sinks and spreads gradually, with no real points of reference to judge relative elevation. We crested a rise and saw the deer at the same time—a group of about eight, so far in the distance that they were mere dark dots in the sea of tawny grass. David cut the motor. The deer seemed to be angling toward us, browsing as they went. As they drew closer, we glassed them against the silver-blue sky and made out antlers on at least four of them; at least two were big mule deer bucks.

I was running out of time, and while I wanted to shoot only a trophy-class buck, preferably a whitetail, my standards were falling.

The deer were headed southwest toward the coulees, into a crosswind. "I think I can put a move on them," I said. "But I'll have to hustle pretty far north and swing back up behind them, from the east."

David agreed that the plan might work; he let the truck roll back gently, far enough to hide us from view. I scrambled out of the cab, leaving everything but my rifle, binoculars, and shooting sticks—a pair of sectional aluminum rods that could be snapped together to form an X that provides a rest for long-distance shooting. I had to move quickly to close the gap and intercept the deer.

I crept back up to the higher ground. The deer were about to wander over a gentle rise. That was good; if I couldn't see them, they wouldn't see me.

Making a beeline diagonally across the CRP, I walked a fair distance north. I began to swing around in a great arc, mindful of the wind. The rise up ahead was steep enough to keep me hidden; from the top, I ought to see the deer—they might even be within rifle range. But I had to move quickly.

Ducking into a crouch, I made my way up the side of the swell, sweating. I swung the rifle off my shoulder and got down on all fours as I approached the top of the rise. On my knees, I saw the long, gentle slope falling away on the other side, empty, and beyond it more of the same.

Perplexed, I looked back toward the road. I couldn't see the truck. I turned to check my back trail but had no clue where it was. I was turned around on the prairie, within perhaps a mile or two of a big honking silver Dodge truck that had inconveniently vanished. It might have been parked in Nebraska, for all I knew.

I was enveloped by a sense of the vastness that lay all around and above me. I looked up at the sky, where the sun was a molten, nearly white pinwheel, harsh and pitiless. I felt a touch of vertigo, and it occurred to me that I'd left the compass and GPS back in the truck.

Compass? GPS? You're within shouting distance of the danged truck, you idiot . . . Or are you?

I got hold of myself. Judging from factors like the position of the sun, I guessed that I'd been overly prudent. Instead of traveling in a semicircle, I was just drifting in a gentle arc, away from the truck, away from the deer. I set a new, aggressive course, which soon took me to another swell, beyond which lay a shallow bowl, and there they were—the herd of deer, about three hundred fifty yards off, where the land began to rise in a gentle, curving hill. I wasn't comfortable taking a shot at that distance in a stiff breeze. I had to get closer, so I dropped to my knees and began to cover ground.

I crawled through the brush, most of it native grasses, alternately using my rifle and free hand to push away the thick growth. It was tedious work, hard on my knees and back, but my senses were on edge. The wind was still in my favor; that was one good thing. Periodically, I raised my head to locate either of the two big bucks whose wide, branched antlers gleamed in the sun.

I resisted the urge to hurry; I'd invested too much energy to blow it now. I poked my head up again. The deer were halfway up the incline; another few minutes and they might vanish over the top. I estimated their distance at close to two hundred fifty yards, a bit of a reach for me; but the location offered some protection from the worst of the wind. I needed thirty or forty more precious yards; it was a race—or a crawl—against time.

And I got lucky. The deer lingered, dawdling up near the top of the rise. I forced my aching legs and arms forward. I lay flat on my back for a few moments to calm myself and gather my thoughts. Then I rolled over and onto my knees and snapped together the shooting sticks, jamming them into the hard soil.

I slipped my 7 mm. mag into the notch where the sticks were joined and dialed the scope all the way up to 8 power. I pushed the safety forward to the "off" position.

My heart was flopping like a fish when I picked up the deer in the scope. They were milling around, making it hard to keep track of the two big bucks. Again, I found what I thought was the biggest buck, walking, until it stopped—right behind a doe, leaving just his neck visible. My throat tightened. I tried to settle the cross hairs on the buck's neck, but a smaller buck wandered into my sight picture. The tension was nearly unbearable; now that I was close to fulfilling something like a lifetime ambition, the small, magical window of my rifle scope was filled with . . . too many deer.

I moved my face off the gun; my hands were trembling. *Slow down*, I told myself. *Don't do anything stupid, even if it comes naturally. This isn't your first county fair* . . .

Two of the deer had already gone over the hill, the rest were bound to follow shortly. I rested my scope eye for a moment and, wriggling into a slightly more comfortable position, shifted the scope just enough to pick up the other big buck— I'd forgotten about him entirely. He stood off to the side, offering an unobstructed shot. My nerves still tingling, I settled the cross hairs just behind the top of his front leg, moved my point-of-aim ever so slightly to the left to compensate somewhat for the crossing breeze, and slowly squeezed the trigger. The rifle went off with a violent crack.

The bullet I shot travels at a rate of 3,110 fps (feet per second). Out on the big empty, it flies free for so long, and with so little to absorb the sound, that the spinning bullet makes a high-pitched, wicked buzz. I quickly jacked another shell into the chamber, but I couldn't find the big buck in the scope. All I could see were the rumps of four deer, disappearing over the rise. And that was the last of them.

I set the safety and absently laid the rifle down in the grass, staring at the vacant space where I'd last seen the big deer. I stood up slowly, reminding myself that I might have hit the deer. A bullet travels so quickly that you can often see the impact in the scope before you even feel the rifle leap and kick back into your shoulder. I had noticed nothing, though, and that buzz—it was a bad sign. A bullet makes a percussive *whap* when it hits home; a whizzing bullet is flying, unimpeded.

I folded up my shooting sticks, wondering if there was any chance at all that I'd scored. I knew I ought to go and look; things happen awfully fast and it's easy to fool yourself, one way or the other. But already, the Blown Opportunity Brass Band and Chorus was marching and blowing its trumpets and tubas inside my head. A sensation like shame burned through me and I couldn't suppress the thought any more than if it had been uttered by someone standing alongside me: *You missed.*

It's not for sure, I told myself, and myself answered: *You missed.*

I stared out across the vast prairie, feeling the cool air on my overheated cheeks and forehead. I fought back my bitter disappointment. I told myself that the shot was no gimme—it was at two hundred yards, plus, in a breeze, from a dodgy rest.

And again, I was taunted by the awareness: *You missed.*

If a psychologist were standing beside me, gently stroking

his beard as he read the body language of my slumped shoulders and pursed lips, read the disbelief in my eyes, he might have counseled me to let it all hang out—to throw my arms up, laugh like a maniac, and address the gods:

I missed! I am such a nimrod! Here I am, halfway through the long deer season I'd promised myself after three decades of catch-as-catch-can hunting, more than halfway through the Year of Our Lord 2008, the year when I promised myself I would pull out all the stops and do whatever it took to kill a big buck, a buck of a lifetime, and . . . I missed!

It was a chore to get myself moving. I had to go look for blood, hair, or any other signs that I'd wounded the deer. I counted the paces but lost track somewhere around two hundred yards. I went through the motions, but that's all I was doing; at least it kept me doing something.

At the top of the rise, I looked out over uninterrupted, undulating prairie, stretching as far as the eye could see. It was an emptiness vast, lonesome, and disorienting. I turned away and saw the truck, a white speck crawling over the horizon. I trudged toward the Dodge, wondering what—if anything—I'd done wrong. Wondering if I'd get another chance.

David, Julie, and I outfitted ourselves for a proper whitetail drive, with blaze-orange caps and bird-hunting vests. We took the truck across the Milk River and followed the rough trail carved out of the side of the steep north bank. In one pinch, the passenger side-view mirror was just inches from the vertical face of the crumbling bluff, while the tires on the left, wallowing over unstable depressions and ruts, were mere inches from the edge of a sheer drop of about sixty feet to the river. "Do you ever think of coming in with a bulldozer and shaving off part of the bluff, to make the trail wider?" I asked.

"Oh no," David replied nonchalantly. "This stuff is way too

unstable to fool around like that. The whole side of the mountain could slide loose . . ."

"But doesn't that mean . . ." I caught myself. "Never mind."

David grinned. "Besides, you wouldn't want just anybody to be able to get down to these flats, right?"

After the pass, the country opened up on either side, with gentle sagebrush flats that extended all the way to the tall cliffs on the north side. We parked the truck and stuffed our pockets with water bottles. We would fan out with Julie in the middle and me on the outside while David busted through the brush along the river, theoretically driving deer in front of our guns.

From my position on the wing, any deer fleeing across the flat would be fair game, unless Julie saw it and shot first. At times, though, all of us had to push and fight our way through dense, towering reeds or nearly impenetrable thickets. It was tough going in the heat; the breeze coming off the prairie was infernal.

We flushed a few pheasants and a mule deer doe with two fawns in an open stretch but had no luck beating anything out of a quarter-mile stretch of Russian olive trees mixed with reeds. We rested periodically, drinking water. David was his usual uncomplaining self; following the twisting riverbank in order to keep any deer from slipping out the back door, he walked twice as far and had to contend with more obstacles.

At one point, David rousted out a decent whitetail buck that disappeared into a small thicket of chokecherry. Julie later walked right by the hide, but nobody ever saw that animal again. The deer were there, though: a mix of mulies and whitetail that kept us paying attention.

We took a short break before we tackled the last and most promising stretch, a pretty, semi-open glade studded with big cottonwoods amid patches of tawny, sun-dappled grass. It offered good shade, water, and numerous escape trails.

We put Julie in the middle; she would walk right through

the woods while I followed the fenceline on the high side with David along the river. Almost immediately, I spooked a white-tail doe; she fled, her white flag switching left and right as she went. A short while later, I thought I heard David cry out; I assumed he jumped a deer as well. I tried to keep an eye on Julie's orange cap, but we lost sight of each other. Twenty minutes later, I came to the end of the glade and sat down to watch and wait for my companions.

Before long, I spotted David pushing his way through the tall reeds. He popped into view and waved. Where was Julie? Ten minutes later, David and I sat together, wondering what had become of his wife. Finally, she emerged, right where she was supposed to be.

"So?" I asked.

Julie had a crooked grin on her face. She said, "I almost stepped on one. It was a buck."

"But I never heard a shot," I said, puzzled.

"Oh," she replied. "I didn't even think of shooting it."

That got David's attention, too.

Julie said nothing; she may not be much of a hunter, but she knows how to tell a story. When she finally explained, it went something like this: she had been walking along, gun on her shoulder ("Minding my own business" is how she put it). Suddenly, she saw a flicker in a patch of brush.

"Wow," she thought. "It's a buck!"

"And you did what?" I wondered.

She looked sheepish, and explained. "Well, I wasn't sure what to do. He was so cute, just munching on leaves, flicking his tail back and forth."

"You forgot that you had the gun?" David said.

"Well, he was looking right at me, for gosh sakes. But I did notice that he had four or five points. That was on one side, anyway."

"Wait a minute," I interrupted. "This was, possibly, a five-by-five Montana whitetail and you did nothing? Is that what you're telling us?"

"If you want to put it that way, yep. I guess so. But what could I do? I've never been that close to a deer. Not a real, live one, anyway. It was really interesting. I do remember thinking, 'Oh, that little stinker. I'll bet he's going to circle around and smell me.'"

I shook my head, waiting for the rest of the story. I'd blown my chance at a great deer; now I had to listen to a cockamamie story about how Julie stood around waiting for a big Montana whitetail—a "little stinker" who was "so cute"—to give her a lap dance.

"And that's just what he did," Julie continued. "Yuppers. I stood there, and after a while he quit staring and he started to walk around, kind of sideways to me, more or less watching me from the corner of his eye. Then he made this funny sound, like a sneeze. And the next thing I knew he was running like all get-out, jumping this way and that, down toward the river."

"Why, Julie," David said, smiling. "That's a wonderful story."

I had to smile, too. Some things you're never going to figure out anyway . . . We sat down on a log; I took out my camera and snapped some nice pictures of my friends. We had a long walk back to the truck, and almost all the way I wondered what a ten-point Montana whitetail might look like, if I came upon the little stinker munching leaves.

David, Verges, Julie, and I went out together on the last day of my hunt. I was the only one toting a rifle; nobody would say it, but this was a Hail Mary—my last chance to kill a big buck in Montana, at least in this, a year of special significance.

Early in the morning, the climbing sun warmed the prairie. But the brush in the dark bottoms of the coulees was still glazed with frost when we chanced upon a dozen deer, most of them bucks. I had never seen so many bucks in one group. They were in the main coulee downstream of the stock reservoir, and four of the bucks were outstanding, including two three-by-three fellows with wide, thick antlers, and an even better pair of four-by-fours.

Traveling slowly, they went around a point and vanished from view. A succession of four tributary coulees lay before us, like gaps in the teeth of a comb, before the main coulee split off into two broad valleys. It was likely the deer were just moving along. We agreed that they hadn't spotted us. We decided not to push them, hoping they might bed down in a tributary ravine.

We returned to the truck to formulate our game plan. Julie would stay with the truck, well in back of us on the prairie, trailing us slowly. David, Verges, and I would steal along the upper edges of the coulees, staying off the skyline as much as possible.

We stalked meticulously for about three hours. We raised a few deer from their beds, but none of them were the same caliber as the deer in the original group. My hopes, which initially had soared, faded.

Eventually, we even stopped talking. The three of us, and probably Julie, too, were thinking the same thing: *They gave us the slip* . . . They might even have watched us pass them by; the land was sufficiently broken, with corners we couldn't quite see around from any angle, and benches with patches of brush carved into the steep sides of every draw.

We finished circumventing the last of the major tributary coulees. All that was left was an innocuous-looking, horseshoe-shaped draw before the great bowl where the main coulee broke up. Getting down on my hands and knees, I crawled over to the edge of the drop-off above the minor draw. The brush near the bottom was thick and seemingly empty—until I picked up the tip of an antler. I relaxed my eyes, allowing them to see through the brush. Sure enough, I saw bits of antler everywhere. It had to be the original bachelor group—the bucks lay everywhere. They were just seventy yards away, almost directly below me.

David came crawling up beside me. In crude sign language, I indicated where the animals lay. Meanwhile, I rolled over just in time to see Verges striding over toward us; he had lagged behind and remained oblivious to our find. We frantically signaled for him to hit the deck, but by the time he did, the bucks knew that something was wrong. Maybe they felt the vibrations of Verges's steps, or maybe they winded us.

The deer began to clamber to their feet. They're never more vulnerable and awkward-looking than when they're getting off their beds, and the process gave me just enough time to find and get the cross hairs on the best buck of the lot. As they scampered off, I squeezed off a round. It seemed a miss, and the prodigious crack panicked the entire group. Suddenly, deer were running helter-skelter, but their options were limited and they didn't seem to know our location. They could run straight up a steep but short pitch to the prairie, but I had that covered. They might follow the curve of the coulee and pass me going the other way on the far side of the ravine, a little over a hundred yards from where I lay.

"He's the third from the front," David called, trying to keep track of the biggest buck.

I shot again—another miss.

The deer chose to follow the U-shaped contour of the coulee; within moments they were circling the back end and coming back toward us across the way. The biggest buck was at the tail end of the string, and he hesitated for a moment at the edge of a rock face that plunged straight down for about sixty feet. He was moving again when I fired, and I thought I saw him flinch before he ran, laboring, after the other deer. They were around the corner in a flash and suddenly all was still.

"I think you got him," Verges volunteered.

"I do, too," I answered. "But I'm not sure. We'd better go have a look."

We waited for Julie to bring up the truck. I picked out a few landmarks around the place where my last shot hit. If the deer was wounded, I needed to find blood or I'd never locate him. He could pile up and disappear into almost any crevice or nook between the boulders, impossible to find. We drove to the point directly above the place where the buck stood when I last fired.

I leaned my gun against the barbed-wire fence and dropped down onto the slope. It was so steep that I had to grab handfuls of brush to keep my footing; below me were nearly sheer patches of almost bare soil and slab stone. It was a long way down if I lost my footing. But I picked up blood on what was clearly the trail along which the deer had run. It was bright, crimson, arterial blood, not the foamy, paler blood that indicates a lung shot.

I'd hit the buck; I was right about that. Now it was imperative to stay on the blood and find the deer. For a moment, I thought of the doe I'd hit with an arrow at Tom Daly's place.

I picked my way along the trail cautiously. Within fifteen yards, I had to negotiate an outcropping of blue and orange stone. Before I got completely around it, I stopped short. The big buck was bedded down, less than twenty yards from where I stood, calmly watching me approach.

It was a disturbing scene, more appropriate to a dream. The buck was mortally wounded. He stared right at me, head still held high, but he made no effort to move. Nor did his large black eyes betray even a hint of fear or panic. He regarded me, mute and regal, with something like curiosity.

I viscerally understood that he was clinging to what little was left of life: to the blazing sun and scent of sage and the sensation of the prairie breeze rippling his gleaming, handsome coat under that deep clear sky. The only things he had ever known. He was serene in his hurt, at once fragile and stoic, caught in a vortex taking him far from everything familiar, things he no longer felt obliged to cling to with all the power of pure animal instinct. It was an excruciating moment, but I also realized I had to kill the buck quickly—and that the gun was back up at the fence.

I backed away, around the outcropping, scrambled up the slope, and grabbed the rifle. When I returned, my hands were shaking as I tried to settle the cross hairs on the area of his heart. From that close range, all I could see was hair. I had to turn the magnification way down and move the cross hairs from his head down to the area of his lungs. I squeezed the trigger.

He seemed to lift off the ground momentarily, then he rolled over, onto his side, and tumbled off the bench. He slid down the slope. The pitch was so steep that David and I would not be able to drag the animal, which weighed about two hundred pounds, back up to the edge of the coulee. So we took a cable and a roll of barbed wire from the truck, and secured one end to the trailer hitch. I slip-slid my way down the slope with the other end, cut slits in the buck's rear legs near the knee, and wrapped the wire around. I signaled David. Verges pulled away, slowly, dragging my buck up to the top of the coulee.

It was tough going; the barbed wire hung up between rocks and in brush, and each time I had to work it free. But gradually, we got the buck out.

He was a beauty—his antlers were about two feet wide, and each of them forked about halfway up, with an additional fork at the end of each beam. The antlers formed a perfect semicircle; if you laid a carpenter's level in the crook of the tallest forks, the bubble would rest right between the marks. The buck had brow tines; short ones, but enough to make him a legitimate five-by-five. He was not a Boone and Crockett caliber deer, but he was a trophy—my trophy. I had to get to work field-dressing him, but all I could do was stare, incredulous.

While cutting him open, I picked out three bullet holes— one more than I expected: the killing shot that blew off the top of his heart. One that passed through his paunch, which explained the way the buck hunched up momentarily at my second shot. The third bullet was the real surprise; it had penetrated up near the hip and come back out through the buck's thigh. So I had hit him with my first shot. No wonder the big deer had been slow to follow the others.

I was elated and washed out. I was glad to be with David and Verges, men who knew all about the ebb and flow of life in the natural world. I clapped my friends on the back and thanked them for their help; we cracked a few jokes and stood around admiring the big deer. The breeze off the plains suddenly felt chill, and it stung my eyes.

One day, one or the other of us would say something like: *Remember that big buck we killed up near the canyon in the northwest corner that time? Geez, that was a good buck. Was that some Wild West show or what?*

I proudly posed for pictures with my deer. But all along, I felt the subtle undertow of tristesse.

I looked at my hands, chapped, nicked, and still tinted red by the blood of the buck I had just killed. A sense of dread mounted in me; I was having some kind of emotional chain reaction. I was a member of the unofficial Big Buck Club, but it was dawning on me that while something great had been given, something precious had been taken away.

It sure was a beautiful deer. If I saw that buck lying in the back of a pickup at the gas pump, I would have looked longingly at the magnificent antlers, pestered the lucky son of a bitch who shot it with questions, inhaled the lingering scent of the buck's blood, ambrosia.

I had anticipated an end to my quest, but since a secret part of me believed it would never come, I wasn't prepared for this emotional buffeting. What was I going to do now? Of what would I dream? I felt my heart hardening, braced to fight against further loss. I had to find something to fend off these feelings. I'd do it all right. I had a trophy mule deer buck, but the elusive monster of my dreams, the Picket Fence and his kindred spirits, were whitetail. And they waited for me back home, that place so distant and different from this elemental and wildly beautiful land.

I wasn't going to lose the thing I love, not without a fight.

The next morning, my last at the ranch, we took the deer over to the Guilford colony for butchering. I would keep the skull and antlers, of course. The rest of the deer would be made into sausage and jerky.

We met a truck on the way over and stopped to visit with Josh Stahl, the patriarch of the Hutterites. Built like a Coke machine, Josh speaks in the guttural singsong common to his people. "A fockin' beautiful day, David, aina? We got a fockin' mess of birds on our land—a fockin' messa huns and sharp-tail, I'm tellin' you . . ."

When we pulled away, David told me about the time Verges bumped into Josh in a waiting room at the nearest hospital. Josh's wife was in for some sort of throat surgery and Josh, visibly upset, exclaimed, "They fockin' cut her from ear to ear, Verges, from fockin' ear to fockin' ear."

Verges himself was in for a procedure that required cutting a surgical canal to help drain his intestines. Josh found the revelation disturbing. He grew agitated. The entire waiting room fell silent when his voice boomed out: "Why they gave you two fockin' assholes, Verges! What the hell you be doin' with two fockin' assholes? Why a man canna have two fockin' assholes, Verges, it canna a happen that way!"

Some Hutterite men, somberly dressed, were building a stone wall around the tidy cemetery of the colony. Brandon, a teenager and hunting fool who does butchering and taxidermy on the side, stood on a concrete pad nearby.

Brandon allowed how it was a "nice buck" I'd shot, but what he really wanted to do was talk about hunting and guns; he had his mind set on getting a .243 Winchester. A few of the Hutterite children had overcome their natural reserve to gather around us, giggling and whispering. The little girls were dressed in the same Spartan garb as their mothers; the boys, lost under their black cowboy hats, gathered around my deer, examining it.

David and I visited with some of his friends, and we ultimately left the colony loaded down with a freshly baked apple pie and some smoked ham. As we prepared to pull out, Brandon asked if we'd scouted the area of Dodge Pass.

"Did you see the great big mulie then?" he asked. "We seen one when we were over dere on horseback one time. He was all graylike, with a body like a fair elk. We seen him so much in the summer that we give him a name—the Phantom."

David and I exchanged glances and turned for the truck. The Phantom, old Grayface to us, would have to wait. We hoped he'd make it through another winter.

PART III

9

Love and War in the Woods

ANDES, NEW YORK, NOVEMBER 5

ALTHOUGH IT WAS FALL, the still-green hay meadows and turbulent rain clouds massed above my Catskill home reminded me that I lived in a temperate rain forest. My lips were still chapped and the skin of my knuckles was cracked, effects of the time I spent on the semiarid prairie. A part of me missed the dry brightness of the plains, and all that seeing room, especially when I studied the looming ridges where fog was caught like cotton in the latticework of naked trees. In the fields, great patches of goldenrod stood like rusting broadswords.

I thought about my mule deer antlers. Brandon would leave them on the stripped and bleached skull and together they would be an enduring monument to something. Certainly not to my own prowess, or skill. They would be an icon of a specific time and place and experience, although it wouldn't take much prodding to get me to tell the story of the hunt. I couldn't dwell on that, though; I felt my own woods calling me, and I wanted to get to know them again.

Hunting is an addiction, and like the most powerful ones, you don't develop it on your first, second, or third taste. It's strong stuff that demands patience and faith, and teaches you to embrace physical discomfort and the need to act from instinct, improvise and make quick decisions. And like a drug, hunting immerses you in an altered state no longer available to the civilized person in everyday life. It heightens, sometimes powerfully, the sense that you're a living creature up against the physical reality of the world. You discover a watchfulness in yourself, an ability to observe, size up, note details.

For the hunter, nature ceases to be a scenic, impenetrable wall around the windshield of the car or outside the living room window. It becomes three-dimensional, a second home that you enter with a sense of familiarity. You live hard while doing nothing, at least not by our society's standards. And it brings you face to face with the only other person usually out there: yourself.

I felt serious spiritual turbulence after my success on the plains, but the afterglow was mellow and left me feeling confident and fit and ready to go out to meet the whitetail.

Rifle season in New York was still about two weeks away, but the rut was gaining momentum. It was time to start using scent, which meant another quick trip down to Mark Finne's place, Spring Valley Sportsman. In addition to his bow-hunting franchise and guiding activities, Finne is a deer farmer. Collecting, bottling, and selling deer urine is a significant revenue stream, if that's the right term for it.

The rut, which peaks in mid-November in the northeast, is prime time. In many states, rifle hunting begins at the tail end of the breeding season to ensure that enough does are bred to maintain deer populations at a level that, in reality, probably is much too high—especially in areas with rich feed, a fairly temperate climate, and enough mankind to create fertile "edge" habitat (where woodlot meets meadow, or, increasingly, housing development). Unfortunately, attitudes toward hunting are often antagonistic in the areas that can most benefit from it.

Deer are driven by the breeding imperative. It's especially true for the whitetail buck, whose iconic antlers are a multipronged monument to the priority of procreation. Antlers mean a lot to hunters, but they serve only one purpose for deer: they're an aid in a buck's drive to multiply. They're used only for fighting, but paradoxically they may also curb fighting, because their size and shape sends visual cues to other deer— rival bucks, as well as does—that help establish a fundamental breeding hierarchy.

Antlers are both achingly beautiful and, by objective standards, deeply weird. They're bonelike, skeletal appendages that sprout like deformities from a buck's skull. Many people are surprised to learn that bucks annually shed their antlers (during the early winter, after the rut) and spend each spring and summer growing new ones, because antlers seem so . . . permanent. They're associated with deer as thoroughly as the shell is with a turtle, the tusk with an elephant, or the horn with a rhino. Yet these baroque appendages, smooth, polished, and finely tapered, are produced annually in a few short months to serve a function for just a few weeks. Then they're discarded.

Unlike a bone, an antler has uniform density throughout. It begins to grow out of a shallow cup called a "pedicle" on either side of a buck's skull. Throughout the growth phase, the antlers are covered in a highly vascular sheath named for a material it resembles, velvet. The velvet carries oxygen and nutrients to the developing antler, and the quality of available feed and minerals plays a critical role in how large the antlers become before the buck, preparing for the rut, begins to strip off the velvet.

In the fall, bucks rub the soft, spongy velvet off their antlers.

In velvet, antlers are spongy and susceptible to breakage. But they harden as the weeks and months go by. Come September, with the testosterone levels of the buck rising, antler growth comes to a halt. The buck soon begins to strip off the velvet by working over saplings and brush. If you catch a buck at this, you may see bloody streamers of velvet hanging like seaweed from his newly exposed, hard antlers. If you're really lucky, you might see the buck eat these bloody stringers dangling from his horns, for their nutritional content is high.

A buck is ready to breed once he's rubbed off his velvet, although does are still indifferent and many of the biological cues and stimuli that influence the rut have yet to be triggered. Like most changes in the natural world, breeding behaviors and biological changes that culminate in the rut are thought to be photoperiodic (dependent on the length of day and strength of the sun, rather than factors such as air temperature).

In the ensuing weeks, the buck will spend much time sharpening and polishing his antlers against saplings, showing a marked preference for trees of a certain size. Whenever possible, he'll conduct these velvet-shedding and antler-polishing sessions in a place where his work is most likely to be seen and interpreted by other deer as a territorial marker. A typical "rub" looks like someone took a knife to a tree and shaved away all the bark, leaving a bright, conspicuous blaze of raw wood.

By mid-October, the buck will spar with his summer companions and other deer, the way my friends Pancho and Lefty had done a few weeks earlier. This phase, beginning with the shedding of velvet, is loosely called the "pre-rut," during which the buck is bracing for the raging biological storms and behavioral turmoil to come.

Next comes the "chasing" phase, which usually begins in late October. The bachelor groups of bucks gradually dissolve and

Bucks will spar playfully or fight in deadly earnest to get in shape for the rut.

184 · WHITETAIL NATION

all bets are off—each buck becomes a solitary creature, with one growing priority. He'll seek out, follow, and hang around does, investigating their hormonal state. The does will begin to produce pheromones, which foreshadow estrus.

As the buck picks up on the pheromones by scent or even taste, his own production of male hormones begins to rise, and he grows even more bold and aggressive. He'll harass and chase any doe that communicates that she may be approaching estrus. Although the window of the rut is small, the does don't reach the peak of estrus on the same day; some may not be ready to stand for a buck until weeks after the first does come into high heat, ensuring that the fawns of the spring will not all be born at the same time.

One bright, still, summery afternoon in late October a few years ago, I was walking through an open field at around 2:00, heading for a tree stand. I heard a crashing in the woods about fifty yards away, and froze. Moments later, a doe hurtled into the field, with a six-point buck in hot pursuit. Neither deer noticed me. I stood, frozen, as the two preoccupied deer ran right toward me and veered off only at the very last moment. Others have been less fortunate; aggressive bucks have been known to challenge and even attack and gore humans.

By the peak of the chasing phase, the buck has staked out his turf—although a doe in estrus, or the prospect of finding one, will often lure him afield. As the chasing phase matures, a buck will also make any number of "scrapes" along his habitual travel route. He'll choose a spot, preferably under a low-hanging bough (beech trees, with spindly branches that grow parallel and spread out close to the ground, seem to be particular favorites) and clear out all the leaves, grass, and woody debris, right down to bare earth, in an area roughly the size of a bathtub.

The buck nips off a branch immediately above the scrape,

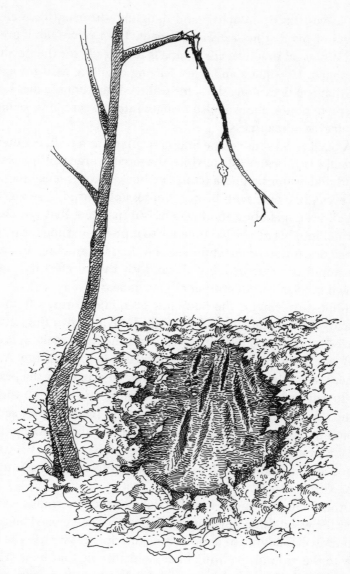

A deer scrape, into which bucks and does will deposit urine and glandular secretions.

but leaves the tip attached and dangling—bearing trace elements of his distinct saliva and scent. It's a remarkably precise, universal practice. His scrape is now ready for the finishing touch. He squats and pees, leaving a calling card for any doe that wanders along the same trail. As a doe approaches her receptive phase, she will also urinate into the scrape to signal her degree of readiness.

A buck checks his scrape line as regularly as a train conductor collecting tickets. Meanwhile, the terrible urge continues to build, like water behind a dam. The buck's neck swells up and his eyes glaze over with brute, irrepressible purpose, subverting all else, including the fine survival instincts that are also burned into his genes. No time for that now—no time for prudence or caution or watchfulness, no time for ambling among the apple trees or bedding down with the comforting gray brown mass of a twin brother or cousin nearby.

Almost overnight, the buck has been transformed from a placid, shy creature into a feverish, bullying, grunting, sex-crazed, and hormonally enslaved beast, bent on making love and war in the most critical two or three weeks of his life. Another reason the hunt is often scheduled to start after the peak of the rut is that rutting bucks, having just one thing on their minds, are far more vulnerable to hunting. If you've ever seen a buck standing along a highway in broad daylight, testing the air for scent, you can be sure it's a buck that has caught wind of a doe and isn't about to let some silly eighteen-wheeler interfere with his plans.

And finally the rut arrives, breaking like an enormous wave over the woods, flooding them with hot does and crazed bucks. A buck will follow a doe approaching full ripeness with his head low to the ground, grunting like the lustful pig that he is. The receptive doe's own hormonal journey has been less dramatic, with fewer outward signs of the inner bedlam, but the intensity of her heat may be even more obliterating.

The doe needs to keep the aggressive buck at bay until she is ready to copulate; she flees, trembling and skittish, because standing still is an invitation to rape; yet when her moment arrives, the need is as overpowering as it is immediate. A doe in high heat will stand for any buck, even a puny spike-horn buck in its first full calendar year of life. Hence the competition among bucks as they seek, fight over, and jealously trail does that are on the cusp of receptivity.

During the peak of the rut, the entire purpose of life—which can be boiled down to the transmission and continuation of an essentially fragile condition, often by the roughest and cruelest means possible—is acted out in a radiant explosion, the imperative singing electric in the blood of all deer. It's not unlike the orchestrated hatch of mayflies that brings the surface of a trout stream to a boil, or the salmon that, one day, flood into an Alaskan river in great, unstoppable waves.

Does torn in conflicting directions by mounting heat will flee bucks. Their suitors will lock horns, sometimes fighting so savagely that their antlers become interlocked, leaving both of them to die a miserable death of exhaustion and starvation, enmeshed in an eternal embrace. They will puncture each other's lungs and necks, gouge out an eye with their lethal brow tines. Thankfully, these grisly episodes are exceptional; one buck usually drives another off before death is ordained, which is a long-term benefit for the species.

I don't have the baseline stats on the average size of a whitetail buck's penis, although the ones I've seen are about four or five inches long. Copulation lasts for mere seconds, but there is no stigma attached to such a brief encounter. The deer make up for what they lack in quality of contact in quantity: during the twenty-four- to thirty-six-hour period of receptivity, a doe will stand for breeding as many as a dozen times.

Given that the sweet spot of the rut is a ten- to fourteen-day period, it's natural to wonder why it's so concentrated and frenzied. It's best understood by working backward. The gestation period for fawns is about 220 days, and fawns stand the best chance of survival if they're born in early to mid-June, when the nutrition and sheltering cover are ample, but they will still have sufficient time to develop body mass for their first winter.

Those deer, by virtue of genetics, will also be the ones most likely to hit the peak of estrus at the same time as their forbears; hence, their own offspring will be the most likely to survive. Over time, natural selection has made the breeding window smaller and smaller, while keeping it large enough to sustain populations and offset any natural conditions that might, for a few days, discourage successful breeding or impact newborn fawns.

In New York, rifle-hunting season begins while the rut is in swing, while in nearby Pennsylvania the hunt commences as much as two weeks later, when the rut is just about over. Bucks will still breed after the November rut, because does that have not been successfully bred will go through another estrus cycle twenty-eight days later. But the majority of the does are finished with procreation for another year by about the last week in November.

My first chance to kill a buck at the farm was on opening day of the first season that I owned it. I had hunted in the morning, without luck, and was fixing breakfast in the kitchen. Doug Stevens, the kindly farmer from whom I bought the place, appeared at the door. He asked me if I wanted to shoot a buck. He explained that he'd gone out for a little drive, and at the big turn he happened to spot a nice little buck bedded down on the brushy hillside, two hundred yards off the road and beyond my neighbor Rick's hayfield.

"Don't you want to shoot it?" I asked.

"No," he replied. "I wouldn't trust my old gun or my old eyes that far, and I think he'd see me if I tried walking closer through the meadow."

Doug is a tough old coot. He contracted polio as a child, and his family remembers how, even as an adult, he sometimes fell on his way to the barn and had to crawl fifteen or twenty yards to the utility pole in order to haul himself back up. Small wonder that he wasn't much interested in belly-crawling across a wet meadow.

"Well," I said, "if you're sure . . . We can share the venison."

"Oh, I don't mind about that," he said. "It would be your first deer here, anyways."

I hopped in Doug's truck and we drove down to the big turn. Sure enough, I could see the buck bedded down near a nasty tangle of briars and thorn apple trees. I glassed the buck; he had a small rack, but he would make a fine first deer at my new home.

I studied the situation. The buck was on the brushy hillside about fifty yards above the back edge of the meadow. From where we stood on the bank, a stone wall and a line of trees ran down through the field. I could crawl along the wall unobserved and get in position for an easy shot.

Rick pulled up while we were formulating the plan; he'd tagged a buck earlier and was just riding around, checking on everyone else. A few moments later, another neighbor stopped and, naturally, wanted to know why everyone was parked along the road, looking through binoculars.

I slung my rifle on my shoulder and dropped over the bank. I got down on my belly and began the long crawl along the stone wall. The meadow was wet; my knees and elbows quickly soaked through. I'd covered most of the distance when I looked back at my neighbors. A few more vehicles had stopped, and one neighbor, Johnny Little, was running through a field to see what the commotion was about, trailed by his five-year-old son, Ryan.

Within range, I edged up and peered over the stone wall, but I had no good shooting lane through the brush. I crawled to a high spot a little farther along, looked up again, and saw the buck easily, eighty yards away. He was still bedded down. And the group of spectators up by the road was still growing.

I wasn't about to scare the buck to his feet; I had a decent view of his vital area. I shouldered the rifle and put the cross hairs on the money.

I squeezed off a round. The buck lifted its head. As I chambered another round, a previously hidden doe popped to her feet, not ten yards from the buck. I got the scope up and when I found the buck, I was astonished to see that he had mounted the doe. They were screwing! I was stunned and deeply torn. Could I shoot a buck while he was in the act of copulation? What might that mean, karma-wise?

It was no time to get all philosophical; I touched off another round.

When the gun barked, the doe slipped out from under the buck and ran twenty feet. She stopped, and the buck ran over and mounted her again.

I aimed and shot—missed again.

Once more, the doe scampered off, vanishing into some thick brush with the buck hot on her tail. I rose. Something was wrong, I was sure of it. My first shot was a gimme, even for a nimrod. How could I have missed? And how could I have subsequently missed—and twice—when the buck was straddling the doe? The only thing worse would have been shooting the doe out from under the buck. I was surprised that hadn't actually happened.

I wished the walk back up to the road would never end. Instead of getting my first buck, I'd just endured a public humiliation in front of my new neighbors. Well, at least little Ryan Little wouldn't be aware of all the delicious, dark resonances of what had just happened; he was only just five. I would make no excuses, let them judge me as they would.

When I reached the crowd, most of them muttered condolences; they averted their eyes and nudged pebbles with the toes of their boots. "This is going to sound weak," I said. "But I think there's something wrong with my gun."

At least nobody laughed; that could wait until I'd gone down the road.

But I was convinced something was wrong with my gear. As soon as Doug dropped me at the house, I jumped in the Deermobile and drove down to see a neighbor, Chuck Vossler. He's a retired physicist, and a gun nut and Second Amendment activist, with a shooting range right behind his house. I was gratified to learn that the gun was indeed off—way off. The bullets I fired landed nowhere near each other, or my point-of-aim. Some barely hit the sheet of plywood to which the target was stapled.

I went home and immediately called Ruger, the makers of that 7 mm. Remington Magnum rifle. By the afternoon, my rifle was on the way to their shop, and forty-eight hours later I had a face-saving—sort of—reply. A tiny sliver of copper, probably from a barrel-cleaning brush, had somehow been fused to the inside of the barrel; in as precise a weapon as a gun, that was enough to make the bullets fly all over the place.

In the ensuing weeks, in true nimrod fashion, I would tell my tale of woe to anyone who'd listen. Nobody cared, at least not about that bit involving the flaw in the gun. It got to the point that I stopped explaining—why ruin a good, hilarious story? And in the end, it was maybe better that way. Had I killed the buck, I would have become nothing more than the heartless guy who shot a buck that was in the middle of doing the thing that man and beast most enjoy.

Here's a postscript: about three hours after my shooting spree, I looked through my window to see Johnny Little and his cousin Steve pull up and jump out of Johnny's truck. They lit out across my lower meadow and returned about half an hour later, grinning and slapping each other on the back.

After my disastrous experience, Johnny and Steve had teamed up to hunt down the amorous pair of deer, and eventually spotted them on my property. Johnny killed it at close range with one shot from his old .30-30.

That's the rut for you. That buck, unlike most, never had a fighting chance.

I pulled into Mark Finne's to pick up some estrus scent. When the rut is coming on, various urine-based lures undoubtedly attract deer. This has given rise to a somewhat shadowy, secretive industry that isn't the least bit averse to marketing its product with the bombastic flair befitting snake-oil salesmen. How can any nimrod resist the lure of "Tink's Fatal Attractor," "Buck Magic," "Crazy Juice Hot Doe," or my personal favorite, "Mrs. Doe Pee's Buck in Rut"?

But ask one of these urinetrepreneurs what goes into his product, and he's more than likely to say, *Come on, buddy, you don't expect us to divulge the secrets and formulas that make our scent draw in every buck from the county, do you?*

Scott Bestul, a writer for *Field and Stream* magazine, took a closer look at the pee-farming industry and came to the same conclusion as many other investigators: the top marketers of doe urine (usually, doe-in-heat urine, which dramatically reduces the amount of urine that can be collected) annually sell about 500,000 bottles (averaging two ounces each) of urine. Deer hunters in the U.S. purchase enough deer pee every year to fill a 660,000-gallon Olympic-sized swimming pool.

But if you do the math, the number of farm-raised deer in the U.S.—theoretically and legally the only source of urine—can't possibly produce that volume of pee. So the industry remains open to charges ranging from outright fraud to alchemy

—with the majority of whitetail fanatics voting with their dollars that it's the latter, with a naive belief in better living through chemistry.

Finne is not a big player in the burgeoning deer pee farming market; he's the first to admit that his urine business is just a small part of his overall operation. It's an outgrowth of his life-long fascination with deer, and his determination to become an expert bow hunter. He was open to walking me through his entire farming operation, including his collection methods.

Walking down to his deer pens, Finne told me how he got started: "A relation of my wife's was raising deer in Illinois, and I thought that was fascinating. I also thought that keeping a few deer will help bring me customers. They'll bring their kids up, so they can bottle-feed the deer while the parents can come into the shop and buy stuff."

Mark's deer herd once numbered over seventy whitetails, but when I visited he was down to twenty-three deer (including ten bucks). They lived on a few acres of land fenced into various enclosures, and a shed about the size of a two-car garage. The largest of the enclosures is where most of his deer spend their time, well-fed and watered, with shade and some browse available.

"It's been a real learning experience," Mark told me. "When deer are born, there's no scent to them—that's one way they stay safe from predators until they're strong enough to run away. They also don't go to the bathroom—because that would leave scent. In the wild, a mother licks the fawn to stimulate it to go to the bathroom, then she eats the feces. So the way to get a little fawn to pee or poop is to take a warm, wet rag and wipe their butts and stuff."

Mark's deer get a blend of feed for optimal nutrition and antler growth. At around five most evenings, he'll go out with a feed can and call, "Here, bucks, here, little bucks . . ." When he needs to capture a deer for veterinarian purposes, he darts it with a sedative.

After a few years raising deer, Mark found that too many people were wandering around the fences and trails near his pens, keeping the deer in a constant state of alarm. Sometimes, the deer would crash into fences and suffer mortal wounds. So he began to discourage whitetail tourism. He also learned that if you put more than three mature bucks into a small enclosure (less than an acre), they would eventually fight—sometimes to the finish. Once rutting activity kicks in, he spends a lot of time moving bucks into separate paddocks, and usually leaves just his best breeder buck in with the does in hopes of producing superior buck fawns.

"At first, I would leave the bucks together and just cut the horns off a few inches up from the base. One day, I did my morning rounds and found a buck lying there, dead. It looked like he had a perfect bullet hole, right behind the shoulder blade. I thought some idiot had shot it from the hill across the road. But I called the vet, had the deer X-rayed, and it was determined to be a puncture wound."

Mark began to de-horn his bucks, cutting the antlers off flush with the skull. But the bucks still instinctively rubbed trees and poles so vigorously that they made a bloody mess of their skulls. Finally, Mark began leaving an inch of antler, which is ample for ritual rubbing and fighting, but short enough so the deer can't seriously injure each other. "What they still do, though, is gang up on one another. One of them will take a shot in the ribs and start limping because of the bruise. Then the others will notice and start to gang up until they kill the injured one."

Over the summer, Mark puts feed in the accessible big shed so that the deer become acclimatized to indoor dining. All of his deer have ear tags, like livestock. As the rut approaches, Mark watches with binoculars or walks the fence, studying their behavior. When the hormones kick in, Mark repairs to a small cubby in the big shed to watch the main room through a peephole. When the deer he's after comes in, he'll drop the pulley-driven deer doors to trap the animal inside.

He gently herds the captive through a series of tiny rooms and a short hallway that leads to the collection room, which is about ten foot square. The floor is made of wooden slats over a stainless steel panel. When the deer urinates, the product trickles down to a small hole at the low end of the stainless steel and collects in a large aluminum roasting pan.

"Getting them in is no big deal; they're pretty well-trained," Mark told me. "I leave them in the collection room for twenty-four hours, with plenty of feed and water. I leave it dark. They're very calm in there—I can put two or three does in there at a time, but every buck goes in solitary. The deer will even lie down in there. By the next day, there's a lot of urine in the roasting pans. Ever see a deer go to the bathroom? It's like a friggin' waterfall. And when they're in heat, they pee a lot more."

The next day, Mark turns the deer out through a different door and filters and bottles the urine, storing it in a refrigerator for sale. Scent works as a deer lure; there's no doubt about that. But any experienced hunter knows that merely using scent and ignoring other factors is a mistake.

"The big thing when using scent is to be clean," Mark explained. "These guys—they buy urine and expect miracles. Going hunting, they stop to pump gas in their hunting boots and eat a couple of hot dogs. They tramp through the woods, sprinkle out a little urine and hunker down, fifteen yards away. Then they say a deer comes in, smells the urine, and runs the other way. I say, 'How the hell could it? It's just pure deer urine. Maybe they smelled the gas on your boots or the mustard on your breath.'"

The urine of both sexes has its uses, and Mark mixes them at times. He told me that the first time he used the urine he collected, he put some on a piece of cloth tied to his hunting boot (in the parlance, a "drag") so it would leave a trail of scent as he walked to his tree stand. He then left the bottle of urine near the base of the tree.

Soon, a button buck showed up and put his nose right on the bottle, then the tree-stand steps. Then, a seven-pointer strolled in, looked up at Mark, and sauntered over to sniff the bottle as well.

I wondered if Mark thinks his deer have a decent life. He said, "They do good. I walk right up and feed them, five, eight yards away. I used to bottle-feed a few of the bucks to make it easer to get them in the pens, but a funny thing happened. The ones I bottle-fed got so used to it that they would get very demanding—especially during the rut. They would come close, then snort-wheeze and come right at me, real aggressive. So I stopped doing that. It's not worth getting a hole poked in you."

A mature buck with good genes (read: big antlers) is worth north of two thousand dollars, and when a deer of the caliber gets to be three and a half years old, Mark will sell him. From about that age on, even farm-raised bucks are simply too wild and aggressive during the rut. Mark sells many of his bucks to a nearby shooting preserve where, as he put it, "Some guy can come up from Long Island, shoot the deer, and then go home that afternoon and brag about it to his brothers-in-law. 'Hey, I shot a monster!' It sounds terrible, I know, but the way I look at it, it's a farming operation—just like raising beef or chickens. They just happen to be deer."

The skies were still a calico patchwork of clouds, and the light wind out of the south made it an ideal time to hunt the one-acre quarry meadow on the ridge behind my house.

This rectangular field attracts deer. I keep it mown, so the blend of clover, timothy, and orchard grass is nutritious. And with a steep bank on one of the long sides and a nice stand of oaks and maples opposite, feeding options abound. The quarry abuts one of the short sides, and the road runs alongside the other.

The road is the one flaw in the setup, because only a degenerated stone wall and scattered trees screen the meadow. So the quarry field is vulnerable to road hunters who have no qualms about shooting from the truck window, even on someone else's land. And the sight and sound of a passing vehicle of any kind, while relatively rare, sends the deer running.

Deer frequent the field to browse or dawdle on their way to or from the oak stand or the big fields below. It's also a place to socialize and bed down for the night, close to the steep downhill bank that serves as an escape route to the deep woods. Before going out, I saturated the wick inside a small plastic container with some of Mark's doe urine. I'd hang the device, wick exposed, on a branch somewhere in bow range, in a location determined by wind direction. I wanted just the scent of the urine wafting down through the woods.

My ladder stand is near the corner of the field farthest from the road, set back among some cherry trees on a level bench just below the edge of the field. Deer usually approach uphill from the woods and wait until near dusk to steal into the meadow. But they can appear from any direction, and I enjoy just watching them across the field and out of bow range in the oaks. Whitetail are browsers; they rarely make a beeline, even for a preferred food source, and seem to enjoy noshing on their way to the main course.

In addition to the doe urine, I had a grunt tube hanging around my neck and a "fawn-in-a-can" bleater in my pocket. The bleat will attract does by triggering their mothering instinct, but bucks also intuit that a bleating fawn means there's

A grunt tube imitates the distinct, hoglike vocalization or "grunt" of a buck.

a doe nearby. The grunt tube is a call that mimics the guttural, burplike vocalization of a buck when he's issuing a challenge, declaring his sovereignty, or in the throes of trailing a hot doe. A grunt will often stop a deer of either sex in its tracks. During the rut, it will often draw in a buck looking for a fight—or a mate.

I climbed the ladder stand and hooked up my safety belt, hung my daypack, bow, and quiver of arrows, and settled in to wait. The clouds were clearing off and soon the sun peeked out. What leaves were left on the trees glittered wetly and occasionally lost hold and spiraled to the ground. It was a cool fifty degrees and I felt the chill of winter in the air. Cooling down, I turned my collar up against the breeze. Somewhere in the distance, a neighbor was running a chain saw. Otherwise, all was still.

Every twenty minutes or so, I stood up to stretch my legs and take in the woods behind me. Then I sat back down, continuing my vigil as the evening descended. I was considering getting down off the stand a little early when I caught a flicker of movement from the far side of the field, among the oaks. It was just a coyote, slipping through the brush. It slinked across the old log road in the oak grove and disappeared.

Coyotes in my neck of the woods are relative newcomers; at first I welcomed their presence, because I still get a shiver up my spine when I hear them howling and yipping. But after I saw a few of their deer kills, I decided to shoot them when I had a chance. Not that it matters much—the creature known to many Native tribes as "God's dog" has weathered some of the fiercest and most horrific of extermination campaigns ever mounted by man and still survived to successfully colonize every state in the lower forty-eight.

The extirpation of larger predators, chiefly wolves, greatly helped the coyotes achieve their manifest destiny—with smaller predators, like the fox, paying the price. The colonization of the northeast by coyotes is an astonishing tale of niche-filling and adaptation by an opportunistic species, but the prey base of small creatures (coyotes are omnivores) is much smaller in the northeast than in the coyote's original range on the prairie. Thus, the eastern coyote has adapted and learned to kill deer, often adopting pack behaviors to get the job done.

Some biologists believe that a century or more ago, pioneer coyotes interbred with remnants of the now extinct eastern timber wolf population to produce the eastern coyote, which is significantly larger than its western progenitors. This would also explain how the eastern coyote made the transition to hunting in packs, like the wolf.

In my rural area, hard winters, coyote predation, vehicle collisions, and hunting pressure keep the deer herd surprisingly small, given the habitat. It might be different if fish and wildlife officials and hunters embraced a more enlightened management regimen, but we get the worst of both worlds: a lower population of deer and relatively poor genetics, because the breeding hierarchy is destroyed.

Suddenly, I picked up the unmistakable sound of deer shuffling through the leaves, downhill to my right. I slowly stood up and gingerly removed the bow from its tree hook. Was it just a playful squirrel out there? But soon a deer darted from brush, into the field, about fifty yards away. It was Lefty, the forkhorn buck I'd last seen traveling with Pancho, the five-pointer. But he was on his own now; during the rut, it's every buck for himself.

I had no desire to shoot Lefty, having brought some venison home from the west. I was hoping that the rut had smoked out bigger and older whitetail, or led one to leave his home range for my property. Once you get beyond that idea that providing meat for the table is the only legitimate reason to hunt, you face a quandary with both practical and ethical overtones, and a sometimes uncomfortable, deitylike degree of power: which deer should you kill, or will you kill, when hunting means more than gathering?

Lefty lifted his head and tested the air for scent; his neck was swollen, and he cut a substantial figure despite his puny antlers. He remained still as a lawn ornament for some time. He was close to directly downwind, but there was little I could do about it. He ducked his head and began to browse through the new grass, tail twitching.

Lefty was edgy; every few moments he lifted his head to look around, moving little. I wanted to see if I could draw him in, or attract any other buck that might be nearby. I blew once on the grunt call. Lefty's head flew up, and he looked in my direction for a spell. Then he started toward me, walking in an arc that put him well upwind. He was coming to investigate, spoiling for a fight.

Lefty headed straight for the bottleneck between my tree stand and a great big mound of quarry rubble. Any deer using this natural travel route to get to or from the field would be in bow range.

But Lefty stopped to crop grass again. Once more, I blew into the grunt tube, and again Lefty reacted sharply. He began walking toward me, not exactly hurrying, but with purpose in his steps, and his head low to the ground. I was goading him into a fight with a buck that didn't exist.

As he advanced, I was tempted to shoot him; my hunter's blood was up. But I'd resolved that issue and was fresh off a great hunt. If I were to kill a whitetail on my own land, it had to be a trophy—or something better, at any rate, than Lefty. I decided to just sit back and enjoy the show.

Dusk was falling, quickly, and Lefty kept coming. At twenty yards, I drew the string while slowly raising the bow. When the let-off kicked in, I settled my twenty-yard pin—it glowed noticeably in the dying light—right behind the joint where Lefty's left leg met his torso.

I've got you this time, I thought, as I eased the string back toward the bow. I wondered how I was going to climb down out of the stand without scaring the living daylights out of Lefty, and also about how long his luck would hold out when gun season arrived and he left my property and protection.

Somebody might shoot him before he had a chance to grow bigger and develop a better set of antlers. All I knew is that it wasn't going to be me.

10

The Million-Dollar Free Throw

FREDERICKSBURG, TEXAS, NOVEMBER 7–11

I FELT TORN, leaving Andes just as the rut was coming to a head, but I had plans to hunt in one of the most storied regions of Whitetail Nation, the Hill Country of Texas. I was meeting up with Mike Potts, a friend from my professional life as a sportswriter.

I'd expected San Antonio to be a quaint and manageable little town, and found it the opposite—a bewildering maze of highways, mega-malls, towering neon lights, and five-acre car dealerships flying American flags the size of Rhode Island. But after hurtling through this kaleidoscope for an hour, I slid into the soothing darkness of the Southern Plains.

I turned onto U.S. 87N, a gentle roller coaster of a road twisting this way and that into the Hill Country, heading for the tourist center, Fredericksburg. I began to see deer—mere shadows betrayed only by the fluorescent green glow of their eyes in my headlights. I slowed to an easy sixty; I was here to shoot a deer, not explode one with my rented Chevy Impala.

I checked into the Best Western on the edge of Fredericksburg and learned that I could get my hunting license that night at a 24/7 Walmart a few miles away. When I got there, the sporting goods clerk, a pretty young girl named Lauren, was checking out a guy who was buying a camo hunting jacket in XXXL. Browsing around, I came across a huge display for something called the "Butt Out." My pal Tom Daly had been right—his nifty anal canal extractor was now an official product. It came in blaze-orange (I'd been right about that), and it was shaped like a rocket ship, but with the three navigation fins up near the nose cone. The other, nonbusiness end ended in a T-shaped hand grip.

I picked up a Butt Out and returned to the register, feeling a little sheepish. Lauren glanced at the object in my hand. "Eeeuuuwwww, you're buying one of those butt things!"

"Strictly for professional reasons," I said, smiling.

"Don't laugh; I was the one who had to open the whole freakin' crate of those things. I couldn't figure out what it was until I read the package and saw the diagram. I dropped that thing like a hot potato. It was, like, *This is waa-a-a-y gross . . .*"

Lauren was a good ole girl, though, so we made a few lame Butt Out jokes and when that was played out, she cut my license. Texas doesn't go for the usual one-buck-per-hunter stuff you get in other states. My nonresident license cost a relatively modest three hundred dollars, and provided me with more game tags than my wallet had business cards from people I don't know and have no intention of ever calling. Among them were *five* deer tags, including two for bucks. Texas has five million deer, or one for every five people. I felt like a king. This trip wasn't such a bad idea.

In the morning, I called Mike Potts. He had houseguests, an aunt and uncle from England, and suggested we meet for lunch in a Fredericksburg beer and burger joint called the Buffalo Nickel, after which we would return to hunt at his mini-ranch, a place he'd named Ardmair House. He had four or five bucks that used his property, and one of them was a fine seven-point specimen.

I would oblige him and kill the deer if I had a chance, but that wasn't the main reason for my visit. I made the trip because Mike had put me in touch with Ted Masser, a neighbor who owned a "high-fence" ranch teeming with monster trophy whitetail.

When I first spoke with Ted, months earlier, he seemed wary of my intentions. I was, after all, a journalist. I explained that I was a hunter, and neither angling for an invitation to shoot a buck in exchange for a little publicity for his ranch, nor was I necessarily opposed to paying for a hunt. Mainly, I told him, I wanted to find out how a top-quality high-fence operation worked—to see if it was something I might want to do.

Ted agreed to show me around his ranch, which is just one of the many spreads that are part of a controversial tradition —hunting on fenced property, usually managed for the optimal production of trophy whitetail deer. The practice is reviled by many as a violation of the semisacred principle of "fair chase." Fair chase demands that we pursue game on a reasonably level playing field, where the animal has a chance to elude the hunter, and it also requires using tools and equipment that give the deer a reasonable chance to escape. It's related to the broader concept of sportsmanship, the willingness to compete on equal terms under agreed-upon rules.

But ethical concepts tend to shift in response to the times. While high-powered rifles and scopes are standard equipment for even the most ethically minded of hunters (traditional bowmen and traditional firearms users could argue that), spotlights used at night are not. In some places, baiting deer (by regularly feeding them desirable foods in a designated area) is legal, as is hunting with hounds. Most of the deer poacher's techniques, including shooting deer from vehicles or helicopters, are considered violations of fair chase, and many of them are forbidden by law, but even that varies from state to state.

I wanted to experience a high-fence hunt, either as an observer or a hunter—I wasn't entirely sure which. I had a fundamental prejudice against high-fence hunting, and while I had paid to hunt with a guide or outfitter now and then, it was never under the tacit assumption that I was paying to shoot (or even get a good shot at) a deer of a certain quality, provided by my host. That was nothing but a canned hunt, and I wanted no part of it.

But what if the reality was different from the popular perception? What if an opportunity to kill a monster buck in the 160 or better B&C class was too much for me to resist?

The only thing I knew for sure is that even if I shot a world-record whitetail on a high-fence farm, it would never go into the B&C book. The wardens of the nation's hunting records refuse to acknowledge deer taken on fenced land, because it violates the fair-chase ethic. Still, I had my checkbook in my backpack. I vowed to go into this experience with an open mind.

Ranches like Ted's spread are entirely fenced; the barriers must be at least eight feet high to keep deer enclosed on the property. But that isn't quite the same as hunting in an enclosure as we might think of it. The most famous high-fence ranch of all, and one steeped in American lore for many reasons other than hunting, is the King Ranch, a Texas spread that encompasses 1,289 square *miles*. It's the largest ranch in the nation. Masser's place, by contrast, is 750 acres, which is still a sizable property. You can hunt a piece of land that size almost anywhere in Whitetail Nation for a long time without killing a deer.

By and large, though, deer living in a fenced area simply can't run far enough, although the King Ranch folks might strenuously disagree. It's also true that if you hunt on public or relatively small parcels of private land of up to a few hundred acres, other hunters have a fair chance of beating you to a deer. And that figures into our ideas about fair play, not just fair chase.

The other objection to game ranches is based on the degree of difficulty we associate with hunting, and in that area many high-fence operations are on shaky ground. Game ranches prosper in direct proportion to the success of their hunter-customers; the sure ticket to bankruptcy is a low hunter success rate. The estimated success rate on a typical Texas game ranch is around 85 percent—or better—and it's mainly because the deer herd is tightly and expertly managed for hunting. Feeding deer is a commonplace practice in Texas, even on small private holdings, and deer become as accustomed to regular feeding as livestock. If you know where they eat, you know where to go with your gun.

A three-day hunt on a high-fence property for trophy whitetail easily drives the needle above $5,000. And while you aren't guaranteed a $5,000 buck simply by handing over a check (at most high-fence ranches, the cost of a hunt is measured by the size of the deer's antlers), your host will almost always put you in a position to bag one, usually right under a feeder that goes off like clockwork twice a day. So the overall impression of game ranches is that they offer you the best canned hunts money can buy. It's pretend hunting.

This much is true: if you play it square, you're looking at the exact reverse of the fair-chase hunting equation; it's much harder for a reasonably competent hunter to *not* shoot a buck on a high-fence ranch than it is to bag one.

In Texas, 97 percent of the land is in private hands, and four million acres or more may now be behind high fences. Public opinion is divided on the wisdom of allowing high-fence game ranches, partly because wildlife in the U.S. (as opposed to Europe) is officially considered a public resource, but a rancher's right to fence his land is considered pre-emptive and God-given—especially in Texas. So is yours and mine, for that matter, even if you own considerably less than 1,300 square miles.

Some high-fence ranches offer hunts for exotic game, including sika deer (a native of Japan), African gemsbok, oryx, and blackbuck antelope, aoudad sheep, and nearly fifty other African and Asian exotic species. These colonists have established a foothold and flourished in Texas. In 1963, when the first census was taken, there were thirteen species of exotics totaling 13,000 animals. The last survey, completed in 1979, found fifty-one species numbering 72,147 animals. The growth in species variety and numbers of animals is attributed to hunter demand.

The introduction of these exotic critters to Texas also has been controversial, because some of the new citizens are, essentially, invasive species. Studies have established that white-tail prefer forbs (weeds or broad-leaf, herbaceous plants) and browse (the leaves of woody plants), and eat very little of what can properly be called grass. Exotics prefer the same food as whitetails, but they're also capable of shifting their diet to grass, something whitetail can't manage successfully enough when stressed to avert malnutrition and starvation.

After I made my plans to meet Mike Potts for lunch, I called Ted Masser, whose gruff voice and short, clipped sentences are eerily evocative of John Wayne. He was friendly on the phone. He invited me to spend as much time as I needed with him out at the ranch over the next two days. Happy to have nailed that down, I met Mike and soon found myself at Ardmair House.

"I can't hunt in these shoes," I said, looking down at my navy blue Crocs, which look (and feel) like Tupperware. I was standing in Mike's living room, looking over his shoulder at three deer, all does, that had already trotted in to feed on corn. The kernels had been broadcast out over the well-trod prairie grass by a feeder that looks like a fifty-gallon aluminum drum perched on a tripod. It was just thirty yards away; the deer were in his backyard.

I quickly pulled on my boots, and we walked out the front door and over to a blind built among the sturdy branches of a black oak towering above the gravel driveway. We climbed the ladder and crawled into a wooden box just big enough for two. Mike, a gun nut and collector, had persuaded me that I wouldn't need to bring my own gun. And because this was mostly a research trip, I was happy to use his weapon, a handsome .30/06.

Now I was between a rock and a hard place. It was impossible to call this hunting; I could just as well go to a Wisconsin dairy farm, walk up on a placid Holstein, and blow its brains out. But I could tell that it meant something to Mike to offer this opportunity; I didn't want to offend his feelings by turning down the chance to kill a nice buck that he might have been saving just for me. This is how they did things in Texas. So be it.

Mike is a British expatriate who married a Connecticut girl, Susie, who's a veterinarian. It wasn't like these people had a low regard for animals, or for life in general. Mike's eleven-acre piece of Texas paradise is part of an intricate network of mostly small, unfenced properties in the midst of the high-fence culture. I guess his place is part of a kind of underground railroad for free-roaming deer, of which Texas also has plenty.

The feeder sits on a quarter-acre level, beyond which Mike's land drops off sharply to a small, densely wooded canyon that partly encircles his home site. There's a high fence at the bottom of the draw on Mike's property line, built by his neighbor. I settled into a camp chair alongside Mike in his blind. We

In places like Texas, where feeding deer is both legal and encouraged, "broadcast" feeders that distribute corn or other feed twice a day (with the aid of an electronic timer) are common.

watched the growing number of deer a scant sixty yards away. Mike had asked his British auntie Anne to stay off the deck at the back of the house, either to keep her from spooking the deer or to ensure that she didn't take a round in her chest. She sat in a folding aluminum chaise by the front door, reading a thick novel.

There were now nine deer, including a spike buck. I asked: "So we shoot right past the corner of the house?"

"Try not to hit the bedroom. The wife wouldn't like it. You know how women are."

I liked that Mike wasn't defensive about the setup. I allowed the .30/06 to rest on the wooden shooting rail. It wasn't like I'd be called upon to make a seventy-yard snap shot at a buck running among pines. A few more deer joined the group. We chatted quietly, watching and waiting for the seven-pointer as the others gobbled up the corn.

Mike is a native of Hartlepool in the United Kingdom. He became interested in target pistol shooting at age fifteen. When he went to visit relatives living on a farm in Scotland, he was introduced to pheasant hunting. "They were the happiest days of my life," he said, "until I came to the U.S."

While at university in Liverpool, Mike worked in a gun shop. He also found work around guns as a loader on big British grouse shoots—those aristocratic get-togethers in which the tweedy "sports" do all the shooting as the skies above them fill with grouse put to flight by an army of beaters advancing toward the shooters over the heath. The action can be fast and furious, a little too much for someone like me, who would just as soon powder clay targets as live birds when I have a hankering to burn up a few boxes of ammunition. The sport at a shoot has at least two guns with him, and the loader's job is to keep passing him a freshly loaded one after the other has been emptied.

Mike jumped on the opportunity to relocate to Dallas, Texas, in 1983, when a gunsmith he worked for was recruited by a dealer, Buckhorn Quality Firearms. But Mike's boss had a falling-out with Buckhorn, and he told Mike, "That's it—we're going back."

Mike, having grown accustomed to the tolerant gun laws and excellent public hunting opportunities in the U.S., shot back, "Oh no, *we're* not."

I heard a strange, whistling sound. "What the hell is that?" "Sika deer," Mike said. "They're over the fence there. Sika have 'whistling teeth.' They use them to communicate."

A forkhorn and another spike buck soon joined the milling deer. Suddenly, though, the demeanor of the does changed. A number of them seemed restless, and they looked back toward the draw, and moments later the seven-pointer Mike had saved for me emerged. His antlers were asymmetrical, with four total points on one side and three on the other. He had strikingly long brow tines that ended at almost right angles, pointing forward. The rack was dark and high. He was no record-book deer, but as good as any whitetail I'd ever shot.

Then things got a little weird. I stupidly asked, "Should I shoot him?"

"I don't see why not," Mike deadpanned.

As I raised the gun, the buck flung out his chest and waded in among the other deer. In order to hit his vitals, my bullet would have had to pass through various parts of at least three other deer—something that the 150-grain tip of my .30/06 was perfectly capable of doing, if I were inclined to do such a ghastly thing.

But I was almost tempted—hell, I had enough tags, because my Texas nonresident license came with five, covering both sexes. How many other nimrods could ever claim to have shot four deer with one bullet?

The bodies shifted and suddenly I had a clear, broadside shot at about sixty yards—a gimme, by any measure. *Well,* I thought, *I sure hope Auntie Anne has a strong heart . . .*

I slowly inched the rifle forward on the shooting rail. I had a final thought: *You've been bow hunting; make sure you don't aim too low.*

The gun bucked, and so did the deer; then it ran off. But I knew they can't go far after taking a double-lung shot. The does scattered, too. I heard a crashing in the brush.

I didn't know what to say.

It wasn't supposed to be so easy, not in my experience, not with a buck the equal of anything I'd killed on sometimes grueling hunts in big woods and bitterly cold weather. Here I was, in shirtsleeves, unnecessarily wearing hunting boots when Crocs would have been fine. I shrugged and said, "Well, that's that."

"It looked like you shot high," Mike said.

"I think I hit him pretty good."

We slowly climbed down from the tree stand; Anne was fine. She looked up from her book: "Well?"

"We got him," I said, but Mike remained silent.

We walked around the corner of the house, my eyes already scanning ahead for telltale blood. The buck was standing about ten feet from the feeder when I shot, but we found no blood or hair there. There was no sign at all.

I still felt confident—depending on where and how the bullet passed through, there might not be any blood until enough had collected to leak through the entry or exit wound.

We began walking in ever-widening circles, starting at the assumed point-of-impact. As the circles grew wider, I found myself thinking: *I hit him. It was impossible* not *to hit him. I could have hit him with a rock.*

We were at the perimeter of the clearing and poking around in the thick stuff when I heard a commotion in the brush. But it was just a jackrabbit running off. Right about then, I made a little speech, something to this effect: *I'm no great hunter, but I couldn't have missed the shot. Besides, I saw the deer buck. It was as easy a shot as I've ever had . . . Mike . . . Do you think I might have missed?*

Mike spared me the indignity of meeting my eyes. He just said, "It happens to everyone."

I felt like I was going to vomit. How could this happen to me? We looked at each other. There was nothing left to do.

At least I had missed clean, instead of gut-shooting the poor thing. This wasn't supposed to happen, not after Montana, not after I'd let Pancho and Lefty walk . . . My inner nimrod cried out for comfort and understanding.

We strolled back to the house. David, Anne's husband, had missed most of the action. He politely asked, "Were you successful?"

The words sounded strange as they came from my mouth: "I think I missed."

In the background, Mike's young son, Georgie, squealed with delight as he watched a Curious George video.

"Oh dear, no deer," David said, trying to lighten things up.

I politely asked Mike if he was sure the scope was zeroed in properly. He said it was, and suggested we take a test shot, just to make sure. He taped a ten- by eight-inch rectangle of white paper to a plywood panel and set it up near the feeder. I shot twice: the holes were both on the left edge of the paper, about an inch apart. The gun was fine.

Mike had been prepared to broil up some fresh venison tenderloins for a celebratory dinner, and now it was going to be chicken and shrimp. When Mike said something about "white venison," I realized that sulking was not an option. The grotesque humor of it all dawned on me. I made some crack about rubber bullets, and David observed that there did seem to be an awful lot of deer in Texas.

"Now you know why there are so many," Mike said.

Georgie came over, and I taught him one of the gestures I did with my own son, Luke—a very light head butt that we call a "doink." Susie, Mike's wife, a triathlete as well as a vet, poured the wine for dinner. She cheerfully said, "Don't worry . . . he'll be back tomorrow."

Georgie lightly tapped his forehead against mine. "Doink!"

· · ·

I sat with my coffee in a rocking chair on the faux-Western covered boardwalk at the front of the Best Western. It was a relatively new joint made of honey-colored logs, and I sat right under a stained glass Texas Lone Star.

It was a chilly morning, with a hint of mountain air in the breeze out of the west. The RV and trailer park across the paved road was well-hidden among trees and brush. The sign in front of the squat rectangular building made of pale yellow corrugated steel advertised "Quilt Fabric." Small homes without sidewalks or gutters lined the road and extended back from it, a comfortable distance from each other. There was no neon anywhere in sight, and I watched pickups laden with machinery, heavy winches, and stock tanks rumble by.

It was a fine morning in Whitetail Nation, and I was in a mellow, reflective mood. Maybe this entire odyssey was less about the search for a monster buck than my own desire to seek out and touch the heart and soul of my country—the nation that gave my immigrant parents a new, better life, the nation whose own history, particularly before the turn of the twentieth century, still has a fierce grip on my imagination, the nation that I love and appreciate, even though I'm as deeply stuck in its contradictions and strange web of consumerism and rampant indulgence as anyone else. I am, like all good Americans, resolutely unfazed by the ironic.

I'd set forth focused on killing a big buck, sure; but I realized that finding one didn't end the quest. If anything, it lured me deeper, and I was profoundly happy exactly where I sat, in touch with . . . something that was hard to pin down. This other thing was no less important than the monster buck, and that only made sense. For I already knew that hunting isn't about killing animals.

So what is it? *A few things,* I thought, feeling the morning sun on my face and forehead. A search for a connection with the old and honorable ways, when killing a big deer was an event and a cause for celebration, not soul-searching. For a deeper understanding of the natural world that had such a shaping influence on my nation's history and my own life. For self-sufficiency and vestiges of the untamed, still lurking and flitting in the shadows in a quiet patch of woods despite the encroachments of civilization.

I didn't have the discipline, nor the purity, of a modern-day Thoreau, nor the protest gene of those folks who just go off the grid, heaving a great big middle finger at a culture drowning in excess and spiraling through a misguided, paranoid search for material comfort and security—a process that probably took form in the empty bellies of hard men and women searching westward, shaped as much by failure as success.

Even the great Davy Crockett, who had died heroically at the Alamo, not all that far from where I sat in the wooden rocker enjoying the sun, knew the kind of spectacular hardship that might leave him with a generationally communicable reverence for property and status.

I'm trapped on the grid and pretty happily so, and maybe that allows me to experience some basic things, including my explorations, with greater wonder and joy.

The Hill Country resembles the African savanna, although I doubt that in the bush of Botswana you'd come across a white plastic shopping bag from Walmart, complete with the trademark yellow smiley-face icon, tangled up and flapping conspicuously on a high branch.

I was on my way to the Masser Ranch. The grasses were golden, but tipped with delicate, pale tones of orange and maroon. The road dipped frequently to cross creeks of clear, blue-green water. There isn't enough dirt out this way to cloud the water, or even to absorb it—hence the flood gauges at every bridge over a creek. Along the way, I passed a number of high-fence ranches, the archways and tube gates at some of them still festooned with Halloween decorations.

Following Ted's instructions, I took my time opening and closing his electric gate, aware that if I screwed up he could lose twenty or thirty grand's worth of buck by nightfall. A long dirt drive led up to a spacious ranch house pleasantly situated on raised ground overlooking a large field dotted with shade trees and containing a deer feeder much like Mike's. It was just one of the many on Ted's property.

Ted's wife, Kathy, an attractive and well-kept woman, welcomed me into the house, informing me that Ted was still out on the morning hunt with two regular guests who live in Seattle, Jim Young and his son Kyle. She offered me iced tea and invited me to sit down. We chatted, and I learned that she was from the Texas town of Comfort, and had started dating Abilene native Ted while they were both students at Southwest Texas University.

Ted was an avid hunter and had been a high school football coach at Alamo Heights High School in San Antonio, in the state where football is king. He bought the 750-plus-acre ranch in 1971, before the original house even had electricity.

For a while, the Massers ran cattle. They also fed deer and allowed what Kathy called "blue-collar hunting." But they were frustrated when they saw how many of the quality deer they worked to produce ended up jumping their low fences, only to be promptly shot on a neighboring property. "When we got tired of being poor, we decided to try something else," Kathy said lightheartedly. "So we began to look at hunting seriously. We improved our feed program and decided to fence the ranch. The payoff has been pretty obvious—one year, the second-best typical shot in Texas was killed right here on this ranch."

A pickup pulled up to the house while we chatted; I saw the

hefty antlers of two deer poking up out of the bed of the truck. We went outside, where I met Ted—a stocky, powerful-looking man with pale skin, a ruddy complexion, and small but striking pale blue eyes. Add the Marine Corps–grade haircut and he fits the image of an ex-football coach to a T. His companions, Jim and Kyle Young, were dressed in camo, and they had about them that relaxed glow of successful hunters. Each of them had killed a handsome eight-point buck in the 130 class.

Ted invited me to accompany them to the machinery shed, where the bucks were hung on a scale while Ted recorded various particulars of their condition and age, starting with their antlers. Ted is closely monitored by the state game department, Texas Parks and Wildlife. One of the numerous ironies in the fair-chase controversy is that many high-fence ranches are at the cutting edge of deer management. It is, after all, in their own best interest to create the best possible herd.

We walked down to the small trailer where Ted keeps his records in a big desk and a bank of filing cabinets, and he entered the pertinent information about the Youngs' deer. A series of deer jawbones lined the wall above the desk, used for determining the age of deer by the most common method, wear on their teeth.

While Ted did his paperwork, he explained that he partners with the state in a habitat improvement program. He gets help and advice from the state as long as he observes certain guidelines established by wildlife and habitat biologists. He said, "If this place were grazed off and our only aim was killing deer, the state would have nothing to do with us. We're not a 'Bubba' outfit—we're more like a bellwether for the state."

Trained biologists tell Ted what he needs to do, habitat as well as killing-wise, to maintain an optimal deer herd. Ted showed me the guidelines for selective harvest, which recommends that he strive to maintain a herd averaging 1 deer for every 3.9 of his

750 acres. The Masser Ranch currently has a doe-to-buck ratio of 1.03 to 1, which is close to ideal, because an overabundance of does—such as exists in states where hunters mainly target bucks—skews the principle of selective breeding.

The guidelines suggest removing "inferior" whitetail in ascending order, starting with the most conspicuously poor specimens—spike or three-point bucks of any age or any deer that have no brow tines. The next target group is six- or seven-point deer that are three and a half years of age or older (this can be tricky, because aging deer by sight in the field is an inexact science at best), followed by mature eight-point deer that are four and a half years or older.

These priorities affect the hunts and rates Ted offers, and they help him produce the maximum number of trophy whitetail for his clients to shoot. "We don't like to price out animals in advance," he told me. "Pricing heads is always a problem and at the end of the day, are we marketing hamburgers or hunts? One good thing about having a price structure in general is that it protects some of the deer that we don't want to see shot."

The cheapest hunt offered at the Masser Ranch is a two-day "management" hunt, for $2,000. It allows a hunter to shoot a buck that scores up to 120 Boone and Crockett points, which compares with the seven-pointer I missed at Mike's place. In most of the nation, that qualifies as a dandy buck, if not exactly a trophy. The next category is a $4,000 three-day hunt for a buck in the 120 to 150 class.

Ted also offers a limited number of three-day hunts for 150-plus trophy bucks, at the cost of $5,000. Just what happens if a hunter doesn't kill a buck opens a vast gray area that can lead to uncomfortable negotiations, and sometimes that happens. But the bottom line is that Ted is in business to provide his customers with quality deer, and he has the animals and professional operation to deliver what he promises.

After Ted finished in the record books, we piled into his truck for a run to nearby Harper, home of Easy Pickens barbecue and Lively's taxidermy, which would mount both of the bucks shot by the Youngs. On the way over on State Highway 290, Ted told us about the axis deer recently shot by his son, Trace.

"How long a shot was it?" Jim asked.

"To hear him tell it, half a mile," Ted said. He was preoccupied fishing around in the console for a picture of the animal while he tried to keep the truck on the road.

"Go ahead," Jim said. "I'll watch the road . . . or we can wait until we get to town."

"Yeah," Ted said. "But that would take the fun out of it."

Jim has hunted with Ted for eighteen years; can you tell?

Harper, Texas, is a sleepy crossroads town that seems immune to the gentrification influenza that has shaped larger Hill Country towns like Fredericksburg and Kerrville. We visited Lively's first. The taxidermy studio is right on the main drag; it's an ancient wooden building with a plate-glass storefront, flush with enough Western character to make a New York set stylist wet his or her panties.

We hauled the freshly killed whitetail off the truck and laid them next to a bearskin left outside to dry in the sun. Inside, I examined the plethora of exotic mounts of species as diverse as ostrich, kudu, and elk. Most of the specimens were shot nearby, on high-fence ranches. When Kyle remarked upon a zebra, his father, Jim, corrected his Anglo pronunciation: "Anywhere you go in Africa, son, they're not called *zee*-bra. They say zeb-*ra*."

Kyle scowled and muttered, "Well, Dad. You're not in Africa. This is Texas."

We went down the road a piece to have lunch at Easy Pickens, where the menu was written on a chalkboard. If you opt for the brisket of beef or ribs, you show the cook hovering over the outdoor barbecue how much you want, and he hacks off the appropriate-sized piece and slaps it—sans plate—onto a plastic tray. Inside, a lady weighs your slab, wraps it in paper, and doles out sides of coleslaw or potato salad, and drinks. The barbecue beans, sauces, and jalapeños are free. We feasted at a long table sitting on benches, family-style.

After lunch, Ted and Jim wanted to relocate a few of the tripod hunting stands. It was a good time to tour the ranch. As we drove a two-track toward an area called Long Pasture, Ted told me that one of the significant sources of mortality on the ranch was fire ants. Because fawns will stay where does stash them during the first few days of their lives, leaving one anywhere near a fire-ant nest is a tragedy.

"The fawn is programmed not to move, and the fire ants will swarm it, by the thousands." Ted's voice filled with emotion. "You'll hear the fawns squall, but they still won't move. The ants fill their nose, mouth, ears . . . they blind it. We're talking about a pretty delicate animal that weighs just a few pounds, so the ants can kill it in just a few hours. I hate even thinking about it, but it's a serious, regular threat."

The Long Pasture area is typical of the Hill Country, which was once dense with buffalo and the domain of Comanche and Lipan Apache Indians. The prairie grasses are good for cattle (Ted still runs a small herd of beefers) but of limited use to the deer, forage-wise. Ribbons and islands of dark foliage break up the landscape in every direction, providing deer with plenty of cover and shade.

The ranch has an abundance of oak—six species in all, including the highly favored white oak—that provide Ted's herd with plenty of protein. As we rolled past a mesquite tree, Ted pointed out a fresh buck rub, and in the shade of the broad, twisted live oak, he said, "If you look at it from this angle, you can see why I sometimes tell kids that I tied a knot in the trunk when it was a sapling and it just grew that way."

We passed one of the hunting blinds, positioned to face a feeder a little over a hundred yards away. Ted strives to create as authentic a hunting experience as his management and business plan allows. He moves the blinds and stands around, but tries to keep them about 125 yards from the feeders, so that his hunters are obliged to make a decent shot. The feeders are programmed to go off at 7:00 A.M. and 5:00 P.M.

"The positive side of hunting out of a blind is that you get to evaluate an animal before you shoot," Ted said. "Some of these guys from Pennsylvania and other places with a lot of public hunting go a little crazy as soon as they see antlers. They want to pull the trigger, right away. We don't like 'ground shrinkage' [which is when the antlers of a dead buck suddenly look a lot smaller than they did when the hunter decided to shoot].

"We also don't like wounding animals, so shooting at running deer is forbidden. We stress clean kills. Our general rule is that if you shoot and we find blood, your hunt is done—whether we recover the animal or not.

"You'll see when the feeders go off and a lot of deer start mingling that people can spend a lot of money in a hurry, with just one shot. We try to coach them through the temptation to just let the lead fly. It leads to problems that we'd just as soon avoid."

"Still-hunting," which is basically the technique of quietly and slowly sneaking through the woods, hoping to catch deer unawares, might seem a viable option for those who don't care to shoot a deer near a feeder from a blind. But Ted won't allow it. He said it's because on a high-fence property, an alarmed deer anywhere near a fence has no option but to run along it, alerting every other deer along the way—thereby affecting anyone else who might be hunting that day.

We stopped to check out a brushy ravine and relocated a stand. As we left, Ted pointed out a handsome young ten-point buck watching us from among some mesquite trees. Given the number of deer at the ranch, I was surprised by how few we saw. But it was a hot day, there's plenty of cover, and the summer bachelor groups of bucks had already broken up. With the rut approaching (the farther south you go, the later it kicks into high gear), the deer were pretty well spread out.

I wondered if the brushy habitat made it easier for a poacher, unable to resist the call of those 150-class bucks, to sneak in and go undetected. Ted said, "In Texas—"

Jim interjected, "Beware any sentence that begins, 'In Texas . . .'"

Ted laughed and explained that in the Lone Star State, trespassing is a serious offense. Get caught with a gun on someone else's property and you're officially a felon. The risk is just too high for all but a hardened outlaw. The high fences also were a convincing deterrent. With so much of the land fencing up, it was becoming harder and harder for someone to just jump out of a truck and slip into the brush to hunt on someone else's land. There hasn't been much outcry about this de facto privatization of game. Either Texas offers adequate opportunity to satisfy the general public, or maybe its citizens have higher regard for property rights than their hunting privileges.

We drove into the Papalote Pasture, where cattle and wildlife still water at a well powered by a windmill (*papalote* in Spanish). Ted is permitted to run one animal unit of livestock (a cow and calf) per twenty-five to thirty acres, but he's duty-bound to make sure that the cows don't graze off the pasture, lest the state decide he's failing to maintain suitable deer habitat. It takes a fairly large herd and a robust hunting program to keep producing trophy bucks while annually removing about 25 percent of his buck population. It's a delicate balancing act, but it yields a sustainable and desirable resource—great deer. Ted doesn't want the cows to get in the way.

Over time, Ted has become convinced that nutrition trumps

genetics and age as a factor in producing great bucks. He feeds anything that contains digestible protein, from commercially pressed pellets to cottonseed. Although he feeds about seven tons of corn a year, he says it's nothing but bait: "It's about as good for deer as potato chips are for you and me, and just about as irresistible."

Ted feeds the corn out of his broadcast feeders until it runs out after hunting season, but switches to protein in January and feeds up to eighty tons of it by early October. Bucks that call on too much of their reserves to recover from the stress of the rut and to survive the cold winter are at a disadvantage in the spring, when antler development begins.

"Antlers are skeletal growths," Ted explained. "And good nutrition in the first few years of a deer's life is critical for good muscular and skeletal growth. Anything over and above what a deer requires goes into antler development or, in lactating does, into their milk. If we were deer, instead of getting big bellies from eating too much, we'd just get bigger antlers. But there's a genetic limit on antler growth, just as there is in height in humans. No matter how much my mama fed me, I would not have grown to six-six. I'd just be the same height and weigh a lot more."

I was coming to understand that beyond the barrel chest, big Texan personality, and gravelly voice, Ted has a born teacher's love of sharing his knowledge. At one point a little later, he pulled over, got out of the truck, and navigated through a patch of prickly pear cactus. He pulled some leaves off a shrub and invited me to put the leaves on my tongue. The taste gave me a strong, tingling sensation. "Neat, isn't it?" Ted said, grinning. "We call that there 'tickle tongue.'"

I asked Ted if he ever missed coaching football. He didn't miss a beat. "I miss the kids sometimes, but I don't miss the administrators or the parents."

• • •

At around four in the afternoon, Ted suggested that I sit in one of his blinds for the evening to observe the show. He left me at the head of a nicely mown trail that led to a blind—a wooden shed about twice the size of a Porta-John—eighty yards away. I ducked inside, opened the Plexiglas windows, and sat in a chrome-framed office chair with a thick black seat cushion. It was oppressive and smelled like hot weathered wood, but a gentle breeze soon cooled things off.

Coming in, I had spooked a few deer that were loitering near the tripod feeder a hundred yards out, across a field of rich, knee-high grass. But within ten minutes, a doe sauntered back into the clearing, and within five minutes a pair of bucks—a six-pointer with wide but low antlers, and a picture-perfect eight-pointer in the 160 class (one of Ted's five-grand deer) joined her. They nosed around, close together. It thrilled me just to watch them through my binoculars.

A sizable doe and two smaller ones came and joined the group, but the largest one soon wandered off into the tall grass at the fringe of the meadow. The big eight-pointer followed her at a slight distance, parting the pale yellow grasses with his wide brisket. He moved with imperial self-assurance. The grass was so tall that the doe disappeared into it, and all I could see of the buck was that enormous set of antlers shining bone white in the late afternoon sun.

The feeder stood deserted, but not for long. Within five minutes, a doe and two new bucks appeared; one of them crowned with extremely tall but spindly antlers, the other a smaller version of the eight-pointer that had gone off with the doe; it might even have been his offspring. The latter rose up on his hind legs and began to nibble on leaves in the copse of oaks right behind the feeder. He was joined by a young four-pointer. I caught glimpses of other deer, back in the shadows in the brush—how many could there be, I wondered—twenty? Thirty? More?

At 5:10, the feeder clanged to life and broadcast corn for about thirty seconds. There was no rush at the sound of the dinner bell. The deer just drifted into the clearing. The next buck I noticed was the largest yet, a nine-pointer with antlers of great mass that would push 170 B&C points. He ran out and began to gobble corn. He kept his nose to the ground, feeding for about ninety seconds. I was looking at a broadside shot at about a hundred yards with a good, stable rest. It might have been a fish in a barrel, but for the "buck fever" factor.

I could imagine how a real estate broker who'd never killed a big buck in his life might feel shortly after he was escorted by a guide to this blind, his belly still full of pancakes, eggs, and bacon. Shortly after the feeder goes off, he's looking at a buck bigger than any he's ever seen, even on television! He's at a little over a hundred yards, in a hut, with a great rest. Does he kill the buck, or die of a heart attack first? Does he flinch and miss, and return home with the word *Jerk* tattooed on his forehead?

It could be a tricky proposition, no doubt about it, which is why some of the hunters who hunt high-fence ranches feel okay about doing it. And those who won't or can't invest a decent amount of time in their hunting know they can go on a three-day trip and be assured of seeing plenty of deer and probably killing a trophy buck. It's difficult not to draw the obvious parallels with paying for the company of a woman.

Other deer joined the party, including an unusual eight-pointer with a very wide but low set of antlers. The big nine-pointer suddenly snapped to attention and surveyed the scene. Deer browsed and socialized all around him. Perhaps he remembered his duties as the herd boss, because for some reason he charged toward the brush where the handsome young eight-pointer stood.

They were partially screened, but I could identify them among all the other deer by their antlers. They began to spar.

It was a brief but spirited tussle; I heard the clicking of their horns and saw the smaller buck grudgingly yield ground as the big fella shoved him backward. The battle ended as quickly as it had started, with the smaller buck running off.

I counted twenty-odd deer milling about, including an eight-pointer whose antlers formed a nearly perfect oval, the tips of the tallest tines on either side almost touching. It was a beautiful set of antlers to put on a wall, but oddly enough I didn't even think about writing out a check and returning with a gun in the morning. The spectacle was riveting. With the significant exception of the feeder, the setting was utterly natural.

I sat studying the deer as they came and went, marveling at the genetic diversity expressed in the varied antler configurations. Finally, I heard the growl of Ted's truck and realized it was time to go.

Mike had coffee on when I walked into his home early the following morning. He was loading his shooting vest with shells when I walked in. He said, "We won't run out of bullets . . . may as well wait another fifteen or twenty minutes."

I wasn't sure how I felt about firing the .30/06 with Mike's wife, child, and elderly relations still sleeping so close to the tree stand: *Good morning, Mrs. Potts. This is your wake-up call. It's thirty-aught six!* But Mike seemed fine with the idea, and I secretly doubted that the big buck would be back.

We soon climbed into the tree stand. Anticipating the morning feed, a handful of does, including one with oddly twisted spikes (hermaphrodites are fairly common in the species) that we dubbed the "devil doe," drifted up out of the brushy canyon. A forkhorn appeared, but bolted when the feeder suddenly went off as he stood beside it. After the machine cycled through, deer poured into the clearing. Soon there were five or six does, two forkhorns, a nice little six-pointer—but no sign of the big fella.

We talked softly in the tree stand, enjoying the scene. Suddenly, Mike said, "Wait. Here he comes. On the left."

I couldn't believe it. I didn't deserve or expect a second chance, but I watched, mesmerized, as the mahogany antlers advanced above the grass.

"Now," Mike said.

But just as I found the buck in the scope, a doe stepped in front of him, and Mike said, "No."

The big deer turned and looked right at us, presenting a perfect neck shot as he peered out from behind the doe. I didn't have the guts to take it; the other deer milling around dissuaded me. The tension was excruciating. I had the sevenpointer in my scope again, but the glass clouded with shades of gray and brown.

"He'll turn again," Mike whispered. "Be ready."

The buck turned, all the way around, and began walking away. For a moment, I had a quartering-away shot, one I wouldn't have hesitated to take under ordinary field conditions. But the corner of the house was a blur on the right side of my sight window and I didn't dare shoot.

As the buck disappeared, Mike and I exhaled.

I dropped my forehead and let it rest on the scope, unbelieving. There were moments when I could have shot, no question. But the tight quarters and abundance of deer made me overthink the situation. And if that happened here, what might happen if I tried to shoot a 160-class buck out at Ted's?

This all was so crazy. Some baroque new form of nimrod torture.

The realization sank in: I'd let the buck . . . walk away.

And while I would never be able to brag about the hardship endured or skill required to kill that buck, I felt I owed it to my host to kill that buck.

"Well, you didn't miss," Mike said.

I saw the humor in the situation. Maybe I just wasn't cut out for this. Maybe we ought to return to the house, have breakfast, and play with Georgie—and that was when the big buck walked back into the picture. He was screened by two does, but he turned and the does remained between us.

Mike grunted, to stop him.

"That was a horseshit grunt," I hissed, as I watched the buck continue on and out of view—again.

Was I under some bizarre spell, the Curse of Ardmair House, or paying off some karmic debt to the antler gods?

Yet almost ten minutes later, the buck came up over the bank yet again, this time turning to give me a clean broadside shot. I took careful aim and squeezed the trigger. The gun bucked and the buck bolted.

"High. Again."

I sat there, stupefied. After a bit, Mike gently said, "I'm starting to wonder about that gun."

But we'd tested the gun. I pored over the options. I felt I'd done everything right. I was shooting off the crossbar, seated comfortably. Was there some kind of cold-barrel issue here; did the gun shoot way high on the first try? Mike also was dumbfounded. His suspicion that I was a lousy shot had morphed into a conviction that I couldn't be *that* lousy a shot.

"I guess it just wasn't meant to be," I said. "We can call it quits and leave it at that."

I'd given up. I was so weirded out that I thought, *Dear God, whatever I did, I'm sorry.*

Mike said he had one more idea. He didn't think the buck had gone very far. He probably had bedded down with the does in the ravine. The deer would hear and recognize the sound of the feeder if it went off again. We decided to reset it, and soon we were back in the stand, waiting, but unconvinced that the buck would come again.

It seemed that we were right. After the feeder threw corn

again, a group of deer answered the call. The buck wasn't among them. My mind was a thousand miles away when Mike said, "There he is."

I saw the buck's head and antlers advancing uphill through the brush, toward the feeder. I said, "You call it."

"Don't worry, I've got plenty of bullets," Mike whispered.

The buck presented yet another perfect opportunity. He lowered his head to feed, and I touched off the shot. The buck jerked his head up, looked back toward the canyon. Unconsciously, I jumped to my feet and worked the bolt. I fired another round, freehand, and the buck collapsed.

Mike and I both whooped, did a little dance in the tree stand, and embraced. I felt like I'd just won the lottery. It was absurd, what we were doing. So what?

"No buck gives Pete Bodo a second chance," I boasted.

"Actually, it was—what—your fifth?"

"Yeah. But who's counting?"

We laughed some more. All I knew was that as fine a whitetail as I'd ever shot lay on the ground about sixty yards away. And that I'd finally done right by Mike.

Mike and I got to field-test the Butt Out on my seven-pointer, and found it worked exactly as advertised. Later, after a celebratory breakfast with Mike's family, we would take the deer to a local meat market, donating what we didn't want for the house to a local food bank for the homeless. Mike would send me the antlers and skull plate for display.

The drive to Kerrville took us past many high-fence operations and palatial ranch homes. Coming over one hill, the panorama in the valley featured herds of African game, including regal kudu, feeding on a plain while nearby a dozen people dressed completely in white played croquet on a bright green lawn alongside a stone mansion.

I had finally killed the buck with a neck shot, and Mike thought it was because I had finally acted by instinct, leaping up to fire a snap shot in one smooth motion. As far as degree of difficulty went, it was a tougher shot to make than any of my previous ones.

Something clicked in my mind as he rolled out his theory. I said, "Remind me again of the proper technique for shooting off a rest."

Mike shrugged and explained that you laid your hand palm up on the rest, settled the fore end of the stock into your hand, took aim, and shot.

The light bulb went on over my head.

I was pretty sure that when I shot sitting down, I hadn't rested the gun on my palm. I just let it sit on top of the wooden rail, holding it in place lightly with two fingers. It was a casual mistake that I'd never made before. But I'd also never hunted under comparably easy conditions before, either. Could it be that the relatively flimsy wooden bar flexed and caused the barrel to jump just as the gun went off?

"Sure," Mike said. "The gun should never rest on a hard surface. It's Marksmanship 101. It's supposed to be in our soft hand. But how come you made good shots when we tested the rifle?"

That I couldn't answer. Maybe I reverted to good form because I had more often shot at targets under similar conditions and reverted to form.

Our chores done in town, we sat on the outdoor patio of a restaurant situated on a bench above the Guadalupe River. The clear, green water sparkled in the morning sun; beyond it, the hills were a fetching combination of red soil and dark pines. We weren't hungry; it was just noon. So we drank beer and talked about our families.

Mike Potts was a good man and so, for that matter, was Ted

Masser. They had shown me a different and surprising face of the hunting culture. I had killed a nice buck, although the element that would most likely stick with me was the absurdity of how it had come to pass.

But I was struck mostly by the way deer hunting in Texas simply had evolved along different lines and was shaped by different values—values inherited, perhaps, from the original cattlemen who settled in Texas in the nineteenth century. Deer can't be domesticated, but these enterprising Texans had come about as close to turning deer into livestock as you can get without actually taming them.

When it came to fair chase, it was almost like the culture ruled it out, although I knew there was plenty of more demanding hunting available in Texas as well as many hunters who were no more interested in sitting in a blind, deciding which of a number of trophy deer to slay, than was I. Like me, they wanted to earn their deer, demonstrating a higher measure of dedication, knowledge, and skill than was required on a borderline canned hunt. Many also wanted a more physically challenging experience.

The deer I had observed and shot weren't as awe-inspiring as their cousins on the Northern Plains, or in the hemlock forests of New York. They didn't have anything like a comparable aversion to man. Deer here were raised, cared for, and all but trained to be shot—but how could I have a problem with the idea of shooting deer? I couldn't deny that high-fence ranches represented the maximum utilization of an abundant resource, and in a way that could only be called renewable. How could I fault that?

And this, too: At the Masser Ranch, I had observed what a deer herd could become under ideal, nearly laboratory conditions. Yet the creatures remained essentially wild, and free to fulfill their full biological potential. Superior bucks, the ones that probably would have done best under any circumstances, lived to be five, six, eight years old in excellent habitat—a luxury that very few bucks enjoyed on most public land that was hunted with any frequency.

Hunting at Masser's wasn't really a fair-chase proposition, but it provided vivid proof of what good management could achieve, and the principles it could export to help improve conditions elsewhere. In fact, those approaches were already popular in some places, including on some public lands where herd quality was determined to have a higher value than satisfying the broad demand for deer to kill.

I also saw the respect and concern a high-fence rancher can have for his deer. Ted makes his living by allowing people to shoot trophy bucks on his property, but his job, and abiding interest, is creating trophy bucks. It's Animal Husbandry 101.

I wasn't sure I'd be a hunter if the Texas brand I experienced was the only option, but I also saw how invested Ted was in his ranch. The last time I saw him, we sat with Kathy on his porch, sipping iced tea in the late afternoon when the feeders in the field in front of his house went off. Soon, the field was full of deer, including half a dozen bucks that would be considered trophies anywhere.

Ted gazed at his deer contentedly and said, "I love hunting, but I could sit here, just watching them, forever."

11

Know When to Fold 'Em

BOVINA AND ANDES, NEW YORK, NOVEMBER 16–19

A NDES WAS PREMATURELY locked in the grip of an early winter shortly before the opening of gun season. Fall has stages, just like spring, but most of us tend to overlook the incremental changes because we don't exactly await the arrival of winter with comparable pleasure. Below the house, meadows that had been green and wet just eight or nine days earlier were now bleached by frost, with an onionskin of ice on the numerous puddles that collected in small depressions and furrows everywhere.

For the better part of a month, I'd been hunting mostly in pleasant weather. I was spoiled, and loath to dig out the woolen gloves, watch caps, neck gaiters, and "expedition grade" thermals that are essential gear for deer hunting in the northeast from early November on. The forecast for opening day called for snow, and unseasonably cold temperatures.

Whitetail deer are essentially cold-weather critters. The greatest deer of all are northern deer—the big-bodied bucks of Saskatchewan, Alberta, Maine, Minnesota, Montana, and Wisconsin. During warm weather, deer are indolent and relatively inactive, at least during daylight hours.

But when the temperature begins to climb into the fifties and above, deer do a lot of their traveling and feeding at night, and hunker down in cool places to wait out the daytime heat. Their coats consist of overlapping, hollow hairs that work much like the down in a ski parka, using trapped air for insulation. As temperatures drop below freezing, deer are energized and, depending on how cold it is, driven to move more frequently in order to generate body heat, feed, and conserve fat.

Opening day is both charming and dispiritingly egalitarian. Unlike that same magic date in trout fishing or baseball, it's no ritual moment enacted in anticipation of the distant, more agreeable days to come. Opening day of deer season is the annual Armageddon for whitetail that have largely been unmolested by humans for eleven months, except for farmers, low-impact bow hunters, and nonlethal recreationists.

For the astute hunter who's patterned his local deer and doesn't need to worry about other nimrods blowing out the woods with noise and scent, opening day is as close as you can get to a sure thing. But because of hunting pressure, usually it's more like a lottery, especially on public or small- to medium-sized properties. A shocking number of fine bucks end up being killed by what you might call the "wrong" people, like your buddy's butthead cousin from Long Island, a two-day-a-year hunter who hits pay dirt despite having staggered into his stand too late, with a pounding headache, reeking of cigar smoke and pepperoni.

When the density of hunters is high, deer have less chance to evade hunters, and are often pushed all day—at a time of year when the rut already has them half-crazed. Opening day can seem more like a roundup than a hunt, although it's always surprising how good whitetail are at sneaking by or around humans, or finding places to lay low. That's why legal hunting is a good population management tool, not an ecological holocaust.

On opening day of my second year in Andes, I quit at around noon on a bitterly cold, snowy day to run an errand I couldn't put off. As I drove my Jeep over the hill and off my own land on a washed-out dirt road, I chanced upon a spike buck standing in the deep drainage ditch right beside the road, not ten feet from my vehicle. He appeared to be cowering, like a lost, frightened dog. I knew there were hunters all around, and I sensed that the little buck had simply run out of options. At a loss for where to go next, he just gave up. I looked at him for a long moment, tipped my hat, wished him luck, and drove on.

It's not uncommon to hear fifty, sixty shots before dusk settles on opening day, but that's deceptive. Some of those rounds are touched off at phantom deer, or because lack of opportunity creates itchy trigger fingers. The things that most commonly get shot on opening day, besides deer, are discarded beer cans, chipmunks, turkey vultures, the occasional coyote, and POSTED: NO HUNTING and yellow ONE-LANE BRIDGE signs.

Deer don't like the sound of guns, and quickly figure out what it means. The ones lucky enough to escape this first, fierce fusillade often become nocturnal. But in cold weather, the deer are hard-wired to move and, no matter what the temperature is, they need to eat. Still, all things being equal, the number of deer killed drops off significantly with each passing day of deer season.

Unseasonably cold temperatures on opening day usually translate to a high harvest, especially when there's enough snow for tracking. Snow also provides great contrast, enabling you to glass even wooded hillsides from a great distance and spot bedded deer. They look like so many raisins scattered among the matchstick trees. So while I found myself wishing it were still

October, with yellow apples hanging on the boughs and crimson pods of sumac ablaze in the afternoon sun, I prepared for opening day feeling good about our chances. Maybe that monster whitetail would come my way; the omens were good.

Although I've always hunted my own property on the first day, I'd agreed to hunt this time with one of my great hunting buddies, Chris Ingvordsen. We would be joined by Tony Cece, a fun-loving extrovert who'd reined in his more exuberant impulses and became an upstate New York state trooper and devoted family man.

Hunting is a solitary pursuit best enjoyed in good company. It was the fly-fishing author Alfred Miller, who wrote under the pen name Sparse Grey Hackle, who first made that observation about his preferred recreation. One drawback to owning your own land, and having hunting buddies who do as well, is that it diminishes the social aspect of hunting. I've felt lonely on the farm at times, hunting alone.

Even the solitude-craving mountain men, the first white men to explore the American West, had famous friendships and fur-trapping or exploration partners. It was Lewis *and* Clark, not Lewis *or* Clark. There's nothing like having hunting buddies you trust, and have known for a long time, no matter how often you've fallen out or how much of a pain in the ass either of you sometimes appears to the other.

Chris owned two prime parcels of land in Bovina, a town adjacent to Andes; one of them was a two-hundred-and-fifty-acre piece of diverse deer habitat we called, simply, "the big hill." For about two decades, Chris was on a mission to turn the big hill into a haven for local whitetail in an area awash in deer hunters, including yahoos and outlaws who preferred to spend their hunting hours driving around in a warm truck, listening to music, bullshitting, and drinking beer, while keeping eyes peeled for deer to shoot through the passenger-side window. These guys are blithely indifferent to posted signs and either private property rights or, in Chris's case, a landowner's attempt at smart deer management.

Over the years, Chris and various friends and guests had shot some fine trophy bucks off the big hill. I never had much luck there, but that was partly because I hunted over that way mostly for social reasons. I had my own land to focus on and worry about, especially early in deer season. But Chris was in the midst of selling the big hill to New York City in a deal that ensured it would never be developed. We might never have the chance to hunt the property again, at least not exclusively. Wouldn't it be something else if one of us dragged a huge buck off that hill on the last day we were entitled to hunt it?

A few years ago, I'd helped Chris build his "secret cabin," a substantial if bare-bones, two-story wooden structure of about 1,200 square feet. It would have to be torn down as part of the deal with Gotham. And his tree stands had to go, too. We were dismantling a rich twenty-year hunting tradition, and determined to celebrate the end of an era with one last night at the secret cabin.

It was about thirty degrees at midday on Sunday when I plowed through the wet snow and slush and pulled in at Chris's house. His parents, Henning and Gisela, immigrated to the U.S. from Denmark (their newly made American friends dubbed them Hank and Gay) and bought the Bovina house and surrounding property in the late 1960s; when Chris inherited it, the young lord of the manor named it Valhalla Farm.

The house is a grand old Victorian, with crooked walls and single-glazed windows so drafty that Chris—who's not real big on creature comforts—ultimately stapled vapor barriers of thick, semitranslucent plastic on the interior side on most of them. Looking out those windows is a little like trying to see after you get a squirt of WD-40 in your eyes.

Chris is a handsome, sturdily built, blond-haired and blue-eyed guy who spent his childhood in Brooklyn, New York, and most of his summers at Valhalla Farm. He learned to hunt with his father, who worked as a banker in New York and did his hunting in the European manner, wearing a jacket and tie. After graduating from Duke University, Chris became an actor and guerilla filmmaker.

I don't mean to imply that he made deep, arty, low-budget flicks featuring incest, drugs, angst, and a great soundtrack by some obscure punk-rock band. He made mostly narrative, action-packed, no-budget adventure or war movies featuring whichever aspiring actors and friends (including me) he could hornswoggle into playing the part of an inscrutable Arab, a sinister Russian arms dealer, or a steely-eyed German World War II submarine captain.

Chris has an incredible talent for making an entire movie on a budget that would be dwarfed by your average PSA spot for a local library. He shot a lot of his footage dodging menacing, pay-to-play representatives of the International Brotherhood of Teamsters, various municipal law enforcement agencies, and other folks who didn't think a guy had a right to just go out and find novel and creative ways to make a movie.

Chris's best movie of all is the unmade documentary about how he worked around the system, a perpetual rebel and entrepreneur who had a simple answer for anyone who wondered if he ever wanted to make a movie that would win the hearts of the Sundance Film Festival crowd: "No."

When I walked through the massive black front door, Chris was kneeling on a worn Persian carpet on the floor in what once had been a formal parlor, his heel poking through a hole the size of a hockey puck in his woolen sock. It was chilly. He took a sip from a cup of stale coffee and studied the aerial master photograph of the big hill, on which all of his tree stands and trails were carefully marked. "Tony's late," he said, without looking up. "When I spoke with him this morning he was already complaining about the cold. How Tony is that?"

I thought it was more sensible than funny. I wanted to leave my jeans and flannel shirt at the house to wear going home, so Chris dug me out some stuff from the vast store of Army surplus-type gear he used in his movies. He came up with a pair of tattered camo BDUs and an old, thin Oklahoma University sweatshirt. It was just like old times, when I'd have to get into some wrinkled and smelly cowboy or pirate costume for a minor role in one of his straight-to-video epics.

"So here's the deal," Chris said. "They've been seeing a nice eight-point crossing by the old barn, and there's supposed to be a legitimate ten running in the swamp—a first-class buck. There's a six with a nice tall rack working the ridge. Last Friday I saw a basket eight [a reference to the small but multi-tined rack of a poorly nourished buck, or a promising young one]. And I know we've got two scraggly fours and a couple of spikes."

"Excuse me," I interrupted. "But where the hell did you get all this bullshit?"

Chris grinned and continued, undeterred: "We've got to remember, the guidos are going to be out in force all over on the perimeter. Fuck them. And I expect the usual heavy pressure on the north side. But that's a good thing, because they'll probably push stuff over to us. The key is going to be digging in and staying hunkered down, no matter how fucking cold it is . . . It's going to be the kind of day when a big buck gets shot. Mark my words."

He sounded like General George S. Patton. He even talked like General Patton, which made a certain amount of sense.

Chris is a student of military history, a guy's guy—and a control freak. He likes to orchestrate every hunt as if it were the Battle of Stalingrad. It leaves someone like me without much to say, even if I'm thinking, *Why don't I just go and sit on that big flat rock in the birches and play it by ear* . . . But the attitude also relieved his friends and guests from feeling pressure to make smart decisions of their own. It's fun to enter Chris's world, which is built on equally strong pillars of logical analysis and something like fantasy.

Chris also loves his deer, and he's put a lot of work into enhancing and improving the habitat on his property. Once again, I was willing to suspend my natural skepticism. One of us might get a cockwalloper; stranger things have happened, although never to me.

I squatted next to Chris and listened to him elaborate his battle plan, which had the three of us strung out across the upper portion of the big hill, close enough to the property lines to get a look at deer driven our way from the adjacent properties, all of which were heavily hunted.

From our vantage points, we would also have a view of various benches and small plateaus on the middle section of the hill. The lower half of the property, all the way to the hardtop county road, would be off limits until the end of the day. There was plenty of space and brush down there for bucks to seek sanctuary. If they were wary enough to remain hidden from the inevitable road hunters, they would survive the day. The chance of that happening was actually pretty good if we didn't go tromping around down there.

I wondered if we wouldn't be better off staying fairly low on the hill, where the cover through a cold, blustery night would be better for the deer, and we could keep an eye on things. But I didn't say anything, and in the end it was guesswork anyway. Whitetail live by patterns, but predicting them with enough exactitude to get a big buck in your sight picture usually involves an unlikely confluence of planning, timing, and sheer luck. The latter is the part you don't read much about in the magazines; you want to sell me a magazine, print an article with the headline: TO HELL WITH SKILL: FIVE WAYS TO GET LUCKY ON OPENING DAY.

Tony arrived at about three, bearing drinks and a humongous bag of snack foods. "Hey," Chris said. "So you finally got the day pass, eh?"

I don't really remember exactly what Tony said, but I'm pretty sure it incorporated at least two references to the male anatomy and had to be funny because that's Tony—a chubby-cheeked, cheerful wiseass who doesn't have a wicked bone in his body. I just shook my head and looked out the window, or rather at the plastic sheeting on it, which was puddled with interesting shapes representing the pine trees, fence, and red osier dogwood bushes outside. I shivered. It was going to be a long, cold night in the secret cabin.

We would need Chris's ATV for the hunt, and somehow Tony got elected to drive it two miles to the big hill property, while Chris and I loaded and rode in his old Dodge pickup. Tony was wearing just sweatpants and a fleece over a T-shirt. At one point on the way over, I looked out the back window at Tony. He was hunched over the handlebars, clutching the handgrips, a grimace frozen (literally) on his face.

At the foot of the big hill, Chris and I loaded his 1940s vintage Willys Jeep (a useful part of his prop fleet) and started up an old log road, with Tony trailing. Those classic old military Jeeps that helped win WWII are absurdly small and light by today's standards; I had to be careful lest I knock a few teeth out with my kneecaps. About halfway up the trail, we came to a short but very steep bank with slabs of slick bluestone under the snow and ice. We tried to climb it three times, with a good running start on each occasion, but failed and nearly rolled the Jeep in the process. It was time for plan B.

We backed down a bit, knocked over a few trees turning around, then went all the way back to try a less precipitous route. By then, the blue of Tony's lips was spreading through his entire face. We bounced and slipped and skidded up the trail until we finally arrived at the secret cabin tucked among the trees. Able, finally, to move his lips, Tony's first words were: "I've never been so cold in all my life."

We got the supplies inside, where the wall thermometer read 25 degrees Fahrenheit and our breath made pretty, billowing clouds in the air. It was getting dark, so Chris and I went to tarp down the Jeep and ATV. While we were at it, Tony burst out of the cabin swinging a giant ceremonial sword that had somehow found its way up there. He waved it around, shouting, "Bong-head Beowulf!"

Whatever the hell that meant.

Chris laughed and wagged his head. If nothing else, it was going to be an amusing—if cold—night.

Inside, Chris finally got the wood stove going, and I fired up two kerosene lanterns. We gathered at the rough-hewn table in the dim light, eating deli sandwiches and chips and drinking beer.

The wind knifed through gaps in the hemlock siding and window frames; now and then a gust blew open the door and sent mare's tails of snow dancing through the cabin while tongues of pale fire flickered in the lanterns. Chris and I speculated on how the stormy conditions might affect deer movement the next morning, while Tony was preoccupied with the eight-hundred-pound gorilla in the room—the temperature. Chris gently tried to explain that enduring hardship was one of the interesting challenges presented by hunting; tomorrow, he said, was going to be all about "survival." Tony looked at him as if Chris were speaking Venusian.

Tony also took Chris's warning to mean he'd better call his wife, Sarah, and his two girls—and not just because he hadn't spoken with them for five whole hours. He also wanted to make sure his life insurance policies were properly filled out. But when he started to fumble in his pocket for his cell phone, Chris offhandedly said, "If you leave right away, you can probably get a hot spot for reception on county Route 7 in, oh, three or four hours."

Tony looked crestfallen, and we ate in silence for another three minutes, at which point we all had the same idea and made a spontaneous dash for the wood stove. We arranged the three chairs right in front of the stove and continued eating.

Pretty soon, I noticed that my left side, which was closest to the stove, was so hot that I feared my cotton OU sweatshirt would spontaneously combust. Meanwhile, my right side was starting to go numb from the cold. I could have bundled up in my hunting clothes, but I didn't feature having them stink of cigars and Italian dressing in the morning.

Tony cracked open his bottle of Sweet Lucy, a bourbon-based liqueur (presumably, it's for an audience that craves something sweeter than bourbon, if that's at all possible). He offered each of us a pull. It tasted like Southern Comfort, only worse, and Chris asked the rhetorical question: "What does it tell you that *everybody* remembers the first time they got drunk on Southern Comfort?"

Well, it was no time for weighty philosophical discussion. Your basic options in deer camp in bad weather are limited. You can get all surly, stomp around in your long underwear, and rail against the gods. Or you can pick a fight with your companions of choice. Or you can just roll with it, seeking refuge in humor. Fart stories and jokes are a pretty good place to start, and from there it's a seamless transition to commentary on the anatomical blessings of certain women, then a short hop to the gender preferences of your buddies, followed by a quick segue to girlfriends or wives—just so nobody gets any weird ideas.

Meanwhile, our supply of Scotch and Sweet Lucy was disappearing faster than an anorexic catwalker. But I'd better stop right there, before I violate the law as inscribed on the ubiquitous sweatshirt: WHAT HAPPENS IN DEER CAMP *STAYS* IN DEER CAMP. Another law of deer camp is: when in doubt, or adequately bored, drunk, or both, break out the cards. Unfortunately, we found it difficult to play cards with our hands in our pockets. By then it was almost nine, the empty bottle of Sweet Lucy was asleep on her side, and we agreed to make an attempt to join her.

Tony and I climbed the ladder to the frigid loft, where we would sleep on either of two Spartan folding army cots. I slipped into my sleeping bag fully clothed, but there was not much difference in the temperature inside. Somehow, an innocent mouse had chewed its way into the bag; I could tell by the small tumor moving around on the surface of the fabric. I tried to grab it, which at least made the lump move south, where it finally disappeared. That was all right; maybe we could keep each other warm.

I realized, to my shock, that Tony had decided to do a little reading—a novel, no less. Some book titled *The Underground People*. But Tony's sudden literary interest was dampened by the poor light from the kerosene lamp, and the fact that reading requires the turning of pages out there in the cold outside the bag. So he gave up on it.

We lay there in the dark, freezing, and for some reason, I just started singing—something I ordinarily wouldn't think of doing in public, even while three sheets to the wind. I sang every line of that bittersweet ballad, "I Was Born to Be a Cowboy."

Moments after I finished, Tony picked it up, choosing the Kenny Rogers classic, "The Gambler." And when he was done,

Chris, who was sleeping on the couch downstairs, let rip with "The Rodeo Song," that timeless, sensitive plaint by Garry Lee and the Showdown: *It's forty below and I don't give a fuck . . . and I'm off to the rodeo.*

Then it was very quiet, and we all lay there, listening to the soughing of the pines while the hardwoods creaked, rustled, and occasionally cracked. The banshee whisper of the wind sliced through the walls. I would probably never spend another night in this place again, or hunt this hill again; a chapter in my life as a hunter was about to close, which is just one of the tolls you pay on your way.

I felt a pang of sadness. But since there seemed to be a chance I wouldn't survive the night anyway, I said to hell with it and wriggled around to get a little more comfortable. And that was when I felt my nasal and cranial cavities slowly filling with fluid, like my entire head was just a plastic reservoir for cranial windshield-washer fluid.

Just seven hours, I thought, *just seven more hours and it will be opening day, and the deer will come pouring down from the ridge, and the snow crystals will sparkle green and blue and yellow in the sun, and suddenly I'd see him, Old Mossy Horn, sneaking through the thorn apple trees and briars, and he'll stop just as I raise my rifle . . .*

My reverie was interrupted by the loudest burst of snoring I'd ever heard. *Son of a bitch,* I thought, glancing over toward Tony, who began churning out an amazing symphony of barnyard sounds. *He's out like a light and happy as a clam.*

A familiar sound penetrated my thick sleep, and I gradually recognized the "Ride of the Valkyries" overture, from Wagner's operatic Ring Cycle. It was part of our morning ritual whenever Chris and I hunted together; sometimes we even took a small boom box on the road, so we could wake to those heroic strains. I checked my watch—it was four-thirty in the morning. I was completely congested; in a mere seven or eight hours, I'd developed the mother of all colds. But I also noticed that outside, all was still.

"Tony?"

He grunted.

"Time to get up."

The nice thing about having a waterlogged head was that I couldn't be bothered regretting my hangover. I slipped out of the bag and negotiated the ladder down to the ground floor, with Tony right behind, no doubt trying to draft in my body heat. Chris had breakfast already prepared: a thermos of room-temperature coffee that he'd brought along last night, and a box of half-frozen store-bought muffins. In no time, I was into my thermals and winter hunting clothes.

"It's eighteen degrees in here," Tony noted. "Let's get the fire going."

"No," Chris said. "We're going low-impact."

"Are you nuts?" I politely inquired.

Tony pleaded, but to no avail, while he hunted up his tooth-brush and paste in the dark. He stood by the door. As he lifted the brush to his mouth, Chris offhandedly said he'd switched out Tony's toothpaste with a tube of Vagisil. It stopped Tony, but he called Chris's bluff. He stepped out to rinse and came back in, declaring: "It's so cold outside that my nuts are up in my hip joints."

When we were all dressed, Chris tucked his medicine pouch into his thermal top and cued up the music. It was time for an-other ritual of ours, the Horn Dance. Before a hunt, we dance around, chanting and singing in tongues while making pretend antlers on our heads with our hands and fingers. Tony, who may be the least-inhibited human being I know, decided that he was above that kind of silliness. He sniffed, "When you fools are done, can someone lend me a flashlight?"

That was no problem—between us, Chris and I probably had a dozen lights of every description. But before either of us could rag on Tony for forgetting something so essential, he produced a plastic shopping bag full of chemical handwarmers, and our view of him changed dramatically. He must have bought a case of them, because Tony passed them out like some rock star's gofer distributing the cocaine. We jammed them in our boots, our pockets, and the tips of our thick hunting mittens, and hurried outside lest we catch fire.

"I don't know about you guys, but I'm going to stay in my stand all day," I declared in a moment of ill-advised bravado.

"Say what?" Tony asked.

He was already thinking about returning to the secret cabin for a nice nap once there was enough sunlight to call it day, and with Chris out in the woods, he'd start a roaring fire.

"I'm serious," I said. "This is my—our—last chance to shoot a monster buck off the big hill. I'm going to get him, or go down in a blaze of glory."

Tony made a corkscrewing motion around his ear with an index finger.

"I'm staying out all day, too," Chris said to Tony. He was just trying to be, what would you call it, nurturing?

Chris passed out the walkie-talkies. A film guy, he couldn't live without those things, which are legal to use for communications while hunting, but not for the purpose of steering others to deer, or as a hunting aid. "Let's try to maintain radio silence unless one of us shoots something or has an emergency," Chris said. "We'll check in, though, around noon. See if we want to make some kind of other play."

Electric blue moonlight lay on the snowy landscape, and great clouds pale as butter were puddled around the moon. I thought of my archer buddy, Tom Daly; it was the kind of scene he might paint. The old logging road weaving through the black maples and birches was paved with moonlight. It was easy, quiet going, through three inches of undisturbed powder. We dropped Tony off at the head of the trail leading up to the Washburn stand, named for a film buddy of Chris who shot a great eight-point buck from it a dozen years ago.

Soon, Chris and I split up. I was going to the Isabelle stand. That one is named for a girl Chris and I had both dated, although not at the same time. That was long ago, and Isabelle had aged better than had the stand. I had to twist this way and that on a combination of steel foot pegs, stubs of branches, and wooden slats covered in slick mildew to get up to the seat, from which I would look down on two scrawny apple trees, a spring, and a heavily traveled deer trail leading to a dense stand of sheltering pines. When I sat down, a nail that had worked its way out of the wooden seat poked me so hard that I nearly jumped out of the stand.

I settled in and plugged a few rounds into the .257 Weatherby. The walk and climb had at least warmed me up for the first time in almost twenty-four hours. My nose was running like a leaky spigot, but I felt good. I envisioned all the nimrods on the ridge above us, moving into position for the hunt, pushing deer over the edge and onto Chris's property. At any moment now, there could be waves of 'em pouring off the ridge.

The seconds and minutes ticked by and slowly daylight crowded out the night, but all was quiet. I zipped up my open collar and slipped my hands into thick mittens. By seven, the visibility was perfect and the air sharp but still. Where were the deer? Where was the cockwalloper buck destined to make our final hunt on the big hill the most memorable of them all?

There was no sign of life—not even a squirrel. You can take stillness either way; as the calm before the storm or, as is more often the case, as the calm before the dead calm. Now and then I heard shots in the distance; the single ones gave me pause, the four- and five-shot bursts suggested that even though the season was all of sixty-five minutes old, somebody already was venting his frustration, or screwing up big-time.

There's a certain cowboy-worthy flair to emptying a gun on a deer, although you may feel pretty stupid if you end up with nothing to show for it but ringing ears. Most rifles hold between three and five rounds, and if you need them all, you probably started with a shot you shouldn't even have bothered to attempt.

Once I was hunting in Pennsylvania with an iconic, lever-action .30-30—the famed gun that won the West. Not only did I empty the five-shot gun; I had time to reload it and get back to work. It was all because a buck unwisely happened to bed down in thick brush on a ledge about eighty yards uphill of the level ground where I sat in my tree stand. The .30-30 has been extolled by many as the ultimate "brush buster," because its relatively heavy, blunt bullets push through foliage and find their target much better than the faster, sleeker loads used in hopped-up rifles like my .257 Weatherby. Contact with a mere twig is thought to send one of those sexy, hot bullets sizzling way off course.

I had a good view of that bedded buck's head and antlers, but the rest of his body was obscured behind a curtain of bri-ars and samplings. I wouldn't entertain the idea of a head shot. The very idea creeps out many hunters, and a deer can live a long, terrible time with his jaw or nose blown off. So I guessed where the vitals would be, judging by the position of the buck's head. Even if I didn't kill the buck with my first shot, it would surely make him leap to his feet, at which point I hoped to have a relatively easy broadside shot.

I fired again, and nothing happened. The buck looked around. I fired again. And again. I might have busted brush, but nowhere near the deer from what I could tell. I emptied the five-shot magazine about as fast as I could work the lever. Whoopee! I felt like John Wayne, shooting at a war party of Comanche. The buck seemed puzzled by the commotion as the lead shredded the surrounding foliage into confetti.

After firing the last cartridge to no discernible effect, I shrugged and fumbled another four cartridges—the last ones I had with me—into the magazine.

What the hell . . . I blasted away, two, three times. When I fired my last shell, the buck's head slowly dropped. A moment later, he slipped off the ledge, rolled downhill, and came to rest at the base of my tree stand, stone-cold dead. I expected to find him drilled full of holes, but the only shot that hit him was my last one, and that had exploded the deer's heart.

I had to smile. It wasn't the story I would choose to tell as a guest at a Manhattan dinner party, but these things happen, too. It isn't always or exclusively about the beauty of the great outdoors, the nobility of the buck, or the sensitivity and skill of the solitary hunter. But now on the big hill I was brought out of my reverie by the sight of a big doe and her two fawns proceeding toward me from about a hundred yards off on the level by the pines.

I watched the woods behind the doe, because the buck is a cowardly charlatan who almost always hangs back and allows a doe to cross a trail or road first. Then, if he senses an all clear, he'll sneak across himself. The doe and her offspring advanced slowly, browsing briar leaves that were still green, although partially covered with snow. I studied them until I was interrupted by the grunt of a buck.

I slipped my trigger hand out of the glove and waited, peering through the trees and over jumbled boulders scattered all around, trying to locate the buck. I finally spotted him moving on a parallel path but about sixty yards downhill from the doe. He was a four-pointer, and he watched the doe's every move while issuing his greedy plaints. He was a mammalian portrait of angst and indecision, and his fear of approaching the doe made me think there must be a big tending buck nearby. The little guy was obviously feeling amorous, but not to the point where he would risk life and limb for love.

The family of three drifted toward me. The buck kept his safe distance but constantly let his intentions be known with burp-like grunts; then he melted into a patch of brush. The family was near me now, but the wind was in my favor; they walked right up to the stand and nibbled a few of the briars at the base of the tree. I remained as still as possible, but my eyes were traveling here and there, searching for some sign of another buck. Eventually, the deer passed under my tree and started up the hill behind my back. I could no longer see them, unless I stood up and turned around—which I wasn't about to do.

Meanwhile, my nose was filling up with fluid. It would sure make a funny, front-of-the-book item in *American Hunter* magazine: *Deer Hunter Drowns in His Own Bodily Fluids While on a Stand* . . . There's a certain cachet to that—just look at those rock stars who became famous overnight after drowning in their own vomit.

The four-pointer reappeared, still trailing the doe at a respectable distance. I doubted that another buck was in attendance; more likely, the doe had been bred and had passed through the estrus phase. If the buck came anywhere near her, she'd cuff him around with her hoofs. But you couldn't blame the little guy for trying.

I was chilled through and feeling miserable. Why did all this seem so important anyway? Maybe I should violate my short- and long-term mission statements. I could shoot the four-point buck, get down from the tree, and be curled up asleep in the cabin by noon. It wouldn't take much to convince Tony to come in from the cold, and I was sure I could goad him into making a fire.

But it wouldn't have been right for any number of reasons,

starting with the fact that for years our pact was that we shot no deer with fewer than eight points on the big hill. Chris was adamant about that. And while we no longer had to abide by that, since he was giving up the property, it still behooved us to go down with our dignity intact. Besides, who knew what else this special day might bring?

Eventually, I turned and saw the family of deer; they had sauntered off far enough for me to stretch out and move about. I cleared my head with a big farmer's blow out of each nostril. A moment later, the two-way radio in my pocket crackled. "This is Tony. Come in, this is Tony. Over."

"You rang, Tony? Over."

The feeble voice was barely audible over the static. "I'm freezing my ass off. It's fucking cold, isn't it? Did you see anything? Over."

"Yeah," I said. "I let a forkhorn go by, and a couple of does. Pretty quiet, though. I'm about to take my shirt off, soak up a little sun . . . Over."

"This is crazy," Tony volunteered. "I've never been so cold in all my life. Over."

"This is Chris. Tony, did you say you were cold? Over."

"I'm going in for lunch," Tony said, defiantly adding, "and maybe I'll start a fire, blast the radio, have a good time. Over— and out."

I laughed, switched off the talkie, and settled back to watch the sunlit woods. On a tranquil, frigid day like this, the deer ought to be moving and browsing. My thoughts drifted like a leaf floating in a brook. Soon a pair of does materialized in the brush downhill and they lingered, nibbling on some of the green shoots and forbs still growing around a permanent seep of water. When they walked, the muscles rippled under their smooth, gray-olive coats.

By noon, I had seen perhaps a dozen deer, a few of which

passed so close below me that I could have hopped on their backs. But I'd seen only that one young buck. I played the "lunch game," choosing 1:00 P.M. as my target time to eat. If I could resist checking my watch until that time or later, I'd allow myself to eat all the pepperoni and jalapeño cheese sticks, since the day would be more than half over.

It was right around noon when I dozed off; thankfully, the stand, while primitive and small, was built into the tree in such a way that branches would keep me from falling all the way out. It never really occurred to me to go back to the cabin for lunch—I knew it would be dark and cold in there, even if Tony made good on his threat to start a fire. He'd have to set the whole cabin ablaze to take the edge off the cold. Of course, this was Tony, so there was always that possibility.

The whole process of unloading the rifle, packing up the relevant gear, climbing down, and trudging back to the cabin seemed like a Herculean undertaking anyway. You know what they say: freezing to death is the least painful way to go; you just slowly stop caring and the rest takes care of itself.

It was hard to imagine that I could spend the entire day, dawn to dusk, without leaving my stand, but I was determined. As Ishi and others well knew, that was the great open secret of hunting. Most big bucks are killed by hunters who had the patience—and guts—to just stay out all day. I might as well suck it up and enjoy my last chance to shoot a buck on the big hill. Or at least endure it.

Once I wolfed down lunch, it eliminated my main reason for remaining alert. I struggled. Where were the bucks? My lids grew heavy, my head felt like it weighed a thousand pounds. I was in a weak, sickly condition, and the sleep monster got me in his deathly grip.

I tried to remain awake, thinking about jobs I'd had. I remembered Walt, a guy I worked for as a short-order cook; he was thoroughly unremarkable, but for his remarkable talent for keeping his profits out of the hands of the IRS and his attempts to inculcate me with his deep cynicism. *Hey, how come I'm thinking about this guy? Hmmm . . . could it be because he had that pretty daughter who I had a mad crush on? Used to come in with her boyfriend. What was I thinking, sculpting that bust of her father Walt from raw hamburger as a special "present" to her? She hated her old man. What was her name again?*

It goes on like that. Deer hunting is a redneck version of transcendental meditation. You go through people, places, and things you'd forgotten, usually for a hell of a good reason. You obsess over silly things. It was in a tree stand that I once got all turned around, mentally, trying to figure out if saying "He has a lot to be modest about" is the ultimate compliment—or the consummate insult. I wouldn't recommend this kind of hunting for anyone who's subject to dark thoughts or feelings of guilt, especially if they're justified. Which probably explained why greedy Walt wasn't a deer hunter.

Oh, so now we're back to him?

Now and then, I'd see a deer. But there was a long mid-afternoon lull. It was just as well; I was probably too zoned-out to operate should the big, huge, giant buck of my dreams come to me, grunting and pawing at the earth. But a part of me still entertained hope . . . so many of the big bucks have been shot under tough circumstances. In unlikely places. By bozos too lazy or cold to move. The big battles in deer hunting are waged between patience and impetuosity, faith and skepticism, even light and dark, dawn and dusk being the best times to get a glimpse of Old Mossy Horn . . . Ultimately, they're struggles with time.

Chris had said that this was the kind of day that a big buck got shot, and I thought he was right about that. Of course,

Chris might already be back at the secret cabin, playing cards with Tony. "Man up," I told myself.

At 3:30, I munched on a protein bar and tried to bite into the apple I'd been hoarding, only to find it frozen hard as a rock; I should have removed it from my pack and stowed it in a warm pocket. Better men than I had died because they made a comparably thoughtless mistake with their food or gear. I was closing in on the ten-hour mark, and it was agonizing. I found little things to do, like straightening out the bundle of parachute cord in my pack, and cleaning the lenses on my binoculars.

But as the melancholy shadows began to fall across the blue afternoon snow, I finally just ached for the day to be over. In fact, I thought it was over; I was just doing due diligence, until I saw a doe and fawn coming down the trail from the cabin.

I felt a surge of adrenaline and reached for the grunt tube dangling around my neck. If there was a buck traveling with them, he was keeping his distance. A grunt might encourage him to speed it up. My heart raced. *Kill a nice buck now and you're a hero,* I thought, enjoying the mental image of Tony and Chris standing there in their long johns on the cabin steps as I dragged the monster into camp. A nice buck now would make it all worth it. It would be my just deserts for being such a trouper.

I blew two deep, slow grunts. The doe lifted her head and looked toward me, stock-still. Her fawn ceased browsing and mimicked her mother's alert pose. But they soon continued feeding, drifting off among the trees. The light was fading fast.

Across the valley, the hillside was black with trees and the ridgeline was lit up by the shredded remnants of a spectacular sunset. Since we were spread out on the hill below the secret cabin, we'd agreed to make our way back down to the Dodge truck separately, unless one or another of us needed help dragging out a buck.

It was a twenty-minute downhill hike to the truck, but I was exhausted, sick and weak, alternately shivering and burning up with fever. Falling out of the tree or breaking a leg on the way down wasn't out of the question, so I proceeded with extra care, even though I could think of nothing more than getting back to the house. Any house. I had done my best on the big hill, one last time. It kicked my butt, one last time. A hunter learns to swallow even the bitterest of pills and move on. There is no "one last time" about that.

I was still sick as a dog on the second day of rifle season, despite having slept a solid fourteen hours. I was in the process of consuming a gallon of hot tea with lemon, honey, and rum when I spotted a green Ford truck belonging to a neighbor—we'll call him Mark—crawling down the road.

Mark is from tough, local stock. He's built like a fire hydrant, wears a bushy mustache, and has the sanguine complexion of a farmer (and the tan to match); he has an affinity for red suspenders, camo sweatshirts, and riding around twelve months a year with a rifle propped, muzzle down, on the bench seat beside him. It's mostly for dusting coyotes, upon which he's waged a bitter, unrelenting war ever since I've known him.

Mark divides his time between working as a carpenter and hunting whatever is in season, with a special fixation on deer. He grew up just a few miles down the road and never had two nickels to rub together. But he got lucky when he married a city girl (we'll call her Barbara), whose family owned a large farm near mine.

Barbara had graduated from a fancy New York art school, but she lit out for the country soon thereafter, improving her status from "flatlander" to "transplant." Barbara loved horses and cats; in fact, they sometimes seemed to be the only thing that interested her at all. When she married Mark, she became a naturalized local, which accorded her special privileges—like the right to say nasty things about the flatlanders and participate in any of the various schemes cooked up to take advantage of those hapless folks.

Over the years, though, Barbara had become antisocial and haughty, forever in some kind of conflict with one or another of the neighbors. It probably didn't help that she never had kids; the isolation and dreary monotony that country life can become caught up to her. But by then she had helped transform Mark from a no-account good ole boy into a man of property and status, if not wealth, even if he does live in constant fear of her wrath.

Mark is also a guy who always waves when he passes you on the road, who always has time to pull over and inquire how things are going with you, and who carefully avoids showing even an inkling of the entitlement he feels as a true native in our rapidly changing, small rural community. Slide off the road in the winter, or a tree limb falls on your roof, he's the first guy there to help and the last guy to leave when the job was done— even if he's still shamelessly holding (or more likely, has spent) that deposit you gave him seven years ago for the gutter job. It's pretty obvious that Mark takes a certain amount of gratification, and a sense of empowerment, from the way he operates.

Over time, Mark became a personage, a well-known figure around town who moved easily—and shrewdly—among locals, weekenders, and transplants. He's a good man to know, and he personifies the local ethos in all respects, including hunting. He happily shoots deer from the truck window anywhere he comes across one, as long as it's daylight, during the official season. He doesn't consider it a violation of the law, except in the most petty, technical sense. Killing deer any chance you get is not just a God-given right, it's a local tradition.

So is putting your wife's tag on a deer you shot so that you can keep hunting, and putting your cousin's tag on the next one, and so on, until you run out of relations or days. So is shooting a deer and quickly dumping its body into the truck, untagged, for the short ride back to the barn, where it hangs "aging" until you get around to butchering it when the hunting is done. You give away a lot of deer meat because it enhances your status, and when you're with guys you know and trust, you tell them truthfully how many bucks you shot that year.

For many people on hardscrabble family farms, protein-rich deer meat has always been a welcome addition to a limited, skimpy diet. The habits bred by that reality are still deeply ingrained, and serve as a higher law than the complex regulations issued by the state department of conservation. I know many guys like Mark, who would just as soon be labeled "outlaws" as give up their traditions; it makes no never mind to them. They're decent, hardworking guys who generally abide by the law; they make great neighbors, and they're always happy to lend a hand. But they cling to a code that takes precedence over mere law and besides, their activities get the city people's noses out of joint—that's a reward unto itself.

I'm all for wise management and the rule of law, but I've also seen hunters at both ends of the socioeconomic spectrum break the law with impunity, justifying it with bromides ranging from "This is the way Daddy done it, so it's good enough for me" to a more sophisticated "I shot it the day before the season opened, but I pay a lot in taxes and I don't get to hunt the way the locals do because I'm in the city all week. I'm not an outlaw; I've got a college degree and a successful business."

I wondered, watching Mark's truck roll up the road, how many bucks he'd shot. Like all canny country boys, he will tell you things, but only up to a point, while expertly mining what gossip and useful information he can from you. The unspoken but firm proprietary claim Mark lays to the land all around his own sizable farm is something that rubs some of our neighbors the wrong way. But he did grow up roaming these same hollows and hills, and in the end ours is not a good place to be an antihunter, or a stickler for legalities. The best you can hope for is that guys like Mark aren't out shooting deer with spotlights at night, or popping the big buck with a pistol during bow season—neither of which Mark would do. As far as I know.

Mark is a hunting machine, and that irritates some of our neighbors as well. For him, scouting and hunting whitetail is a year-round avocation, yet he's never ventured farther afield to hunt than the Adirondacks, a four-hour drive from Andes. And those weekend nimrods who count themselves lucky to shoot a buck every third or fourth year, while maintaining their property and paying their taxes, wonder if their hunting is so poor because of Mark's deadly efficiency with bow and gun, combined with his resistance to any cooperative management techniques that might improve the herd.

Mark is, above all, a "natural," a guy to whom hunting is second nature and who's as secure about his hunting ability as Brett Favre is about throwing a football. He doesn't agonize over the whys and wherefores of it, and he has supreme confidence in that familiar "I know what I know" way. The hunt is in his blood, and has been for all of his life; his knowledge, woodcraft, and instincts are first-rate, and he's sensible. The only hope for any of his hunting rivals is that the weight he's been steadily putting on has left him less and less inclined to leave the truck.

For my part, I decided long ago that I'd just as soon have Mark hunt my land with my blessing than without, because he was going to do it, one way or another. He'd get his deer every year, and as many—or few—as his ethics, tags, or conscience allow. I've hunted with him often on various plots of land, and always enjoyed the experience. I've learned a lot from him. And because of Mark's local status and proprietary feelings about our resident deer, the local outlaws know better than to come messing around in our parts. He's like the game warden, driving our roads at dawn and dusk just about every day of the year just, as he says with a sly grin, "poking around."

We're dealing in ambiguities here, but that's the reality of deer hunting in the rural United States: the simple life is much more complicated than it may appear, or than the way it's generally characterized. Traditions like "frontier justice" may no longer be a fact of rural life, but when it comes to deer hunting, the grip of law is tenuous at best, often unenforceable, and no real match for general community standards. Parties with conflicting or competing interests (management-conscious landowner versus live-off-the-land local) are obliged to find ways to work it out, man to man instead of lawyer to lawyer, or they're doomed to spend all their time trying to outfox—or bust—each other.

I was determined to tough it out and hunt. After a light soup lunch, I took some cold medicine and started for the quarry meadow. I dutifully applied doe-in-estrus urine to a felt drag and tied it to my ankle, so I could leave a trail of scent for any wandering buck. I packed my grunt and fawn-bleat calls, the latter a small plastic cylinder about half the size of a can of Campbell's soup. To activate it, you place the tip of one finger on a small hole on one end and slowly turn the can upside down.

The Deer-in-a-Can doesn't always bring in a deer, even if one happens to be near enough to hear it. I've experimented often with calls to observe their effect on deer, and the results are unpredictable. Even during the rut bucks will sometimes ignore an aggressive grunt, but we all live for the few times when a bleat or grunt brings deer charging through the brush, or tiptoeing over to investigate, as had my pal Lefty some weeks earlier.

What's become of Pancho and Lefty, I wondered. Were either or both of them hanging in Mark's barn?

Overnight, the snow had crusted up; it was like walking on potato chips, eliminating the still-hunting option. Given that deer have acute hearing, walking on crusted snow is enough to bring you to tears. Your best option is to get somewhere, quickly, and sit still and wait. But I took a circuitous route anyway, hoping that I'd leave scent for a buck that might cross my track after the sound of my passing had faded.

I've always wondered what determines which way a buck will go when he comes across scent made by drag. Absent doe tracks (now there's an item yet to be invented—the doe-track maker!) and the scent the hoofs deposit, a randy buck could go either way on a scent trail. Maybe he'd follow the trail back to the house instead of the way I'd gone. I always left the remote handy, should one decide to watch a Steelers game while I was out.

I made my way up to the quarry meadow, one careful and annoyingly loud step at a time. All the while, I was getting chills. At the meadow, I decided against getting into the tree stand, choosing instead to hunker down behind a big round bale of hay at the edge of the field. The road lay about seventy-five yards to my right. It wouldn't be long until dusk, when the deer might pop into the meadow to paw up some feed. The snow had already been dug up in many places for just that purpose.

I allowed some time for peace to return to the woods, then took out and deployed my fawn bleat: *Baaa-a-a-a-a-a . . .* I repeated it after a few seconds. The sound was loud in the thin, cold air. Evening tones colored up the sky, and I sensed the hardness of winter coming on; soon the woods would become a giant, tightly stretched drum skin, echoing every sound back

Typical deer tracks. Big bucks often walk in a splayfooted manner, and their tracks are significantly larger than those of does.

into a well of stillness. I looked across the meadow at the stand of oaks; now that I carried the rifle instead of a bow, anything there would be within range.

The light faded, and the silence matured. I had only a few minutes of shooting time left, so I decided to get creative. I blew twice into the grunt tube, waited a few moments, then issued a single fawn bleat. I watched the oaks across the way, but when I heard the telltale crunch of snow and frozen leaves, it came from behind me, on the bank below where I sat, somewhere between me and the road. It was quite a ruckus, whatever made it didn't give a hoot about being heard; it was hard to imagine it was anything but an agitated deer. And that suggested a buck, perhaps even a buck and doe, still in breeding phase.

I snapped to attention and fingered the safety on the rifle. The next commotion came from a little closer. Soon a doe jumped out and stood at the edge of the meadow, looking back into the woods down over the bank. She was skittish. I was sure a buck lingered somewhere behind her, reluctant to show himself in the open until he knew it was safe.

I watched and listened hard. I thought about grunting, but the deer were close now and it might tip them off. Besides, all the indications were that the deer were coming up to feed. It was just a waiting game. But dusk was coming on, quickly. I had to make a play. I took out the tube and grunted, twice.

The doe locked up, fully alert. She looked toward me, and back over the bank again. Then she went crashing off, downhill, into the woods. It sounded like she was not running alone.

"Idiot," I cursed myself, sure I had spooked her with my aggressive grunting.

But directly I picked up a faint rattling that quickly grew louder, and then the squeal of rusty springs. It was a vehicle of some kind coming up the road. Within a few moments, I saw the truck—an old, blue, two-tone pickup that I didn't recognize. The string of amber running lights atop its cab were already on and glowing. As the driver reached the flat hilltop, he slowed to a standstill and sat there, unaware of me, scanning the meadow—my meadow. He was obviously looking for deer.

Son of a bitch, I thought, knowing it was the truck, not my grunt, that had spooked the deer. *Useless, no-account, bottom-feeding, road-hunting, outlaw son of a bitch. Thanks, shithead.*

12

A Nimrod's Lament

GALILEE, PENNSYLVANIA, NOVEMBER 26–28

I F YOU WANT to see big deer and plenty of them, seek out the river bottoms. It's a useful bit of folk wisdom, because of the importance of water to all game species and the foods they eat. Wayne County, Pennsylvania, while less than a two-hour drive from my farm in Andes, is a different world when it comes to whitetail.

The rich Delaware River bottom lands constitute a more temperate, broad-valley climate. And a potent combination of traditional agricultural activity and significant vacation-home development come together along the river to drive the white-tail population through the proverbial roof. I struck my roots as a hunter in Pennsylvania, albeit in a more rural area farther west, in the Susquehanna drainage, where life was harder for everyone, including whitetail.

Way back then, my wanderings with the .22 often took me a few miles over a wagon track to the home of Farmer Taylor, a kindly man with a rosy complexion and watery, pale blue eyes. They contrasted sharply with his dark blue coveralls, which were infused with the *eau de manure,* and which he appeared to wear every day of his life. Sometimes, a mahogany vein of Red Man chewing tobacco could be seen at the corner of his mouth. His wife—if I recall, her name was Fran—had mousy, unkempt hair, and she always wore a wrinkled dress that hung limp and gray on her beaten-down shoulders.

One fall day, when I got tired of pushing weeds and clover through the fence of the sty for the Taylors' companionable, squealing pigs, I wandered around the corner to their old sap house. In the half-light inside, I beheld the long body of a deer, a spike buck, suspended upside down from a steel rod inserted through the thin skin right below his knee joints. The belly of the deer was slit open and his insides were cleaned out, the cavity propped open with an eighteen-inch length of stick.

I was awed. The deer looked enormous. The barn cats had already cleaned the floor of the blood that had dripped slowly from the buck's mouth and nose for a few hours after he was hung. I touched the buck; it swiveled gently. The coarse, gray-brown hair was so perfectly distributed and densely packed that it felt less like the hair of an animal than a slick, aerodynamic coating. I peered inside the body cavity. It was like the hull of some great ship, the skin stretched tight over the stavelike ribs, the flesh a deep, rich maroon with a hard, glossy finish.

That was nearly fifty years ago, but I remembered it vividly on the way to Wayne County, near the town of Callicoon (on the New York side of the Delaware River), where I've hunted for most of my adult life. Until recently, the area was overrun by deer. From the 1970s through the '90s, you might see fifty, sixty deer—the vast majority of them does—on a typical opening day. And it was like that in many other parts of the state, too. Among the big three deer-hunting states—Pennsylvania, Texas, and Michigan—Pennsylvania has the largest number of hunters. Pennsylvania was also the poster child for disastrous deer management policies.

That began to change when Dr. Gary Alt, a renowned bear biologist and avid deer hunter, agreed to take over Pennsylvania's deer management program. Alt took the job partly because he had come to recognize a woeful truth: Pennsylvania was overrun with whitetail, and a holocaust loomed beneath the veneer of the hunter's paradise. Deer were steadily eating their way toward an ecological catastrophe of which they themselves would be the final victims, after they stripped the earth of habitat for various ground-nesting creatures (including birds), and driven entire species of flora to near extinction—all while encouraging invasive species that would prosper because deer won't eat them.

The deer population had exploded out of control because, rather than in spite, of hunters. This was disturbing news for any hunter or wildlife manager who understands the vital role recreational hunting plays in society. The best defense hunters have against animal sentimentalists is the critical role hunting plays in managing the staggering number of large, undomesticated mammals that share our landscape. Hunting is the best and most economically productive way to maintain a genetically viable, appropriately sized, renewable deer herd. Even people repelled by the idea of hunting must ask themselves, *Is it worth destroying the environment and corrupting a species just because I'm personally uncomfortable with the idea of hunting?*

But hunting regulations in Pennsylvania had worked to exacerbate rather than ameliorate the problem. The deer population spiraled out of control in such a breathtaking manner partly because Pennsylvania's wildlife management was driven by politics rather than science. Ironically, it's similar to the problem you have in the "animal rights" community. Pennsylvania's management policies were determined by political appointees, not disinterested wildlife managers. And the state Game Commission, which sets hunting regulations, was not only prohunter, it was more responsive to popular opinion than the advice of wildlife biologists.

Alt discreetly avoided fighting with the politicians who set hunting regulations but, acting on his experience and training as a biologist, he collected data, crunched numbers, and demonstrated that the Game Commission had failed to serve the public interest. Analyzing deer populations, the forest ecology, and hunting habits and regulations, he came to some harrowing conclusions about the impact of deer on the landscape.

A forest is meant to be dense; one of the first things that strikes a pilgrim in true wilderness is the general impenetrability of almost any forest. Alt knew that the woods weren't supposed to look like a pincushion festooned with trees; you aren't supposed to be able to see for a hundred yards through the woods, even in February.

To illustrate his concerns, Alt fenced a small parcel of land in the middle of typical Pennsylvania deer habitat, and within a year or so, the fenced area looked nothing like the surrounding woods. It literally resembled a box stuffed with vegetation, set down in an otherwise sparsely wooded clearing.

Alt identified the main problems that set the stage for disaster. Hunters were obsessed with killing bucks, partly because the conventional logic always demanded that you spare the does. After all, they're the ones that annually replenish the buck population, even as they add to the surplus of does. The rallying cry for hunters has usually been "more deer," rather than "better deer." There was no demand for a healthy, sustainable deer herd, not for any reason. By contrast, wildlife managers in places less wary of annoying voters already were formulating strategies meant to improve the herd, either with antler-size restrictions on bucks, or laws encouraging higher doe kills.

Like most hunters, even antler-obsessed Pennsylvanians wanted venison for the freezer for the winter, so the state had

an official "doe day(s)" at the end of the regular gun season—
never mind that killing a large number of does that had *already
been* bred was an enormous waste of, among other things, good
buck semen.

Pennsylvania's policies eventually created doe-to-buck ratios
that bordered on the surreal—15:1, or worse. That's a sure-
fire recipe for overpopulation and poor genetics, because it allowed even the least fit of bucks to breed successfully—and often. They and their inferior offspring then were able to further
reduce the available, quality forage. Poor nutrition eventually
punishes the strong as well as the weak.

Alt grew up milking cows in the Pennsylvania town of Moscow, so he had street cred at home. I interviewed him at a high
point of his battle against the status quo in 2002, and he framed
his case this way:

"Raising more deer than the land can support has been the
biggest mistake in the history of wildlife management. We've
been doing it wrong for seventy years, and that's one reason it's
been so hard to show that it's just plain bad for everyone. The
ecosystem is pretty complicated, but good deer management
really isn't. Mostly, it's about getting the right number of deer
of the right age and the right sex in the right places."

This was the same mantra recited by Ted Masser at his high-
fence ranch in Texas. Basically, that goal can only be met by either protecting bucks, killing far more does, or—the best-case
scenario—a combination of the two. If you allowed more of the
dominant bucks to assert themselves in a breeding pool that
had significantly fewer does, the genetics would improve, because the fittest of bucks would do most of the breeding. The
general attempt to create the ideal deer herd is called "quality deer management," and it isn't easy to pull off on the public
scale unless hunters back the idea.

One of the main tools of QDM is antler restrictions. The

most convenient, if still inexact, way to determine the potential or quality of a buck is by antler size and configuration relative to age. A typical QDM approach calls for killing bucks only if they have three or, in some cases, four tines on at least one antler. This can be a nightmare in the field, but it's not just the best way—it's the *only* way to protect the right bucks.

There's an additional, cultural problem posed by QDM. The brotherhood of hunters always includes a fair number of nimrods—many of them crusty, cantankerous old blowhards—who believe that the QDM models are a secret plot by fancy pants "trophy hunters" (as opposed to down-home folks who want to share a traditional experience with, say, a grandson). The debate has populist versus elitist overtones, although the battle lines are drawn less along socioeconomic than philosophical and ethical lines. The romance of Grandpa taking little Billy out to bag his first deer is undeniable. But shouldn't every little shaver also learn the principles of herd management and ethical hunting?

In any event, Alt knew that scores of hunters in his state were self-appointed deer "experts" who would resist QDM on the grounds that it was vaguely "un-American" (remember, Alt's from Moscow . . . just sayin'). But it was just un-Pennsylvanian. Alt was prepared to lay out the science and the facts, and to answer the entrenched gestalt with a question: *In a world where old-fashioned values—and hunting—are being challenged or overturned left and right, even by the courts, how are you going to justify hunting as the best management tool when it's clearly not working?*

Alt recognized that he had to win hearts and minds before he even thought of trying to implement QDM principles. He eventually convinced sixty state legislators to cosponsor some two hundred public meetings that enabled him to lay out the rueful news on the deer herd in a last-ditch effort to avert the pending ecological disaster—and deny antihunting forces with some of their most potent ammunition to use against hunting.

"It was like running for governor," Alt told me. "I think I've been within twenty-five miles of virtually every Pennsylvanian, and we had an average audience of over five hundred people at these presentations. We never ended a meeting until everyone who wanted to make a comment got a turn at the microphone."

Alt ventured forth well-armed, with some thirty thousand copies of a video laying out his case—with help from dramatic documentation of comparative (healthy versus overbrowsed) habitat. It was a tough, frustrating, and at times scary job—in some places, Alt was denounced as an "environmentalist." He sometimes wore a bulletproof vest, and one boozed-up kid warned before one meeting: "They're going to carry you out of here in a body bag tonight, and I'm not going to do a thing to stop them."

But by the end of his tour, Alt had convinced an impressive 80 percent of the state's hunters and legislators that QDM was both necessary and right; the basics of his plan went into effect in 2002. The most noticeable effect of the enlightened regulations has been a marked decline in the doe population. The naive dream that within two or three years the woods would be teeming with cloven-hoofed behemoths with eight- or ten-point racks remains unrealized, but the average buck has improved.

Great big bucks remain rare, stealthy, reclusive critters. Ever was it thus, irrespective of QDM—or any of man's other machinations.

Given what I'd been through at the secret cabin for New York's opener, the Pennsylvania trip shaped up as spring break without the beer bongs and bikini-clad, tattooed coeds. The weather was clear and barely crisp; you could count the seconds before a leaf falling from a branch hit the earth. But the weather report on the eve of opening day called for falling temperatures—and rain—for the opener. Nothing new in that: for some reason, opening day in Wayne County often presents bizarre conditions. The ideal crisp, cold morning, with perhaps a little fresh snow, is a rarity.

The boys were in the woods out back at my buddy Chris von Strasser's Deer Hill Farm property when I arrived in mid-afternoon. Chris had found a load of buck sign around a sloping, two-acre field, and decided that the third member of our party, Tony Blumka, ought to hunt there. They were trying to get Tony and his "climber" tree stand set up for the morning.

Chris is an amazing shot—I once saw him break something like ninety-three out of a hundred targets on a sporting clays course. He's also excellent with a rifle and has hunted extensively in Europe, the British Isles, and Canada.

He can also be impatient: on a turkey hunt once, he grabbed my pump shotgun by mistake in the predawn dark, forced a three-and-a-half-inch magnum shell into it, and then borrowed my knife when he couldn't shuck out the oversized shell. He broke the tip of my knife trying to pry the shell out of the chamber and dismissed the whole incident in cavalier fashion, saying, "Don't worry, I'll buy you a new one!"

Most of our crowd forgives him such bonehead moves because—well, because he's a buddy, an experienced hunter, and a generous, jovial guy. So I just looked on, amused, as Chris rushed this way and that, hurrying to get Tony's new stand up. It turned out that in his haste, he'd dropped and lost some critical pieces of the climber (a category of portable stand that enables you to jack yourself up and down almost any relatively straight tree trunk). He decided that Tony didn't need to get that high off the ground anyway. Six feet would be good enough.

Tony shrugged and tried out his perch. I immediately thought of that legendary scene in the "rockumentary" *This Is Spinal Tap*—the one in which replicas of the Stonehenge slabs are lowered onto the stage, but turn out to have been accidentally constructed on a miniature scale. I tried to keep a straight face as I asked, "How's the weather up there, Tony?"

Tony, though, is a good sport; he too has hunted all over the world, which is the kind of thing you can do when your father amassed the world's finest collection of medieval art objects. Tony deals in those artworks now, his home and gallery taking up most of a regal townhouse on Manhattan's Upper East Side. But unlike similarly fortunate New Yorkers, he doesn't go in for the Hamptons, Martha's Vineyard, or Telluride. His vacation place is a log home in the Pennsylvania woods, where he can hunt with bow and gun on weekends. It's not Tahoe, but Lake Wallenpaupack—where Tony is also part owner of a marina.

When they finished, Tony fired up his GPS and marked the location of the tree stand, even though the roof of Chris's house was almost visible beyond a small knoll, and surrounded by towering pines.

When you hunt, you live the dream. The hook-and-bullet press flourishes from hyping the latest products (*The GPS— Every Hunter Should Have One!*) and advising you how to do things most hunters (as well as those editors and writers) have neither the time nor desire to accomplish. They include scouting extensively before the season, or hunting for shed antlers after the season, in order to find a big buck for the following season. They advise you to cut the shooting lanes at your tree stand months in advance, or to hone your skill with the bow for hours, while fully dressed for hunting and perched in a tree stand . . . in August. It sure sounds good—on paper.

We walked a few hundred yards back to the rambling Deer Hill Farm house to clean up before leaving for our annual pre-hunt dinner at the home of Stan Petlan, a hunting buddy over in nearby Callicoon. We discussed a game plan for the following morning. I hoped to go to an area called the sixty acres, which consists of two long fields (one mown for hay and the other gone to seed) separated by a tree-lined stone wall. Both fields peter out into a cul-de-sac filled with hemlocks in the lap of a semicircular ridge featuring rock ledges, dense briars, boulders, and deadfalls. It's ideal whitetail habitat.

Chris was amenable to that—he's in the habit of freelancing on opening day. Still-hunting is the oxymoronic term for creeping through the woods very, very slowly and quietly, looking and glassing, hoping to come upon deer unawares. Three years ago he glassed up a nice bedded buck while still-hunting and shot it as the oblivious buck lay on its bed. It was a fine achievement that required good scouting, great patience and stealth, and excellent shot placement.

With just the three of us hunting some three hundred acres, the deer wouldn't get too stirred up by human activity in the predawn hour—a critical edge on opening day. But the habitat at Chris's farm attests to the problems that concerned Alt. The great, horseshoe-shaped basin behind the house is almost entirely bare of brush or saplings. The boughs on most mature trees are stripped, right up to the browse line, about six feet off the ground. The only good news is that the defoliation has allowed more sunshine to enter, and briars have proliferated.

I can't remember missing an opening day in Pennsylvania since I started hunting there about thirty years ago. And nothing beats hunting on opening day as a guest on land you know well, because nobody can track you down in the woods, although cell towers are robbing us of even that reliable haven.

By the time we arrived at Stan's home high above the Delaware, our friends were deep into the cheese dip, beer, Scotch, and pigs-in-a-blanket. Stan, a Czech, owned a high-end restaurant specializing in his native cuisine in the heart of Manhattan for most of his working life. He retired decades ago, but despite his advancing age, he still insists on hosting the dinner.

Each year, it's exactly the same menu: a classic, European hunter's feast of roast duck with homemade dumplings, gravy, and red cabbage, with unlimited wine. Each year, I tell myself I'm going easy on the hootch because I want to be on my A game, and each year I break my vow of temperance and usually find myself pontificating about deer genetics, cartridge properties, or Jessica Simpson's physical endowments well before the dessert course—which includes that wickedly strong Czech spirit, slivovitz.

Over three decades, our group has had a steady core of perhaps a dozen men, with periodic newcomers or guests. Stan is the elder statesman, but for a long time the driving force was the late Joe Freda, whom I always thought of as a pillar of American virtue and values. Unassuming, reserved, almost pathologically even-tempered, Joe was a smallish, neatly groomed man; most people were shocked to learn that he'd been a distinguished fighter pilot in World War II. After the war, he started the eponymous realty company that's now been taken over by his son, Tom.

In this case, the apple fell some distance from the tree, because Tom is a garrulous, thrill-seeking, impetuous guy. But neither he nor Joe ever missed any of Stan's dinners, and two years ago Tom brought along his own sixteen-year-old boy, Jesse. The Fredas thus became the first family to have three generations in attendance.

Beyond that, the group has included two corrections officers (they work downstate, at the big jail at Fishkill), two airline pilots, a Wall Street wunderkind, a carpenter, a writer, an investment banker, and an art dealer. I know next to nothing about a few of these fellas; but come hunting season, we're like long-lost brothers.

During cocktails, we talked about recent hunting trips—covering Montana, Saskatchewan, Wyoming, the Yukon, and Kazakhstan. Tony Blumka was the guy who'd hunted in the latter nation, and I was astonished to learn that the elk in that rugged, steep country are genetically identical to our own Rocky Mountain elk—the theory being that elk ancestors went wherever continental drift took them when the original mega-landmass broke up, and our present continents began to separate.

We had further cause for celebration because Vanni Fuller, one of the prison guards, was taking his own son out for his first opening day, an event for which the boy had been practicing with his single-shot .30-30 for months. "He can put a bullet in the boiler room at fifty yards, nine out of ten times," Vanni boasted. "And he's under strict orders not to shoot at over that distance. We're hunting in some thick hemlocks, though, so the shots should be close anyway."

We drifted off to dinner; the conversations invariably returned to the next day's hunt, or past hunts. We devoured the ducks, ripping leg bones and wings from the perfectly crisped bodies; if Stan had any dogs in the house, we would have been throwing the bones over our shoulders to them. As the feasting slowed, someone uttered the familiar words: "So, Greg, didn't you hunt New Brunswick once and miss a chance at a real slammer?"

We began tapping silverware against our wineglasses, calling out for Greg Senft to tell his story. It's a story Greg first shared with us two decades ago, and he told it so well that each year we insisted on hearing it again. Pretty soon, the retelling became an annual rite.

It takes Greg about half an hour to get through the story, which might be called *A Nimrod's Lament*. The basics are that

Greg had been taken into the backcountry in New Brunswick by a guide who turned out to be a lazy sack of shit. The hunt had been a wet disaster. On Greg's last day, the guide just dropped Greg off in the woods and suggested that he still-hunt over to another road, where the guide would pick him up before dark.

So Greg set out, alone, discouraged by his prospects, until he stumbled upon the fresh tracks of two deer, one of them leaving the big, deep, splayed print of a monster buck. He was clearly traveling with a doe.

Still-hunting, Greg tracked the deer for hours through swampy bottoms, thick forest, and dense alders. He eventually came to a place where he had a rare, good view ahead, and sensed that the deer were bound to emerge into the small clearing. He positioned himself, focused on the clearing. He heard drops of rain fall from the trees onto his cap. He was vigilant, locked-on in full predator mode, ignoring the odd sound made by someone running a chain saw or something far in the distance. He saw a movement in the brush and eased off the safety. Now there was an odd crashing sound, and not far off.

A moment later, the doe showed a portion of her body, hesitated, but stepped out in the clearing. Greg's heart was pounding; he saw tan in the alders behind the doe, but he couldn't put antlers on it; he fought the urge to take a wild shot into the brush.

At the same time, he recognized the foreign sound; it was some kind of vehicle, plowing through the alders. He debated for a moment, just long enough to catch a brief glimpse of a tall, wide rack of antlers as both doe and buck, no doubt frightened by the approaching truck, plunged away through the brush. Momentarily, a pickup crashed through the last of the alders and came to rest alongside Greg. The three-hundred-pound guy inside turned his face to the window, grinned at Greg, and asked, "Seen anything?"

Over time, Greg has mastered the art of building the suspense of the tale with embellished details, hand gestures, and pregnant pauses. Mere hoof prints have become giant depressions in the moss, with steam still rising from them. He describes the droplets of water glittering on the alders, and the part where he pauses to clean his scope with Kleenex and checks his sight picture.

As Greg narrates the story, we act like a bunch of purple-haired teenagers at a screening of the *Rocky Horror Picture Show*. We interrupt Greg with the same old questions, catcalls, and observations. We quote parts of the story we've committed to memory. At each turn, someone calls out, "Then what happened?"

When he's done, we have a moment of silence for Greg, and it's all any of us can do to keep from leaping up and shouting, "Greg, I love you, man . . ."

For the Nimrod's Lament is an epic, Jungian tale of woe, the story of a typical hunting shit-show that each of us has experienced, in one form or another, more than once. I'd experienced something like it just days earlier, up by the quarry meadow. We savor and drink from this cup of woe, the towering injustice of it lingers, bittersweet, upon our lips.

Then we start on the slivovitz.

Opening day in Pennsylvania is the last of many opening days in any given year for most of my crowd. Pennsylvania's abundant herd makes all of us optimistic; and the only reason we don't kill a pile anymore is that even before the Alt era, we leaned toward restraint and tried to do the right thing.

I've never really gotten over being anxious before any opening day, and Pennsylvania's was no different, especially now that my chances to kill a monster whitetail were dwindling. Maybe it was a stupid goal to set for a specific year anyway; it was a little too much like going to a party or social affair vowing that you'll meet the girl of your dreams. It doesn't happen that way; it happens, if at all, when you least expect it, and even then you've got a few thousand ways to screw it all up.

In my mind's eye, I had looked forward to being a lean, mean, monster whitetail killing machine by the time the Pennsylvania season rolled around. And once again, I found myself lying in the dark, staring at a ceiling that I hoped would stop spinning while outside the window the pine boughs rustled and sighed.

I was lucid enough to know that I'd neglected my due diligence (*spare batteries?* Check. *Clean field glasses?* Check). My stuff was piled haphazardly in the corner of Chris's gun room. I'd shot a trophy mulie, and a fine Texas whitetail; it wasn't like this year was chopped liver. Heck, I'd been sick, and I was still disappointed by the lack of action on the other Chris's big hill. *This is no time to go soft,* I told myself, fearing that I was running out of steam. *You've got to pull yourself together and hunt like you mean it for the next two days. You may never have another season like this for the rest of your life.*

Gradually, I drifted off to sleep, but I woke up frequently. The next thing I knew, I heard Chris and Tony padding around downstairs. I threw some water on my face, brushed my teeth, and made my way to the kitchen. I dawdled over coffee. This venturing forth into the dark, cold, expiring night, dressed like a wooly mammoth and bearing a gun—I loved it, but I wanted to put it off for a bit. Why? What was I thinking?

Nimrod! Loser! Coward! I consoled myself: *It's just nerves.* Star football players sometimes fall to their hands and knees and vomit before big games, too.

Fully dressed for the end of November and wearing a fanny pack the size of a beer keg, I could barely move. But when I stepped outside, I realized something was wrong. It was warmer than I expected, and a fine mist of rain swirled around the corner spotlight on the garage. Oh, I was vaguely aware that a warming trend was in the works, but this? Wasn't it just over a week ago that I feared I would freeze to death to the grotesque soundtrack of Tony Cece snoring?

I unzipped my wool hunting jacket and thermal top, climbed on the ATV, and drove the gravel roads to the sixty acres. I slowly walked the fenceline to the Texas tower, convinced at various times that there were three, five, or nine deer out in the field ahead of me, running as wild as my imagination.

The Texas tower at the edge of the field was serviceable enough, but a porcupine had eaten the plywood roof over the summer, and that meant no protection from the weather as long as I sat there. And the mist was turning into rain.

This promised to be a tough hunt, but no worse than the 2006 opener, when the weather was comparable, but the ground was covered in five inches of snow. I hunted that day up on the Moon Rock, a lunarlike plateau of moss and lichen-covered bluestone high on a ridge. Chris had cheerfully told me back then that he had seen five rack bucks on the property just a few days earlier; there ought to be one hiding behind every rock.

And there might have been, but for something I realized as I struggled to find the familiar trail to the Moon Rock by the green glow of my flashlight. The warm air was melting the snow, turning it into a dense fog that covered everything. I couldn't have seen a Cat bulldozer at ten yards in a hayfield, never mind slender, dark deer sneaking between the black trees.

About forty-five minutes later that day, I perched about twenty feet up in the tree stand, wondering what I was doing with my life. I realized there wasn't going to be anything remotely like daybreak; if anything, the conditions were getting worse.

Large, fat raindrops fell intermittently; they exploded on my head and shoulders, or pinged off the steel rails and steps of the stand. The visibility was all of twenty-five feet. When the rain let up, I thought: *This is bound to lift. The deer are gonna move onto the Moon Rock and into other clearings to escape the dripping boughs at any moment* . . .

I thought of poor Tony Blumka, who was hunting with us that year as well, sitting down in the Texas tower in the sixty acres piece.

At first light and dusk, the sixty acres is a hotspot. But in the fog, Tony could throw a bullet farther than he could see. It was tough luck, but better him than me. The minutes crawled by. I reminded myself that during bow season, on this very Moon Rock stand, I'd watched four different bucks, chasing does.

Every so often, the sky would brighten a bit, rekindling my hopes. But just as soon, the gloom descended again. Chris's words rang in my ears: *I've got at least five rack bucks running around . . . one of them is a very nice eight!* Ha. And here I sit, wet, chilled, thinking grim thoughts.

Some time around noon, I saw it—a patch of brown barely visible in the fog between a couple of dark, wet tree trunks. I yanked the gun off the hook and fumbled with the scope caps, but when I looked again there was nothing. I grabbed the binoculars, as if they would help me see through the fog. It had been a deer for sure. It was traveling alone, so it might have been a buck, maybe a big buck, probably a B&C buck, or the new Pennsylvania state record. Heck, it might have been anything—now that it was gone.

Moments later, I heard a muffled gunshot from somewhere near the sixty acres. *He missed,* I told myself. Two more shots ripped the stillness. *Pure desperation,* I muttered, breaking out my M&M's. I fell into a funk, staring at the birch stump nearby. Suddenly, it was transformed into Pocahontas, the Indian princess. She was wielding an ax and looking right at me! What light remained was fading fast.

When I climbed down from the stand, I felt numb. Somehow, I had made it—I had stayed on the stand on that desolate Moon Rock most of the day. But I was chilled through and mentally fried, eager to get back to the house to wash away my disappointment in the shower. Opening day had gone by, and I'd seen—maybe—one deer.

I traversed the Moon Rock without using my light, for it was familiar ground. I found the cleft between two massive formations of ledgerock, where two natural stone steps led down and out to the trail that would take me back to Deer Hill Farm. I descended a series of benches. Surely the trail was just ahead.

But as I pressed on in the fog, I found myself wallowing through dense briars that tore at my jacket and pants and—this is the one that always infuriates me—repeatedly snatched the hat off my head. I realized I wasn't going to hit the trail. How silly of me!

I backtracked to a place that looked familiar in the soupy dusk and set off again, careful not to change course too dramatically. But something didn't feel right. *This is nuts,* I thought. I know where I am. I've been here a hundred times. But by then it was dark. I suddenly realized it, and the hair on the back of my neck went prickly. I broke out in a cold sweat. Furiously, I plunged back in and plowed ahead.

Sweaty, cut up, and parched, I lost it. I flailed at the briars in anger. I kicked my way through a mess of blow down and fortunately caught myself one step before I walked over the edge of a ten-foot drop-off with a nasty tangle of blow down right below. This couldn't be part of the Moon Rock, I realized. I was way off course.

Everything looked familiar, but I recognized nothing. The beam of my flashlight was little help; it traveled all of two feet before dissolving into an otherwise pleasant lime cloud.

It dawned on me that I might have to spend the night outside. There was no chance I would die of starvation, exposure, or at the hands of bloodthirsty savages. My fate was actually going to be worse: we were all gathering at Steve Renehan's, about ten miles away, for our formal posthunt dinner. Even if my friends decided to leave for Steve's without me, failing to show up for dinner would alarm them. They would organize a search party. I wasn't worried that they wouldn't find me. I was worried that they would.

They would console me ("It can happen to anyone on a night like this!"), but every one of them would be thinking roughly the same thing, *Jay-zus, but you are one world-class dipshit! How the hell did you get lost at the Moon Rock!*

I started hollering, at the top of my lungs: *Chris . . . Tony . . . Chris . . . Tony.* I quickly tied my flashlight to my walking stick, so I could hold it aloft, like a beacon. Eventually I heard the growl of an ATV in the distance; that would be Chris and Tony, looking for me. It wasn't too far off, and I began to slash my way toward them, hollering and waving. They had to hear me, how could they not? When I heard Chris turn off the ATV, I knew it would be okay.

An hour later, I stood by Chris's truck, admiring the thick-bodied seven-pointer lying in the bed. It was no B&C buck, but it was a good one nonetheless. I would have been proud to shoot it, but it was Tony who did it, on the sixty acres. He told me how:

"Once in a while, the fog lifted a little and the sky brightened, just for a few moments. Just long enough to see a little more than before. One of those times, I looked up and the buck was just standing there, not even a hundred yards away. I shot him, and then he turned and ran toward me. So I shot him again, and he still kept coming. The third shot dropped him, ten feet from the Texas tower."

I absorbed his story fully. I wanted to take every particle of useful knowledge and deer intelligence out of it, digest it, learn from it for my own benefit. But really, there was no useful information to abstract. It was a simple, crazy story with a happy ending, the kind that's always reserved for the other guy.

This year, though, it was to be me in the sixty acres, and maybe an even bigger buck would materialize out of the fog. The conditions were better, no doubt about it. *Keep the faith,* I told myself, although the steady rain was beginning to soak through various exposed places as well as my thick brown-duck hunting pants. Now and then the visibility improved, but it was never better than ninety or a hundred yards, a paltry distance in those big fields.

At noon, I decided to descend and still-hunt my way back into the hemlocks, where I could at least roll in under a tree to eat my lunch. The weather took the pleasure out of still-hunting; the conditions for creeping around undetected were ideal, but the rain and humidity constantly fogged up my binoculars and scope. Disgusted, I finally gave up.

I found a hemlock on a mild rise along the course of a running spring. The earth was level, dry, and carpeted with moss. I thought about making a fire, but I wasn't really cold—just wet. I ate lunch, nursing my disappointment. Then I set my fanny pack against the trunk of the hemlock for a pillow and went to sleep.

I awoke in the mid-afternoon, still wet but basically comfortable. I'd seen nothing in the woods; my best chance in the afternoon probably lay with the Texas tower. I still-hunted back to it, climbed in, and continued to watch the twin fields. At about 4:00 P.M. the rain ceased, and I watched a small group of deer emerge from the tree line to my left. They began feeding at the edge of the field. Because of the poor visibility, I couldn't tell if any were bucks, but I knew for sure that none of them were big-racked bucks.

I made sure my gun and grunt tube were close at hand; things could get interesting, and fast. On a clear day, the shadows would be long, and various critters—squirrels, chipmunks, wild turkeys—would be afoot, but a pall lay over the silent land, the only sound the occasional splat of a raindrop. Another group of deer appeared, farther down in the field—or did it? It was getting hard to tell in the failing light.

The first group of deer continued moving toward me, and I saw that one of them was a scraggly little three-pointer. Under the quality deer management regulations, it was not even a legal deer. It reminded me of the last buck I had killed at Deer Hill Farm, in the first year of the QDM regimen.

That, too, had been a rough opening day spent on the Moon Rock, but instead of warm rain and fog, it featured bitter cold and bright, glittering sunlight, with gusts of wind up to twenty-five miles per hour.

The cold knifed through three layers of my high-tech clothing that day, and at times I shivered uncontrollably. The maple tree to which the ladder stand was lashed swayed in the breeze, and I huddled on the small platform, cursing the sick joke of a day. *What's the worst thing that could happen?* I wondered. The answer was all around me: trees, some bigger than the one I occupied, had been snapped like toothpicks in past windstorms on the exposed plateau. But I rode out the periodic fierce gusts, always hoping—idiotically—that each one was the last.

At around noon three deer slipped up onto the Moon Rock from the steep bank beyond it. My eyes were watering, so it was like looking into a little whitetail kaleidoscope, complete with flaring blue and red and green reflections.

Suddenly another deer barged into the scene, and I immediately knew from his body language that it was a buck. He just oozed command and natural entitlement. I got the scope up and saw that the buck had three points on his left antler. Something didn't feel right, but I told myself: *If you shoot this guy, you can get the fuck out of this damned tree and go get warm.*

I squeezed the trigger, the gun went off, and all four deer froze. The deer were only about sixty yards away, but I had missed. I worked the bolt, laid the cross hairs right behind the buck's shoulder, and touched off another shot. The deer kicked like a mule while its companions fled over the bank. The buck I hit ran after them.

I gave myself a few minutes to calm down and gather my gear. I felt certain my second shot had been right on the mark. On the ground, I examined the place where I thought he'd stood, and found the divots he left in the moss when he bucked. But there was no blood—not even hair. It was only about thirty feet to the edge of the plateau, and it was easy to follow the buck's tracks.

When I looked over the lip, I saw him piled up in the leaves. His three-point antler poked up out of the leaves. I was surprised at his bulk, which suggested that he should have developed a much bigger rack of antlers. When I grabbed the spindly antler and lifted his head, I saw why something hadn't seemed quite right. He was missing almost all of his right antler. But the way he'd stood, broadside, made it hard to tell. The antler had been broken off about two inches above the base, probably while it was still in velvet.

Only later did it dawn on me that I had accomplished something unique. Not only had I *not* killed a "Booner," I just might have secured a record of sorts—for the *smallest* buck killed in Pennsylvania in the Alt QDM era. It would certainly be a difficult record to beat.

I dragged the buck out to the Moon Rock and slit one of his ears; I filled out and attached the buck tag with a plastic cable tie. I rolled the buck onto his back and lashed one hind leg to a tree, to keep the appendage from flopping around while I field-dressed the animal.

I stripped down to just my thermal top and laid my bulky clothes aside, out of the way. I was no longer cold. And even though it was a three-point buck lacking an entire antler, I felt proud, calm, and satisfied. I pinched the soft, snow-white underbelly of the animal and, pulling it up, I inserted the tip of my sharp knife. Careful not to puncture the intestines, I slit the skin all the way up to the breastbone. The tightly packed organs began to bulge out of the incision.

I made a few quick cuts to free up the innards and slid the pungent mass out onto the ground. The body cavity was partially filled with blood. I sat down on a rock and touched the blood on my knife with the tip of my tongue. I'd convinced myself somewhere along the way that the gesture somehow bonded me to deer and brought me luck. I smoked a cigarette and watched the steam rising from the gut pile and the warm body cavity, like incense.

One day, when my son, Luke, is of the right age, I'll sit him down and tell him: "Son, your daddy hunted for most of his life and in the Year of Our Lord 2006, he probably killed the smallest buck that will ever be taken legally in Pennsylvania for a long, long time."

I'm pretty sure that, unlike the son of some big football star or tennis player, my own son won't find the idea of following in his father's footsteps too intimidating a task.

When I wandered back to reality from the ghost trail of memories—so many rich whitetail memories!—it was almost completely dark, and a deer, or what I thought was a deer, stood just twenty-five yards from my stand, at the edge of the black hemlocks, in a pose worthy of the hood ornament on a 1959 Dodge DeSoto.

Hard as I tried, I just couldn't tell if it was a buck or a doe, and by that time it didn't seem to matter much. Another opening day had ended, it was different from the ones that had come before and, I hoped, different from the ones that would come later.

I was soaked through. My bones were creaky and cold, and I felt raw. I tied my pack to the haul-cord and, after emptying the gun, I clipped the rifle on above the pack. I lowered my gear to the ground, wriggled through the trapdoor, and took my time walking back to the ATV. The wet air smelled rich and fertile. The lights were on in the milking parlor of a barn on a distant hill; somewhere over that way a dog barked.

Back at Deer Hill Farm, I learned that neither Chris nor Tony had tagged a buck, either. We cleaned up and piled into Tony's car for the fifteen-minute drive over to Steve Renehan's house.

Years ago, Chris had sold a beautiful, four-hundred-acre mountaintop he owned for a decade near Deer Hill Farm to Steve, who worked on Wall Street. The only building on the parcel at the time was a decrepit, two-room hunting cabin with the roof stove in by a broken tree limb. But that's where Steve hunted with his dad and three of his brothers for a few years, as he planned and built his beautiful log home.

Steve's opening day dinner has become a ritual feast as well —it was the place we compared notes and worked out who won our ten bucks per man "big buck pool"—worth, some years, a whopping two hundred bucks. Steve's home is in a remote spot, but on the way it seemed that all the lights were on in Whitetail Nation—almost every house or cabin, modest or impressive, was humming with activity.

Steve's preferred mode of transportation is his Ford pickup, and he'd just as soon wear flannel shirts and jeans as a dark suit and power tie. He smokes the best cigars, but stubs them out in ashtrays he makes himself, from tin soup or bean cans with the labels carefully peeled off.

As we drove up, our headlights picked up the shimmering

blue-green eyes of a dozen or more deer, placidly feeding on Steve's lawn meadow. The house was lit up like a cruise ship. At the parking area, two deer hung, head down, from the enormous maple tree, their bellies slit open with the hair on either side black with matted blood. One of them was a beauty: a typical eight-pointer with thick main beams that curved gracefully and almost touched at the tips. It was a 140-class buck, shot by a guest of Steve's brother Jamie. It was a legitimate trophy—the whitetail I had hoped to shoot at some point in this season.

Inside, the air was blue with cigar smoke and a cacophony of voices. Dinner was in full swing, the serving island in the kitchen crammed with platters of ribs and brisket (flown up from a Texas barbecue joint), bowls of vegetables and chili, and bottles of wine and esoteric brands of Scotch and bourbon. Todd, another of Steve's brothers, was holding court there. A dozen guys were sitting around the dining-room table nearby, others lounged by the mammoth stone fireplace, plates in their laps, beneath handsome mounts of deer, elk, and trout.

I quickly learned that our entire group of about twenty hunters—some of them highly accomplished—had killed a total of three bucks. And Tom Freda, who arrived late, told us he missed a buck to rival the eight-pointer hanging outside.

But the numbers hardly seemed to matter, and almost everyone had some kind of story to tell, or freely indulged his instincts for pontificating about what he—or someone else—shoulda, woulda, coulda done. It was the kind of scene I imagined taking place in a saloon in a Wild West mining town: big men talking loudly, drinking copiously, and packing down enormous amounts of red meat. I kept waiting to hear the sound of someone smashing a whiskey bottle, or the bark of a six-shooter.

A little later, I walked outside with Steve to take a closer look at the big buck hanging in the tree. We talked quietly about the elegant configuration of the buck's antlers; they were at once ancient weapons of war and fetching ornaments. The ash of our cigars glowed faintly in what had become a softly misting night.

"Are you bummed out that someone else shot it?" I asked.

"No way," Steve replied. "I'm just happy somebody got him. Look at the mass in these antlers. And the best thing is that there's an even better one still running around. We saw him all summer."

Steve is more than a good bond salesman who became successful beyond his wildest dreams by the time he hit forty. He's a natural leader: decisive, forthright, disciplined, tolerant, and loyal to his friends. He's well-mannered and friendly, and although he's not a big man, he exudes command and a wiry, tensile strength. And he's lucky to be alive.

As a college kid, Steve and two companions got into a bar fight with a trio of hoods in a rough neighborhood of Philadelphia. One of Steve's friends was beaten to a pulp, and his friends carried him out to his car. After dumping him in, they turned around to see that the other guys, not having had enough, had trailed them to the parking lot. One stood behind Steve, one in front. Steve kicked the guy in front of him in the nuts and whirled around to throw a punch. All he saw was a gleam of light on the blade of a knife.

The hood, who turned out to be a convicted felon, stabbed Steve three times in the chest, puncturing a lung and piercing the right ventricle of his heart. Steve collapsed in the elevator at the hospital, and an alert intern split his chest open and gave him the on-the-spot heart massage that kept him alive.

"Not that it matters," I said, "but it's amazing, how big an investment this buck hanging here represents."

Steve laughed. "I never think about it that way. I just love this shit—all of it. I've loved it since I was a little kid in Connecticut, where there was still one farm left at the end of our road. That was Old Man Morgan's place. He was a solitary guy, but he liked me and gave me free rein to hunt and fish on his big property. I kept those rights, because when I shot a partridge or caught a trout, I'd often clean it and give it to him. He liked that. I was out there at Old Man Morgan's sunup to sundown some days. My priorities changed only when I had to go out and get a job."

The story of Old Man Morgan made me think of Steve's dad, Pete, who had died not long after we lost Joe Freda. "I miss your old man," I said. "I can still hear him hollering, 'Goddamned kids!' He prefaced every sentence with it."

"He was some piece of work. But we were a handful."

Pete Renehan was a tough Irishman who bought a small trucking company soon after he left the Marine Corps and had six kids, five of them boys. By the time Steve bought his mountaintop from Chris, Pete was pretty much retired. Over the ensuing years, Pete became the unofficial caretaker for Steve and two of his brothers, Todd and Jamie, who also built homes on adjoining Renehan properties. Pete brush-hogged the fields, maintained the trails, planted food plots. He loved to sit on the porch on warm summer evenings and drink beer, watching deer that came out to feed.

Pete also hunted, at least in theory. I can't recall him having shot anything in the fifteen-odd years that we hunted together. That wasn't due to lack of opportunity—or grit. We gradually figured out that he was a double agent. He reluctantly trudged out the door on opening day, carrying his ancient, lever-action .30-30. We came to believe that when he saw a deer, he ran toward it, holding his hat and waving his arms, screaming, "You guys, get out of here! My goddamned kids and their buddies are going to pop your reckless asses if you don't stop farting around here!"

It wasn't like Pete had no stomach for the visceral realities of hunting, either. This was a tough, hardworking, black-and-white kind of guy who, when Steve was a teenager, knocked him out with a wicked right cross—for sneaking a beer. Steve maintains that by the time his youngest brother, Jamie, came along, Pete would just shrug when Jamie, driving his first car, jammed on the brakes and a pile of beer cans came rolling and clanging out from under the seats.

One time, Jamie came home from high school bloodied after a fight. Pete sat him down and said: "I have just two questions: Number one—did you start it?"

When Jamie said no, Pete said: "Okay. Number two—did you win?"

Jamie nodded yes.

"Good," Pete said. "Now go get cleaned up before your mother sees you."

On one hunt at Steve's, I shot a buck early in the day, field-dressed it, and returned to the house to clean up. As I set the gun down on the porch, I happened to look out across the meadow and saw a great buck—one that was the equal of the eight-pointer now hanging, so many years later, in front of Steve's home.

I knew Pete was in the house (he always came in to cook breakfast; I think he was trying to protect the deer by luring us out of the woods with the smell of frying bacon), and I rushed in, yelling, "Pete, Pete, there's a monster out on the lawn. Grab your gun."

I heard his muffled voice coming from one of the bathrooms on the second floor: "I'm sitting on the throne, for chrissakes, *you* go ahead and shoot it."

I'd already used my tag, of course, and we never saw that buck again.

We talked about Pete a little bit more, the big eight-pointer slowly rotating where he hung between us, a silent third party to the conversation. Then it was quiet, but for the vaguely audible, raucous laughter coming from the house.

I realized that I missed my own father, Frank, who died about thirty years ago. I used to think he wasn't much of a dad until, with a little age, it occurred to me that maybe I wasn't much of a son, either. Over time, though, I came to realize that he tried hard and did his best, which is about all you can ask.

I have just one clear memory of going afield with him at the old, abandoned Pennsylvania farm of which we once were part owners. The property, a respectable two-hundred-plus acres, was not unlike the place I eventually bought in Andes, and where I hoped my own son, Luke, would someday live the dream.

One day when I was about twelve, Dad asked if I wanted to go along deer hunting. I don't think he really knew what he was doing, but his desire was deep and natural. I didn't have to be asked twice.

We eventually walked a wagon road through a patch of woods, beyond which lay the fields of a neighboring dairy farm. In today's evolved jargon, it would inevitably be called a bedding area, or a transition zone, but to us it was just woods, interspersed with thickets of rhododendron and other brush.

A magnificent buck exploded out of one of the thickets up ahead, taking us utterly by surprise. It leaped across the trail; my father raised his shotgun and managed only one shot before the buck vanished into the woods on the other side.

Dad knew enough to look around carefully, and he found some blood on the carpet of leaves. I remember the red brightness of it, the glistening droplets leaping off the yellow and brown fodder underfoot. We tracked that deer, finding just enough blood to keep going, and that was the adventure of it. For we followed an erratic, faint trail that led us to places I didn't recognize, and where I saw memorable things: a pair of orange newts on a cushion of bright green moss; trees that a big buck, perhaps the very one we'd hit, had raked over with his antlers.

From the moment we set forth, I was emotionally keyed up to find the buck, but I also felt a measure of fear and apprehension. This was a big animal; the woods in places were awfully dark. We followed the blood as best we could, and my confidence remained undiminished until night began to fall and we finally gave up. I remember how dejected my father seemed as we trudged back toward the distant amber lights of the farmhouse. It was a long, long walk in the dark; we were both tired and spoke little.

I can't remember my father ever going deer hunting again, and I don't know why. It's one of the questions that I, a hunter as well as a son, wish he were still around to answer.

Standing by the big tree at Steve's, alongside the great, emptied-out buck, it occurred to me that maybe I was still trying to find that first whitetail buck, and that he'd been kind enough to leave me a blood trail that wouldn't end until my own time ran out.

And if I were lucky enough, maybe my own son would pick up that trail and follow it through Whitetail Nation the way I had, even if he labored under the same delusion: that he was looking for something as concrete and specific as a set of antlers that scored 160 Boone and Crockett points.

My hunt for the monster buck had led me in a big circle, back to my beginnings, through fields filled with the greatest rewards of all: high drama and base comedy, physical hardships and spiritual rewards, a beautiful Montana buck to leaven the disappointment and the frustrations experienced along the way. And memories, all those memories that can't be scored.

I had witnessed the pink-and-lavender sunset in the Mon-

tana coulee country, waves of golden Texas savanna grass, shimmering in the sun. I froze in more than one tree and slept while
being rained on. I saw deer arching away in graceful bounds,
dissolving like apparitions in the dusk. That monster whitetail
is still out there, where he belongs. And where I know I belong
as well. Maybe my own boy would join me out there, one day, to
continue the hunt. I should be so lucky. So should he.

Afterword

I would hunt for a few more days in Pennsylvania, but winter was asserting its grip and, ashamed as I was to admit it, I felt burned out. It had been a memorable year, a two-month hunt during which I had killed two bucks that were handsome trophies, one of them the hard way, in Montana.

Some big bucks were still said to be running the hollows and ridges of my haunts in New York and Pennsylvania, and I wished them well. The morning I returned from Pennsylvania, I met Chris Ingvordsen and his girlfriend, Billie, for breakfast in Andes. He told me, "The guys over on Cape Horn [on the other side of the big hill] shot *five* eight-pointers on opening day—the newspaper had a picture of them, hanging on a meat pole. All five of them.

"We probably pushed those deer over when we went up to the secret cabin with those two vehicles and all our stuff. That's probably why it was so slow for us. We should have been much more low-impact going in, but . . . what are you going to do?"

Chris was in a black mood. He had seen a few stripling bucks on the big hill, but no monsters. The road hunters had been out in force. They crawled along in that familiar, sinister fashion, in vehicles ranging from rusted-out, shit-box sedans to well-appointed half-ton pickups equipped with gun racks, steel toolboxes, and ladder racks. The parade was never-ending.

Once in a while, I went out to scout around. I wondered if the deer I'd seen on my property had survived, now that the weather kept many hunters indoors and rifle season had dwindled to the last few days.

Although the weather turned frigid, I roused myself for one final hunt. At daybreak, I stole past my big barn, down to the corner of the meadow where a huge maple tree, entirely bare, still presides. I began to work my way through the brush on the slope behind the maple and into the woods. I looked back at my little house with the wood smoke drifting up from the chimney, where my wife, Lisa, was playing with Luke.

I slowly worked my way through the woods, up to the quarry meadow. It was a joy, making slow progress through the silent woods. The skies were flat gray, with light snow falling so gently that I was able to track individual flakes as they drifted down. I carried the Weatherby, but didn't expect to see much. Although the one thing I know by now is that . . . you never know.

Up near the quarry gate, I found some footprints in the snow; somebody had been tromping around in a small area. Through the trees I saw the pond a few hundred yards below, where the steep wooded slope ended and the big meadow began. I filtered down through the woods and among some hemlocks I'd planted years ago. They had grown and survived the hungry deer, winter after winter, and now had branches above the browse line. They would make it, of that I was sure.

As I still-hunted around the perimeter of the pond, I noticed a curious mass of brown in the outflow. I walked down to it, a queasy feeling growing in my stomach with each step.

The truth was inescapable; the dark mass was the carcass of a deer.

The animal had a big body, and it lay with its neck out-stretched and resting in some yellow grass while a trickle of frigid water flowed along his back and a fine coating of ice encased his hoofs and part of his tail. It was a buck, a five-pointer that I recognized as my old friend Pancho. The light dusting of snow on his coat suggested serenity; somehow, his lifeless body still expressed some vestige of dignity.

Pancho could not have been dead longer than forty-eight hours.

His eyes were open, opaque, the same color as the bluestone in the quarry just up the hill. I found the entry wound, on the rear of his back near, or on, the spine.

What a terrible shame; what a waste of a good deer, I thought.

I emptied my gun and set it against the tree. My hunt was over; I was done for the year. I would go back for the ATV, drag out Pancho and—what? I'd look for a nice, quiet, out-of-the-way place to lay Pancho to rest, someplace where at least the coyotes could make some use of his meat, someplace better than this cold, dark ditch where the frigid water ran over him.

I felt mournful, but I had a hedge against that feeling once the moment passed. For I'd learned, hunting, something that is a lot more comforting than it might sound—something that people, including many who revere nature from a distance, don't or won't understand. Life in the natural world is as cheap as it is beautiful. There's no other way to put it. Nature is boun-tiful and abundant, less like a delicate Swiss timepiece than an enormous, wanton, roaring, and churning wheel in which death and life are commingled, relentlessly and on the move, tumbling end over end.

Bison once thundered across the Great Plains in such numbers that hundreds of calves and stragglers in any given herd often wallowed and drowned at fords turned into quagmires by the thousands that went before. And in Newfoundland, capelin still fling themselves by the billions onto dry land as part of their spawning ritual. Only one in every ten thousand eggs survives, but then each female alone carries as many as fifty thousand eggs and requires three male mates. The mortality rate for each generation of spawners is north of 99.9 percent, which still leaves plenty of capelin . . .

It seems wasteful, it's borderline horrifying. But it's the reality of the natural world and that's something to celebrate, even as our appreciation of nature and wildlife multiplies. Pancho certainly died for someone's sins, but I don't think they were mine. And there would be more of him, many, many more of him, unless some cataclysmic event halted the process. Under the right circumstances, there would be even better specimens than Pancho. The driving force, so evident during the rut, would see to that.

I hoped that Pancho at least had managed to breed before he was destroyed, for he fulfilled an important requisite for survival with his sheer bulk. I liked to imagine that Pancho had some luck during the rut. His antlers showed signs of use; one was broken off at the tip, although I had to look closely to tell. And as all deer hunters know, it's all about the antlers. May his offspring have better ones, and reign supreme in the woods for many more autumns to come.

Glossary

Bed down—What a whitetail deer does when it isn't feeding or traveling to or from feeding areas (or breeding during the rut—see below). Bedded deer will frequently explode from right under the feet of a hunter in heavy brush, which is one of the better reasons to always hunt with the safety on until you're ready to shoot.

Booner—A whitetail or mule buck deer that qualifies for entry in the Boone and Crockett Club's book of records (minimum score: 160). Not to be confused with "boomer," a Volvo-driving, gun-fearing, Meryl Streep–loving, fifty- or sixty-something member of the baby boom generation of the 1940s and '50s. (Boomers, when encountered in a coffee joint, may be inclined to use strange code words for "small," "medium," and "large.")

Broadhead—The metal, often multibladed tip of an arrow. Belongs to the same family of lethal instruments as the box-cutter, utility knife, and razor-blade. Broadheads are effective on human beings as well as deer, as any happy-go-lucky nimrod who ever tried to screw one into the tip of his alu-minum- or carbon-fiber arrow shaft while watching a music video featuring Lady Gaga can attest.

Buck—A male whitetail deer. The male members of many species, including our own, are called bucks. If you're wondering why the male elk, of a species in the same family as the whitetail deer, is called a "bull," but the male American shad (a fish) is called a "buck," you're asking the wrong guy.

Caliber—A numerical designation (as in .30 caliber) corresponding to the diameter of a bullet at its thickest part. Not to be confused with the Dodge Caliber, the ugliest automobile ever created by the geniuses of the American auto industry.

Climber—A cleverly engineered, two-part, lightweight, and portable tree stand that enables a hunter to climb and descend a suitable tree; especially favored by bow hunters. The garages of Whitetail Nation are full of three-hundred-dollar climbers that hunters are too fearful (or prudent) to use, although they sounded like a good idea at the time.

Compound bow—A bow made from graphite, aluminum, and other materials so resistant to flexing that engineers had to think up a complicated cable-and-cam system to enable most hunters to pull back the damned string.

Coulee—A word used loosely to describe a drainage zone with sharply pitched sides or walls. Derived from the French word for the verb "to flow," or *couler*, in the period during which France produced mountain men and fur trappers. Who knew?

Doe—A female whitetail deer, which is generally of less interest to hunters than is the buck, but of more interest to the buck than is the hunter.

Forbs—Herbaceous flowering plants (including milkweed and sunflower) that are not graminoids (grasses, sedges, and rushes) but constitute a significant and highly nutritious part of the whitetail deer's diet. Right up there with *pedicle* as a word frequently used by deer camp know-it-alls.

Ground blind—A permanent or temporary structure that offers concealment and scent suppression for those hunters crazy enough not to want to spend hours and hours on end perched on a tiny, swaying, wind-and-rain-lashed platform in a tree (aka "tree stand").

Haul-cord—A line or rope a hunter uses to raise and lower his or her bow, gun, backpack, or other articles to or from a tree stand. Prone to hanging up on lower boughs or bark—when not left behind in the truck in the first place.

Kill zone—The area on a whitetail deer where a well-placed arrow or bullet ensures a swift, humane kill, because it ensures damage to vital organs. If you're wondering how a kill can be "humane," you're reading the wrong book.

Longbow—The most primitive kind of bow, it can be little more than a shaped stick with notches at each end for the bowstring.

Mule deer—Common name for *Odocoileus hemionus,* a close relative of the whitetail deer (and thought to have descended from it), found west of Missouri. So-called because of its ears, which are significantly larger than those of a whitetail. Appearance-wise, the mule deer is easily distinguished from the whitetail by its bifurcated antlers. Each antler, as well as its tines, ends in a fork, while the whitetail has two main beams with single-point tines growing vertically out of them.

Pedicle—The part of the deer's skull from which the antlers grow, easily mispronounced as "pedicure" after your seventh Dewar's on the rocks.

POA—Point-of-aim. This is self-evident, but gun nuts, like the United Nations personnel they despise, just love speaking in acronyms.

Prusik hitch—A knot made from a small length of rope and attached to a longer line, used for safety when climbing up or down from a tree stand. The Prusik hitch slides easily in either direction on the safety rope, but locks up on the main rope in the event of a sharp tug. A sharp tug usually indicates that a camo-clad human being has fallen out of a tree twenty-five feet above the ground.

Recurve bow—A bow with tips that curve away from the archer, enabling him to get more power from a shorter bow. Think of it as a variation on the "male enhancement" theme.

Rut—Go ahead, tell me you don't know what it means . . .

Safety—The cute little doohickey near the bolt on your rifle that your idiot cousin always forgets to put in the "on" position while stumbling along in the dark right behind you.

Smoke pole—Informal name for an old-fashioned, single-shot, muzzle-loading rifle, because the cloud of smoke left by the primitive firing system is so dense that you half expect to see Jethro Tull emerge from it. Many states now have special, supplemental seasons during which only primitive firearms may be used.

Tag—A small paper or plastic ticket that most states require a hunter to affix to a deer immediately after he has killed it, and certainly before a game warden spots said deer lying in the back of a truck or hanging from a maple tree, lest the hunter find himself in his familiar habitat: deep doo-doo.

Trophy buck—In order to make the venerable Boone and Crockett Club record book, the closest thing to an official trophy designation, a whitetail with a "typical" rack must score 160 points using the official B&C points-scoring system. Keep dreaming! I say any deer you hang on the wall to replace that photo of you and your wife on your honeymoon in Branson, Missouri, may be called a trophy buck.

Typical and nontypical antlers—A whitetail's antlers are usually symmetrical (typical), with nearly identical tines rising like pickets of a fence on both of its main beams. Each antler is basically a mirror image of the other. However, many deer have somewhat asymmetrical antlers (due to genetics, diet, or injury to an antler during the growth phase). Deer with extreme nontypical racks might cause you to drop your rifle and run, so always hunt with the safety on.

Whitetail—Most common nickname for *Odocoileus virginianus*, North America's most common deer, found in all but five states in the U.S.—a good reason to cross five states off the list of places where you might want to live someday. The popular name derives from the conspicuous, dazzling white underside of the tail, which the deer uses to "flag" others of its own kind when it senses danger, or when it just wants to give a hunter in the distance the animal world's equivalent of a middle finger.

Windage—An esoteric term for left-to-right (and right-to-left), used in adjusting the reticle, or crosshairs, in a rifle scope. Also, a rough measure of certain hunters' inability to provide the short version of a profoundly boring hunting-related story.

Windicator—A crassly commercial term for any number of products, including yarns and powders, meant to tell a hunter the same thing that the village idiot hanging around in front of the courthouse can—the direction in which the wind is blowing.

Acknowledgments

Publishing industry personnel are usually buried at about the point in the acknowledgments where the eyes of even the most devoted of readers have glazed over, but I really want to thank Susan Canavan, my editor at Houghton Mifflin Harcourt, for venturing where so few mainstream book, magazine, or newspaper publishers dare go these days—into the realm of the blood sports, particularly hunting. Susan and my literary agent, Scott Waxman, are the ones who made this book happen; I happen to be the lucky guy who got to write it.

Special thanks to those men and women whose friendship, new and long-standing, helped me gather much of the material in this book. They include, in Saskatchewan, Canada: Paul Pospicil. In New York state: Thomas Aquinas Daly and his wife, Chris Daly, Chris Ingvordsen, Mark Finne, and Doug Stevens. In Montana: David, Verges, Julie, Roald, and Maia Aageson, along with Ross and Rhonda Ritter. In Texas: Mike and Susie Potts, and Ted and Kathy Masser. In Pennsylvania: Chris von Strasser and Steve, Todd, and Jamie Renehan. And lest I forget, Susan B. Adams and Neil Amdur, both formerly of the *New York Times*, who were surprisingly supportive of my desire to write about hunting despite the so-called enlightened nature of that newspaper's readership and editorial policies.

In the course of a lifetime, a guy has surprisingly few real hunting buddies, and I'd like to remember several who are no longer—in some cases, surprisingly—with us, including my own father, Frank, as well as Joe Freda, Pete Renehan, and that towering figure in conservation, Jim Range. I don't know much about great men, but in my eyes all of them in many ways fit the bill. I take great comfort in the fact that Freda's and Renehan's offspring are out there running around with guns in the woods.

My wife, Lisa, put up admirably with my sneaking away to hunt (not always without a little lively debate, but we've all been there, right?), and my son, Luke, will be shooting his Red Ryder BB gun by the time you read this. In fact, I've already said those fateful words: *Watch out, you can put someone's eye out with that thing!*

And to everyone who lives in Whitetail Nation—I'm proud to be among you.